keeping it real

my autobiography

keeping it real

my autobiography

jodie marsh

metro

Published by Metro Publishing Ltd,
3 Bramber Court, 2 Bramber Road,
London W14 9PB, England

www.blake.co.uk

First published in paperback in 2006

ISBN 978 1 84454 528 5

British Library Cataloguing-in-Publication Data:

A catalogue record for this book is available from the British Library.

Design by www.envydesign.co.uk

Printed in the UK by CPI Bookmarque, Croydon, CR0 4TD

1 3 5 7 9 10 8 6 4 2

Papers used by Metro Publishing are natural, recyclable products made from wood grown in sustainable forests. The manufacturing processes conform to the environmental regulations of the country of origin.

Jodie Marsh is represented by SEM Group
98 Cockfosters Road, Barnet EN4 0DP
Tel: +44 (0) 20 8447 4250

For my mum Kris, dad John
and brother Jordan

Foreword

Why?

Why not...

Contents

CHAPTER ONE
Baby Marsh

So there I was: naked, screaming and covered in a thick, gooey substance. I was supposed to be born on Christmas Day 1978, but I was two days early. The nurses came round in the evening and sang Christmas carols holding candles in little lanterns. My mum cried her eyes out (to this day we both cry if we hear 'Silent Night'); I, or so I'm told, screamed at the top of my lungs.

I was never going to be an easy child. I was very intelligent and was walking and talking at nine months. I had an enormous thirst for knowledge, constantly asking questions and one of my greatest interests was reading. I had a collection of books that my parents bought me and I would go and select one, take it to my mum and ask her to read it to me. Many a happy hour was spent sitting on her lap being read to and looking at the pictures. At two years old I could recite *Little Red Riding Hood* and other children's stories. It wasn't that I could read properly, but I had memorised the words from when my mum had read them to me – she tells me she was amazed to hear me do this and decided to teach me to read. She used a series of flash cards with different words printed on them. By the age of three I was reading books that were aimed at five-year-olds. When I started infant school, the teacher told Mum off for teaching me to read. She should have left it to the teachers, apparently, as I was now too advanced for the rest of the class.

I was extremely demanding as a toddler. I had a mind of my own and knew how I wanted things to be done. When I decided that I didn't want to sleep on my own any more, I marched into my mum and dad's bedroom on several occasions and demanded to sleep with them in their bed. I told them that it wasn't fair that there were two of them and only one of me – why should I have to sleep on my own in a room when they had each other to cuddle up to? I was hyperactive and didn't need much sleep anyway – only about three hours a night. Mum despaired and the doctor prescribed me Valium (which seemed a bit extreme – my mum was horrified by the idea and never gave it to me). I screamed constantly when I was awake, wanting affection and attention.

While my mum was pregnant with me, my parents set up a building company and when I was three, my brother was born. My parents called him Jordan – yes, very funny, I know, but he was bloody called it first! He wasn't planned, which is still a source of great amusement to me and many friends. On the down side, my mum always says that the reason Jordan was an accident was that she thought she couldn't face having another after me! Still, the name 'accident' stuck. Sorry, Jord, now the whole world knows!

When I was five we moved into a beautiful big period

house, where my family live now. Set in five acres of land in the Essex countryside, the house has five bedrooms and parts of it were built in 1240. It's most definitely haunted, and my mum and I still won't go in to what we call the 'old rooms'.

My life throughout junior school was extremely happy. I went to a quaint little Church of England village school called St Peter's, where I was top of the class in pretty much everything. I loved writing and drawing and I got on well with all my teachers. On my first day at school I met a girl called Naomi, and we were to remain best friends for the next nine years. Naomi and I were complete tomboys. I was fortunate that my parents bought me a petrol-driven mini Range Rover, a small motorbike and a quad bike. When we bought the house I also inherited a pony called Cheeky. All of our free time was spent climbing trees, driving the car, riding the bikes, horse-riding and generally playing in the mud in the fields that surrounded the house.

I wasn't scared of anything. I remember a time when I pushed my brother out of a tree house my dad had built us. It was ten feet up in the biggest tree in our garden, and you could jump out of it holding on to a swinging rope. I had been doing it for years, but my brother was always scared of it. One day he stood up there for half an hour with the rope between his legs, afraid to jump. Eventually my dad said, 'Go up there and give him a little help.' I took that to mean 'push him out', which is exactly what I did. I thought he would hold on to the rope; he didn't – he fractured his skull and broke his arm. He still jokingly shouts at me for that!

My brother and I had everything children could ever wish for, and, although in most people's eyes we may have appeared spoiled, my parents always instilled in us the importance of hard work, manners, politeness and respect.

We were very happy children. Of course, we fought, like all brothers and sisters do, but we loved each other and we loved our parents. We knew that not all kids had the wonderful things that we had, and we knew that our parents had had to work hard to get them for us. We always appreciated the value of things and – apart from a couple of Cindy dolls which weren't as pretty as Barbie and some Micro Machines – everything we had was thoroughly respected and well looked after.

I became a vegetarian at the age of nine after years of hiding meat underneath vegetables or pushing it around my plate. I wouldn't eat it because of my love for animals, so my mum, realising she was wasting her money, finally gave in and let me become a properly recognised veggie. I could be a handful for my parents because of my strength of character and stubbornness. They loved me dearly and didn't have a bad word to say about me but realised early on that they would have difficulty in having a say over what I did. From the age of three I chose my own clothes and put on my mum's lipstick. I was a born show-off and played up to any camera that was pointed in my direction.

We had a million and one pets, including a pot-bellied pig called Peggy Sue – one of the best pets, we all agree, we've had – dogs, rabbits, hamsters, gerbils, cats, guinea pigs (which multiplied by the dozen – by the time we had 35 on our hands we ended up giving them to the farm next door), a snake (much to my mum's horror), tortoises, a donkey (which we rescued when it was on its way to the glue factory), angora goats (which chewed through everything, the cheeky things!), birds, Cheeky the pony and other horses we acquired along the way. Our house was like a sanctuary for injured or homeless animals, and we loved it.

I wanted to be a vet until I was about eleven and realised that I wouldn't actually be able to put an animal to sleep. Nevertheless, I was always fixing broken wings of birds that had flown into the house (I was a member of the Young Ornithologist Club) or nursing hedgehogs back to health after they had been attacked by foxes. I was an extremely happy and balanced child – intelligent but fun-loving, loud and silly yet caring and thoughtful. Like all other little girls, I loved Barbie, Sylvanian Families, Madonna, Michael Jackson (I even wrote to *Jim'll Fix It* to ask if I could meet Michael) and Bros (yes, I wore Grolsch bottle tops on my shoes!). My parents were wonderful and encouraged my brother and me to learn and achieve as much as we could. Over the years I tried my hand at ice skating, dancing, piano lessons (I gave up after reaching grade eight – my brother was a hundred times better than me and he couldn't even read music), saxophone lessons and singing lessons. I don't think any child could have wished for a better start in life.

Everything changed, however, when I went to senior school. Having realised my academic potential, I was encouraged by my parents to take the entrance exam for a posh private school in our home town. I passed with flying colours. All my friends from St Peter's – including Naomi – were going off to the normal comprehensive schools in the area. I wanted to go with them but, not wanting to disappoint my parents, I didn't really voice my opinion. I just pretended to be excited at the thought of going to Brentwood School where I was going to get the best education. I'll never forget how nervous I was on that first day. Would I make friends easily? Would I be clever enough? All the things you think as a child in a strange place for the first time ran through my head, and

I wanted to cry and run home to the safety of my mum's arms. Instead, I soldiered on like a little lost soul. I kept my head down and got on with the work, wanting to impress the teachers in the same way I had done at junior school. For the first year or so I buried myself in my studies and did very well. No one really noticed me – I was an ugly duckling and quite shy. I had broken my nose playing hockey when I was nine and it had been left to heal naturally, so by the time I was eleven it was crooked and out of shape. Not that it was a problem for me: I was so immersed in schoolwork and concentrating on doing well that I hadn't given my looks a second thought – until I started being bullied, that is, and my life became a living hell.

Brentwood School was made up of a girls' school and a boys' school. We only mixed at lunchtime and break time. I quickly realised I had nothing in common with the other pupils. It cost ten grand a year to go to the school, so, although all the other pupils had money, hardly any had respect or manners. It was a different world. At the age of thirteen, I was asked out by one of the most popular boys in my year. He was arrogant – everyone liked him because they were in awe of him – and he was one of the loudest and biggest boys in the year. I made the mistake of turning him down, telling him politely that I really liked him but that I just wanted to be his friend. From that day on, the bullying began.

The first year wasn't too bad. I had fallen in love with the school clown, Dave Milner. Dave was a chubby little Jewish boy, extremely funny and well liked, and we became best friends in the first year at school. I warmed to Dave the moment I met him. His personality and laughter were infectious. He was the kind of person I could have spent time with every day for the rest of my life and never have become irritated. Young as I was, I adored him, and understood what falling in love with somebody for what was on the inside meant. Dave didn't have a bad word to say about anybody and always managed to find a funny comment about even the darkest situation. He was part faithful, soppy dog and part comedian. Warm, cuddly, loud and hilariously funny, I fell in love with him. I spent a lot of time outside of school with Dave. We would go to each other's house and play silly games in the fields surrounding us. 'Run-outs' were favourites and hide-and-seek in the dark at the house of a mutual friend called Tom was another. We shared a love of hip-hop music and spent many hours in record shops together buying Cypress Hill and House of Pain records.

Dave and I loved the outdoors. We would go for long walks in the countryside and he loved being at my house, riding the bikes and climbing trees. One hilarious day, during school holidays, my parents were at work and we had run riot round the house. We organised a series of wrestling matches in the lounge and were throwing each other round the room and smacking each other with cushions. At one point, a friend of ours threw my brother's best mate on to a sofa. He landed with such force that the back of the sofa snapped clean off. In a state of panic, we spent the afternoon calling furniture-repair places from the Yellow Pages, trying to find somebody we could afford to come and fix the sofa before my parents came home. Between us we had about thirty quid – it wasn't going to happen. Dave stayed to face the music and, when my parents hit the roof, we sat and took the telling-off together.

I wanted to spend every spare minute of my life by his side, even during lessons, and, when we were separated, I missed him. A few months into our relationship as boyfriend and girlfriend, we lost our virginity to each other at fourteen. We had been doing everything but have sex for a while, and felt confident that we knew what we were doing. My first time was exactly how I would have wanted and hoped it to be. It was in Dave's bedroom. There were four of us at his house that weekend – us and our friends Neil and Carlee – and we were staying over. We were all lying on the beds in his spare room chatting when Dave asked if I wanted to be alone with him. 'Yes,' I said, and we left our friends where they were. I remember feeling exhilarated and excited as Dave pulled a condom out of his bedside drawer. I knew I was ready for it and loved him with all my heart. We had built up to this moment for so long that I knew it was going to be great. Over the months leading up to this, we had tried lots of different things and we knew how to turn each other on, so we weren't nervous about doing it – we just wanted each other.

The whole experience was perfect. I still even remember what he smelled like! As he entered me, I felt like I never wanted it to end. I gasped in excitement and lay back to enjoy the sensation of him inside me. I loved his circumcised cock, it was smooth and clean, so finally having it inside me was blissful. It truly was exactly as I imagined the first time should be. Dave was loving and caring; I felt happy and special. It didn't last that long – maybe only five or ten minutes – but it was amazing. We lay cuddling for a while, then went downstairs to the kitchen where Carlee and Neil had relocated to and made a cup of tea. I remember whispering to Carlee that

I was no longer a virgin. She sat open-mouthed for a full five minutes before managing to get me in to the toilet to tell all!

My dad came to get me and Carlee in the morning and I sat uncomfortably in the front passenger seat on the way home, thinking stupidly that he would somehow be able to tell that I was no longer a virgin. It was a painful journey but, once back at mine, Carlee wanted the full story and I gave it. I told her how great it was and how much I loved Dave, and she was happy for me. We squealed and giggled for the rest of the day, not fully believing that I was no longer a virgin. The time I spent with Dave I remember only fondly.

Dave encouraged me to be naughty, and we often bunked off school to be together, much to our parents' dismay. They tried to stop us seeing each other, but that only made us worse. Sometimes we went missing for whole days at a time and they'd find us hiding at our friend Tom's house where we'd been making love all day. Once we'd started having sex, we shagged like rabbits everywhere we could – friends' houses, my house, his house, fairground rides, fields, alleyways and even once in the school toilets. I loved everything about him – the way he looked, the way he smelled, the way he tasted. He was perfect. I was still doing well at school, even with the taunts and the time I missed through bunking off under Dave's bad influence. Life couldn't have been better – until the day I caught Dave with my best mate in *my* house on *my* sofa.

CHAPTER TWO
Broken

Dave and I ended the day I found him with the person who had been my best friend since I'd been five. It was the summer holidays. My parents were out and Dave and Naomi were practically living at our house. Although we were at separate schools, Naomi and I had remained firm friends and saw each other as often as we could. We had started going to an under-18s nightclub every Tuesday night, and had discovered the joys of short skirts and make-up together. She got on well with Dave, and the three of us spent a lot of time together.

I had been upstairs on the phone in my bedroom for quite some time. When I came downstairs, I thought it sounded unusually quiet. As I opened the door to what was known as the playroom, Dave and Naomi jumped apart, half-dressed, and started scrabbling for their clothes. Not only had I walked in on my boyfriend about to cheat on me, but he was doing it with my one and only best

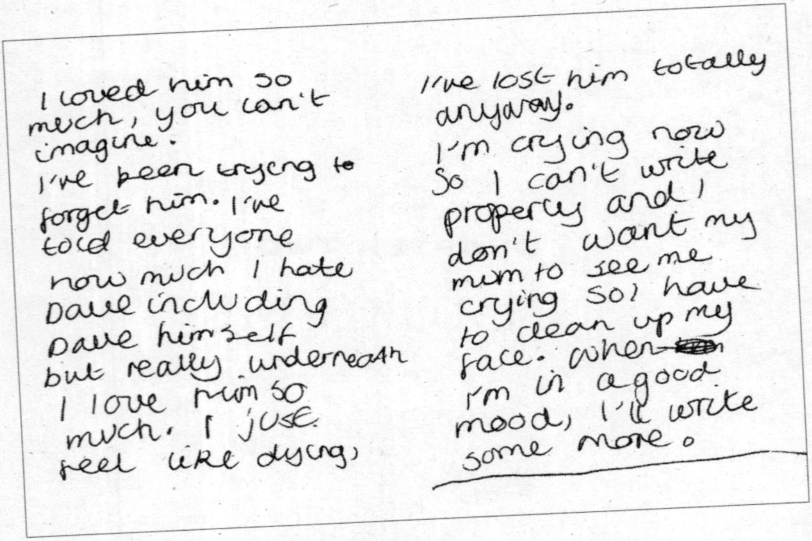

I loved him so much, you can't imagine. I've been trying to forget him. I've told everyone how much I hate Dave including Dave himself but really underneath I love him so much. I just feel like dying, I've lost him totally anyway. I'm crying now so I can't write properly and I don't want my mum to see me crying so I have to clean up my face. When I'm in a good mood, I'll write some more.

My diary from early 1993 reminded me of my feelings when I finished with Dave.

friend of nine years, and in my fucking house! Intense rage overcame me and, through tears of heartache and anger, I picked up every movable object in the room and threw it at them, screaming at them to get out of the house. They left in the torrent of my abuse and tears.

I never spoke to either of them again. I heard through others that they dated for a week, only for Naomi to end it with him because he was 'fat and ugly'. The bitch didn't even want him anyway. I cried solidly for a week. The pain was a physical one as I wept for my first true love and the loss of my best mate. Reduced to a snivelling wreck by the two people I cared most about, I lost a little bit of faith in the human race. I didn't really have anyone to turn to except my family, and I yearned for the day I would forget about both of them.

After the immense pain I felt from having my heart well

and truly broken, I put my head down once more and threw myself back into my schoolwork. It was then that the bullying really kicked in. Everybody in my year turned on me on the say of the popular boys and I got called every name under the sun – freak, ugly, big nose, geek, boffin. It became so bad that the couple of girlfriends I did have at the school were scared to be seen with me for fear of being picked on too. One was overweight and one was black, and they suffered the taunts of 'elephant' and 'the bearded lady' until they stopped being seen with me.

I became a complete loner. I moved around the school silently and had abuse shouted at me every day. I went to lunch on my own but even gave up on that when the boys started throwing food at me as I sat and ate. Instead I hid in the library at lunchtime, trying to pretend I had some important work to do. As I walked down the main road within our school, the boys would kick footballs at me. I can't tell you how much a hard football hurts when it is smacked into your cheek. The tears used to sting my red face but I still never said anything. The 'cool' girls in the school also took the side of the boys and would spit in my pencil case or PE kit when my bag was left in the locker room. I have never felt so miserable as I did at school. I believed every word they said. I felt so worthless and ugly, and at one point I actually wanted to end my life over it. It's easy for me to look back now and think that it wasn't really that bad but, as a child or young teenager, you don't realise there's a big wide world out there. You think that this is your life and it's never going to get any better. I honestly believed that I was a freak with a big ugly nose and no friends. I thought I would never have another boyfriend and that all my life I was going to be a freak who people laughed at. If I knew then what I know now, things would have been so different; but I didn't, and the self-hatred and pity I felt completely took over my life. I became withdrawn and depressed. Every single night I cried myself to sleep, wondering if the taunts would ever stop and wondering what I had done to deserve them in the first place.

I was so ashamed I couldn't even bring myself to tell my parents for ages. How do you say to someone who loves you, 'I'm being picked on because I'm so ugly'? Being bullied is the most lonely and horrible thing in the world. Unless you have been a victim of bullying, you will have no idea of how desperate and low you feel. Think of the one physical thing that you hate most about yourself and then imagine that a group of people publicly shout it at you every day of your life. For example, if you're overweight and feel ashamed of that, imagine walking down the street to loud taunts of 'fatty' from a big group. Imagine having no friends whatsoever and, no matter how many times your mum tells you you're beautiful, you don't believe her because you know that, deep down, you *are* overweight. Imagine that nobody will help you or stand up for you, and imagine that you can't see a way out of the situation. Then imagine that it happens every day for four or five years. It is a very dark and terrifying place, and I still bear the emotional scars of being there today. As an adult, I know that bullies are nothing more than cowards who take their own insecurities out on those who are weaker than them. As a teenager, I felt that the bullies were correct in what they said. I *was* ugly. I *was* a freak. My nose *was* bent out of shape. And I didn't see any way of turning my life around and making it all better again.

When I was fifteen, on a joint visit to the hairdresser's,

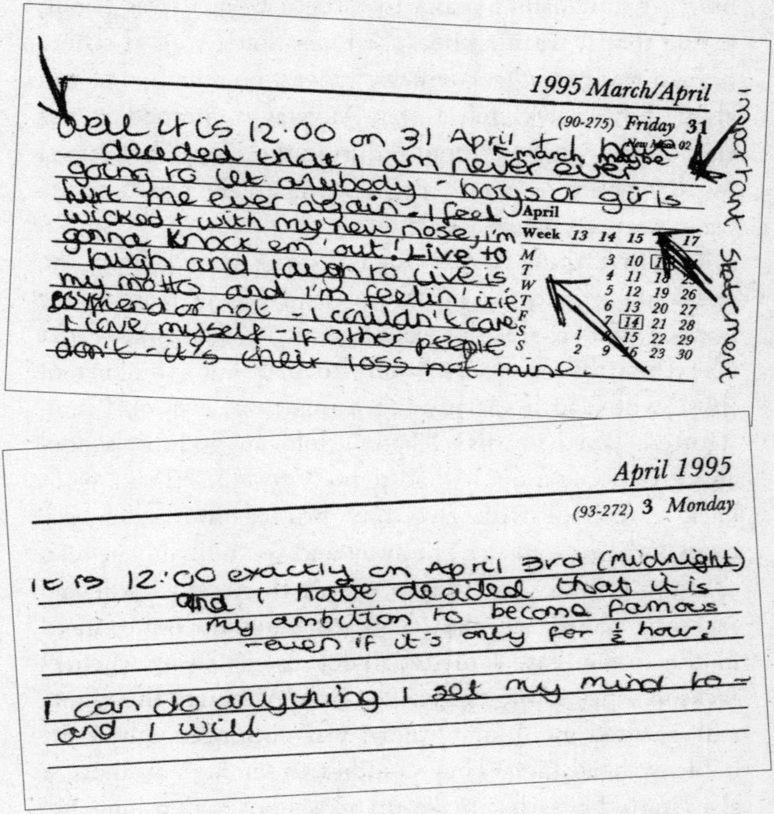

1995 March/April

(90-275) Friday 31

New Moon 02

well it is 12:00 on 31 April *march maybe + I have decided that I am never ever going to let anybody - boys or girls hurt me ever again. I feel wicked + with my new nose, I'm gonna knock em' out! Live to laugh and laugh to live is my motto and I'm feelin' irie boyfriend or not - I couldn't care I love myself - if other people don't - it's their loss not mine.

important statement

April

Week	13	14	15	16	17
M		3	10	17	24
T		4	11	18	25
W		5	12	19	26
T		6	13	20	27
F		7	14	21	28
S	1	8	15	22	29
S	2	9	16	23	30

April 1995

(93-272) 3 Monday

it is 12:00 exactly on April 3rd (midnight) and I have decided that it is my ambition to become famous - even if it's only for ½ hour!

I can do anything I set my mind to - and I will

I felt full of confidence when I'd had the operation and determined to make my mark.

my mum stopped me in the street outside and asked me if I would like to have my nose done. My parents had looked into it and discovered a procedure called rhinoplasty whereby they could straighten my nose. She said they knew how miserable I was and that they were willing to pay for it if it was what I wanted. Looking back now, I know that it must have been very difficult for her to say that to me. I had slowly opened up to them about the bullying, but hadn't really told them what it was about, saying that it was just because I was doing well at school (which was partly true anyway). I was too ashamed to talk about how ugly I felt I was. Anyway, I jumped at the chance and within a month, during the Easter holidays, I was lying on the operating table with a feeling that my life was about to change.

The first thing I did when I came round from the operation was to ask my mum, who was in tears at my bedside, for a mirror. Looking in it, I checked that everything had gone according to plan and, thinking of those who had made my life a misery at school, I said, 'Gutted, you bastards.' I hadn't told anybody at school about the operation – I had nobody to tell. When I went back to school with two tiny bruises on my cheeks, everybody noticed straight away and the bullying, instead of getting better, got worse. I was then called Michael Jackson, rubber face, plastic face; they told me not to stand in the sun in case I melted. They used to sing Michael Jackson songs to me as I walked past. Although the taunts still irritated me, I knew that I was no longer ugly and I held my head high. They couldn't upset me any more. I also started wearing make-up to school and rolling my skirt up a bit shorter than was allowed. Every morning was spent in the headmistress's office having my face scrubbed with a wet flannel – I'll never forget the sound of 'MAAAAARSH!' bellowing down the hallway when coming out of assembly each day – only for me to reapply the eyeliner and mascara five minutes later in the toilet.

Nevertheless, I did extremely well in my GCSEs, even with the constant bullying, and got all A*, A and B grades in eleven subjects. I can still understand Latin and recite whole paragraphs of Shakespeare. I'm not as stupid as I look! Two weeks into starting my A-level course, a boy punched me in the lunch queue and my parents took me out of the school that day. The guy who did it was sixteen or seventeen by then and about six foot tall – so not a small boy. None of us could take it any more. My parents had been up to the school every week at some points, chatting to the headmaster of the boys' school, asking what could be done about the bullies. But the school said there wasn't enough to substantiate what happened – they couldn't do anything. Life's a bitch. When I finally left that day, I wrote the headmaster a letter telling him that I felt he had failed me. I had so much anger inside of me from the years of suffering at the hands of these bullies and the fact that he had never done anything to stop it that I had to release it somehow. He wrote back to me telling me that I was a troublemaker and that I had caused all my own problems. It was a final kick in the teeth and made me want to show all of them that I was worth something and could be someone one day.

I went on to finish my A levels at South East Essex College in Southend. I did OK, but could have done better. I felt so badly let down by the education system that I knew I wasn't going to go to university and leave the only good thing in my life – my family. So instead I bunked off lots and went down to the sea front with some boys I'd made friends with. My days were spent dreaming of the time I'd be rich and famous.

I had visions even when I was five years old that one day I would step out of my house and be photographed. I remember seeing a Page 3 girl in the *Sun* and thinking that I wanted to be like her when I was older. She was so glamorous and beautiful. I also used to buy all the girlie teenage magazines like *More* and *Just 17* and fantasise about being one of the fashion models on their pages. I had done this for years but it was only at college I felt like I might actually stand a chance. At Brentwood School I kept those fantasies well locked away in the back of my mind, knowing that people would only ridicule me even more if they found out. I knew I was way too ugly at school to do a job involving my looks, but now men were paying me lots of attention, and I felt good.

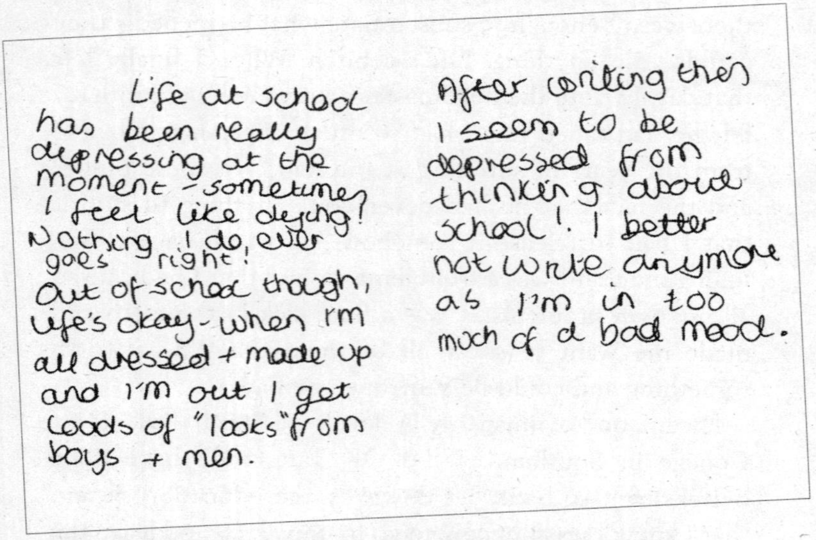

Life at school has been really depressing at the moment - sometimes I feel like dying! Nothing I do ever goes right! Out of school though, life's okay - when I'm all dressed + made up and I'm out I get loads of "looks" from boys + men.

After writing this I seem to be depressed from thinking about school! I better not write anymore as I'm in too much of a bad mood.

I confided my most secret thoughts to my diary as I realised that my life could be better – outside school.

CHAPTER THREE

Mr and Mrs Slippers

After I had my nose job, I led a double life. At school I was a freak and a loner; outside of school I had a big group of friends who were older than me, and with whom I went to nightclubs. I was going to places like Ministry of Sound and partying until seven o'clock the next morning. My parents trusted me – I've always been very anti-drugs as well as very headstrong, so they knew I had my head screwed on. From that age, when house music and pills were big, I watched people being carried out of clubs on stretchers and decided that I never wanted to be like that. Drugs have always been a big no-no.

Clubbing was very glamorous back then, and my group of friends was definitely the group to be seen with. We all tried to outdo each other with our outrageous outfits, and literally anything went. I went out one night, at the age of sixteen, in what Christina Aguilera later went on to wear in her 'Dirrty' video: a pair of black PVC chaps and a tiny pair of black knickers. I'm telling you this in response to all the people who have slated my outfits and said I've only done it for publicity – you're wrong. I've been doing it ever since I knew how to. The more outrageous the outfit, the better. I came up with all sorts of mad costumes – see-through plastic trousers, pink fluffy bras and full bondage outfits complete with whips and chains were all part of a normal night out for me. My parents, although not the slightest bit outrageous themselves, loved all our weird outfits and my mum even helped to style me for nights out, plaiting my hair into Medusa-style coils and helping me to sew fake fur on to wonder bras. They knew it was just a bit of fun and always took loads of pictures of us before we went out.

At one point I was seeing a guy called Mark, who was ten years older than me, and he was really into swinging and orgies. For a few months he had been on at me to have an orgy with him and one night I found myself instigating it. A group – me, Mark, a girlfriend of mine and a few boys – were at mine and had been drinking all night in the lounge. My parents had gone to bed and we moved outside to the barn so as not to wake them. We took a load of alcohol with us and played 'truth or dare' which got quite sexual, as it usually does in my company. One of the other blokes said that he was feeling quite horny and I invited him to pleasure himself in front of us. He did so willingly. One thing led to another, and before I knew it I was being shagged by one bloke while I sucked the other one and, next to me, my mate was having sex with Mark. Let's just say we had the time of our lives. It lasted, all in all, for about five hours and we swapped partners over and over until none of us could take any more. We all piled into a huge king-size bed in a spare room in the house and managed to grab a couple of hours' sleep.

I awoke to Mark shaking me in a state of panic, tears streaming down his face, demanding to know how I could have done this to him. 'Done what?' I asked.

'Slept with other people!' he shouted back at me. We argued for about an hour until he left, and I never saw him again. For goodness sake! I'd only been with him for a couple of months, and that whole time he was begging me to have an orgy with him. Well, I did, I loved it and it's his fault. So there.

I realised that there was a big wide world out there to discover, and was taking full advantage of that. From how I'd been at school to how I felt now was an incredible change. People have scoffed at my parents for letting me have a nose job at the age of fifteen, but it was the best thing I ever did. It was like the child I'd always been, who was happy and larger than life, had been suffocated all those years I was bullied; then I'd had a simple operation which had resurrected that child. I was back to being the confident, bubbly girl I was before senior school and I was loving every minute of life. Something I also took notice of was that the more outrageous or skimpy my outfit was, the more attention I got from men and therefore the more confident I felt. After so many years of feeling ugly and worthless, it was pretty damn good to be looked at in a sexual or an appreciative way by men, so I played on it even more. I knew, and still know, that these feelings I have and the way in which I play on them are really just the old scars from the bullies. When I put on an extremely skimpy outfit, it was almost like I was hiding the real me. I gave off a glow of confidence when I entered a room and I held myself well. Men became almost scared of me and girls hated me. In my head it was OK, because I knew that they were probably just jealous that I got more attention than them. The outfits were like a barrier between me and the outside world. I almost felt that, if I dressed as differently as possible and *made* everyone look at me, I could cope with people pointing or staring. I brought it upon myself but, hey, whatever my motives, I enjoyed the attention so I carried on doing it.

At college I got my first taste of photography, although to start with I was behind the lens. For my work experience I went to be a photographer's assistant on the TV show *The Big Breakfast*. That's the type of person I am. I always wanted to be the best and make the most of myself. Everyone else went to work in clothes shops or offices and saw work experience as a chance to bunk off from doing any real work, school or otherwise, but I saw it as a chance to get somewhere. I was photographing Gina Lee Nolin and Mariah Carey. The photographer I was working with told me I should be in front of the lens, not behind it. I told him how it had always been my dream to be on Page 3 and he encouraged me to go topless for a set of pictures, which I then sent off to the *Sun*. They replied with a 'thanks, but no thanks' letter, which I now have framed in my house. I didn't take the rejection too well, to be honest – I didn't go to pieces or anything, but it was embarrassing and, until I did actually make it to Page 3, I didn't tell anybody about sending the pictures in.

While I was still at college, I also took a part-time job working at a nightclub in Romford called Hollywood. One day the DJ called me to ask if I would come and do the guest list on the door and host the VIP room. He said that the staff had discussed me and thought that I had the right image and attitude to do it. Turned out it was the perfect job for me. I was paid £75 a night to stand on the door for an hour looking outrageous and then go in and look after any VIPs who turned up. A picture of me in a sexy little Santa suit was printed on 150,000 flyers for Christmas and distributed around the whole of Essex. For my birthday they gave me the whole upstairs of the club for nothing to have a party, and even printed the invitations (again with my picture on) and gave me a case of champagne for my guests.

The female bar staff, who were on £3 an hour and weren't even allowed a free drink, took a serious disliking to me. Six of them beat me up one night at a club down the road. I was there on business, meeting with the manager to discuss doing a joint promotion, and they jumped me as I was leaving the club. I got away with two black eyes, all four of my car tyres stabbed and my whole car scratched to pieces with a key. I went to the police station the next day, where I was told there wasn't a lot they could do. Apparently, the only thing that amounts to anything in court these days is GBH, which means broken bones; as I didn't have broken bones, my attack would only be classed as ABH or common assault, which isn't so serious and would amount to no more than a slap on the wrist for the girls who had no other convictions. What he was trying to tell me was that I was wasting my time. Again, life's a fucking bitch. I left Hollywood after that. Well, actually, I stayed under the watchful eye of the doormen who had been told to look after me, until the night a club official locked me in his office, got his knob out and told me to suck it. 'If you come anywhere near me with your shrivelled cock,' I told him, 'I'll bite it off.'

It was at college that I started seeing my second long-term boyfriend, Dean Clark. He had been one of my group of friends since the days of my nose job and it was only natural that we became an item – I never really fancied him, but I loved his personality and he had become as close to me as a brother. Our sex life was a bit pants, to be honest, but we had sex regularly and it was OK, even if it never blew my socks off. I'd had a better time sexually when I worked at Hollywood and used to shag a DJ in the booth or in the office while the club was open.

I cared about Dean regardless and wanted so desperately to be in love again, the way I was with Dave. I tried to convince myself that Dean was 'the one'. He was three years older than me and, at six foot three, a very big bloke. He made me feel safe, and encouraged me to follow my dreams. Like a lot of young people, he had been lightly experimenting for years with pills, acid and speed, as had the rest of our group except me and Carlee, but he had a lot of other issues. I told him I would only get with him properly if he let me help him. He agreed that he would and moved into our house. With the aid of my mum, and some considerable time, he went back to being on top form, and we had a year and a half of happiness where my mum and dad jokingly called us Mr and Mrs Slippers because we spent so much time sitting around the house cuddling instead of going out. I thought that was what couples were supposed to do, and I enjoyed it.

For my eighteenth birthday, my parents bought me a miniature chihuahua whom I called Pixie. I had wanted one for years and they had finally given in to my whinging. She was what's known as a teacup – the smallest type of chihuahua you could get. In fact, we all thought that she might have been one of the smallest dogs in the world. My dad always said we should have measured her properly and sent the details to the *Guinness Book of Records*. I picked her myself. She was one of two left and was so small and fragile-looking I wanted her the minute I saw her. The breeder told us she was the runt of the litter, but, what she lacked in size, she more than made up for in personality. She was one of the most human dogs I had ever known (apart from Paddy, but more about him later); she wanted to be carried everywhere and Dean and I treated her like a human child. She never left my side. I even bought a Barbie rucksack for her to sit in. I honestly think that Pixie sometimes forgot that she was a dog. Because we treated her like a child, she grew used to the lifestyle and was never interested in dog toys or playing. The only thing she ever played with was my make-up, which she would run over and steal as I was applying it and hide it down the corridor, loving making me get up to retrieve it. Pixie was the absolute light of my life. No matter how down I was feeling, she perked me up and always made me smile.

I think the fact that Dean was so good with Pixie made me stay with him longer than I should have. It sounds strange to say it, but we were like a little family and I didn't want to ruin that. I just breezed through life in a little bubble of happiness, thinking I had it all. I think deep down I knew that Dean wasn't going to be the man I married, so it was with a slightly fake smile that I said yes to his proposal on New Year's Eve during a family holiday in Barbados. He went down on one knee on the stage in the hotel in front of all the guests and asked me over the microphone if I would marry him. He had bought a beautiful whole-carat diamond ring while we were out there and presented it to me that night. Although I didn't really feel like he was 'the one' and our sex life was boring (or rather I didn't want to have sex with him), I still revelled in the fact that I was engaged. It made me feel special and confident that I wasn't ugly. Someone wanted to marry me, so I couldn't be! We flew home and had a huge engagement party with all our friends and we all got very drunk. I had the feeling his mum and sister weren't too happy about the whole thing. His dad was sweet and had always been good to me, but both his mum and sister were like the nosey neighbours from hell. They used to sit in their front room drinking tea, smoking fags and gossiping. Every time they heard a noise outside, they would hold the net curtain a little bit to the side to see who was doing what. Curtain-twitchers. They didn't like me too much because, although they never said anything, I know they thought I was a rich little daddy's girl with a posh house and a flash car (my parents had bought me a Suzuki Vitara just before my seventeenth birthday). Their sarcastic comments and bitchiness towards others gave me a pretty good indication of how they felt about me.

When Dean went back to his old ways a few months later, it was all I needed to end it for good. I had never felt comfortable in his house because of his mum and sister (which was why I made him move into mine). I wasn't interested in his lifestyle and I didn't particularly want sex with him by then. It was over for good and I once again took up the partying.

CHAPTER FOUR

Boxing Beauty

It was only a few weeks after splitting with Dean that a programme I had filmed when I was with him was on TV. *Friday Night Fever* was about clubbing. and the producers had come to Hollywood and asked for some 'mad' clubbers to appear on the show. The management immediately put me forward and I had a little guest spot. I enjoyed my first five minutes of fame and thought nothing more of it.

By the time *Friday Night Fever* was shown, I was working in a bar in Romford called Connex, a trendy little place where people would come for a drink before going out clubbing. I was the promotions manager and worked all day and all night for terrible money. Still, I enjoyed the responsibility and the lively atmosphere. The night after my show was screened, I put the boxing on the big screens of Connex. I watched it along with the punters and thought nothing more of it until the following night. Who should enter but Garry Delaney, professional heavyweight and the very man I had watched fighting the night before. He walked into the bar and straight up to me. We struck up a conversation immediately. 'I saw you on TV last night,' I told him.

Garry smiled. 'Well,' he replied, 'I saw you on TV the night before.' It was clearly meant to be. That night the fire alarm went off and – feeling naughty – instead of staying around I legged it to my car with Garry and we decided to go clubbing. It was a Sunday night and the best thing on was at the Cross Club in Kings Cross where I had been quite a few times before. We partied the night away.

When my mum and dad met, they fell in love at first sight. I had always enjoyed hearing that story, and I had always hoped that the same would happen to me. We had only known each other a few hours and Garry was already acting like my boyfriend. I really felt it was the start of something special. He held my hand all night and kissed me lots. Garry was even bigger than Dean – six foot four and weighing about seventeen stone of pure muscle. When he wrapped his arms around me while we were sitting on some steps at the end of the night, I felt like nobody could ever hurt me again. I stayed at Garry's that night and spent the whole of the next day with him. While we were lying in bed that morning, he turned to look at me. 'Do you think it is possible to love someone at first sight?' he asked.

'Yes,' I replied, and told him about my parents and it was then that he told me he loved me. It seemed like the perfect match. The beauty and the beast. The brains and the brawn. Jodie and Garry. I liked it – no, I loved it. He was a professional boxer, and he was nine years older than me. He was big, gentle and soft. Most importantly, he believed in love at first sight. I told him I loved him too.

Garry was managed by Barry Hearn. Things weren't going as well as Garry had hoped for and within two days of meeting him, I took a termination document to Barry's office. Considering I was now without a job, having walked out of Connex that night never to go back, I took on the huge responsibility of looking after Garry's career. I read up on as much about boxing as I could find. It was decided that I would be his manager and we would just use promoters to get him fights.

Our first official date as a couple came four days later. I drove us to a nightclub in London called the Imperial Gardens which had been a favourite haunt of mine for a while as it played happy house music but was still quite underground. My parents had just bought me a brand new Vitara and I was happy to drive. We had a good night dancing and chatting to people when all of a sudden things turned nasty. A bloke looked at me as if trying to chat me up, and before I knew what was happening, there was a scuffle and then Garry ran out of the club. I followed to see him driving off in my car (he had been looking after the car keys as I didn't have a bag). He'd had a drink or two. My first reaction was to run after the car but, when he carried on driving, I just stood in the middle of the road and sobbed.

By this time the DJ, a friend of mine called Tony, was also out on the street with me. He put an arm around me and told me to come and wait inside. He said he would take me home and that he needed to explain a few things to me. But at that point Garry returned and took me off with him.

In the morning, Garry went back to being the person I had met four days earlier. He got up from the sofa where he had been watching TV and came over to me. I was still curled into a corner of the other sofa and he swept me into his arms and broke down. He told me how much he loved me and how sorry he was. He told me that his ex-girlfriend had left him recently, after ten years together, and that they had tried for a baby. As a result he was confused and upset and that's why he had flipped after having a few drinks. I couldn't cuddle him back. I was upset, but at the same time I felt as though I had been given a gift – the gift of protection. As long as I was with this man, nobody would ever hurt me again.

From a comment Tony had made to me the night before, it was obvious that Garry had a reputation around Essex and London that I had not known about. If I was known as this man's girlfriend, I thought to myself, I would be safe from all the horrible people who had picked on me over the years. Coldly and calculatingly I decided to give him another chance. I wanted to be with him, even with any flaws. For a while we spent a few blissful weeks lying in bed at his house in Hornchurch where I had practically moved in. I have never liked my own company as my brain is generally in overdrive, so I was glad to be with someone 24/7. It gave me somebody to talk to and bounce ideas and dreams off.

We got to work on a plan for how he was going to become the next Lennox Lewis and put it into action. I had seen him fight so knew he had the ability, but I thought he needed more of a gimmick to gain publicity and raise his profile – at that time all he had was the nickname The Hammer and the fact that he always boxed in claret and blue shorts as he was from West Ham. I had followed Prince Naseem's career for some time, so I knew that one of the reasons he was so well known was simply because he was such a character. Naz put on a show. People didn't just go to watch Naz fight, they went to see him perform. They loved the way he somersaulted into the ring and danced around cockily.

First off I went to a well-known ex-boxer's shop in the East End. He was called Charlie Magri. I ordered a new pair of shorts to be made to look like a skirt in the traditional claret and blue, and a pair of brand-new Adidas boxing boots that came right up the leg. I wanted Garry to stand out and look trendy. Hell, if David Beckham could wear a skirt, then so could Garry Delaney. Then I took him to the dentist and we ordered a clear plastic gumshield as opposed to the horrible coloured ones that so many boxers have. I also set about ordering a few T-shirts for myself: one said 'Boxer's Babe', one said 'Delaney's Girl' and a third had a picture of Garry on it from a previous win, holding his hands up as a sign of victory. Underneath it was the word 'Untouchable'. It looked like I was saying that Garry, as a boxer, was untouchable, but in reality I meant that I, as his girlfriend, was untouchable and that was how I felt.

After just a few weeks of being with Garry, my confidence grew. Word had spread around Brentwood and the surrounding areas of Essex that I was with him, and we were the talk of the town. Garry became my rock. I felt so safe when I was with him. I loved sitting in pubs in Brentwood with him, knowing that people were looking and talking about us. They can talk all they want, I thought to myself, but they're not going to abuse me to my face ever again.

A few weeks later, I decided it was time for Garry to meet my parents and I brought him over to the house. I wasn't worried that they wouldn't like him, as Garry was such a charmer. He was very well mannered and had such a way of speaking that most people really warmed to him. He came across as a gentle, lovable giant. We had a nice few hours with my parents and afterwards I drove him home. Later that night I came back to the house alone to get my parents' verdict. Both smiled (which I now know was forced) and told me he was lovely. The only negative comment came from my dad. 'I've known a few boxers in my time, Jodie,' he said. 'They always seem a bit heavy, even outside of the ring.'

'Don't worry, Dad,' I said. 'He's a big softie.' It seemed to put his mind at rest, and they accepted him as my new boyfriend. That same week, Garry took me to meet his family in East London. We met his mum and three brothers at a working men's club down the road from their house. They seemed very nice and were very friendly to me.

I set up a meeting with the boxing promoter Frank Warren. We told Frank that the contract between Garry and Barry Hearn was over and that Garry now wanted somebody to promote him. We told Warren exactly what we wanted money-wise and what we hoped to achieve, and he agreed to promote him.

Garry had moved down to cruiserweight, as he couldn't compete with the big boys at heavyweight – he was around fifteen stone and the big heavies were fighting at eighteen or nineteen stone. A fight was arranged and Garry began training. I helped to arrange sparring and spent many an hour at the gym watching him train. I got hold of a copy of the Boxing Board of Control rule book and a huge record book detailing every fighter's record of wins, losses and draws. I have a photographic memory, so I quickly memorised many of the cruiserweight division's stats. For a good month or so the guys at the gym refused to take me seriously or even talk to me. I was a laughing stock, the only girl in a hardcore East London gym spouting to anybody who would listen that I was Garry's manager and had big plans for him. My break came when one of the best boxing matchmakers in the country came and sat at my table in the canteen one day. He asked how much I knew about boxing and I told him to ask me a question. He put two boxers' names to me and asked what I thought of it as a match. I immediately recited their records, even down to how many knockouts each guy had had, and told him I thought it was a very good match. I knew I had impressed him, and from that day on people took me seriously.

Although our relationship was not always good, in a way, though, I did grow to love him. He certainly knew how to pull my strings. He was very big on flashy displays of affection and often came home with little presents for me, or whisked me off to fancy restaurants for dinner. Everybody raved to me about how wonderful he was, and even my parents seemed to have taken to him like a son. Deep down, however, I knew that things were far from being right. I also knew that it would break my parents' hearts if they ever found out that I wasn't happy, but somehow I felt like I couldn't live without him. I didn't feel strong enough inside to face the world alone, and I still felt that my bullies could in some way harm me if he was not by my side.

My dad's building company had built me a house in the grounds of my parents' home. I designed the interior and bought all the furniture. I had realised I wasn't ready to move out completely, having lived at Garry's for a while, when I missed the closeness I shared with my family. The house was built upside down: my bedroom, dressing room and bathroom are downstairs and the whole of the upstairs is an open-plan living room, kitchen and dining room. I loved it. It was my own house and space, but right next door to my parents. Garry and I moved in. It meant I lived as I would have done in a new house. I did all my own washing and cleaning but, being within walking distance, I could slip in and out of my parents' house as I wished. The house became known as 'the flat' and many a happy night was spent in there with friends.

A few months later, a friend of ours arranged a birthday party at Hollywood. I hadn't been back since the night one of the staff got his cock out in the office and I had no real desire to return. I told Garry all about it, and also about the girls who beat me up and who still worked there. Garry, being Garry, told me in no uncertain terms that we were going to the party. I got ready and drove us to the club with a feeling in the pit of my stomach that something bad was going to happen. When we got to the door, the manager greeted us with a smarmy, if slightly hesitant smile. Through gritted teeth and with a fake but menacing smile, Garry squeezed his hand so hard that he very nearly crushed every bone in it. The manager let out a little squeak and we walked through into the club with Garry muttering, 'One down…'

About an hour into our night, all the girls who had beaten me up – who were now on a night off and very drunk – started crowding round us. I nervously pushed up against Garry and hoped they'd go away. The atmosphere was tense, like when a big fight is about to kick off: looks were being thrown around and the odd insult from the girls was shouted in my direction. Garry pushed me behind him as they closed in on us and, quick as a flash, drinks were being thrown and the girls were on top of Garry, throwing punches and trying to get to me. I ducked under a rope to where the upstairs of the club was closed off. As I ran up the stairs, I turned round and saw two doormen escorting Garry away. I mouthed to him and pointed that I would see him outside, then ran upstairs, through a fire exit and down some stairs which brought me out into the car park. I ran to the front door of the club to see Garry in the foyer talking to the doormen and getting irate that we had been attacked and soaked by the drinks that had been thrown. I tried to tell him that we should leave, but he was having none of it. While he waited for the head doorman to come and sort it out, one of the nasty girls came running down the stairs holding her face and shouting that Garry had hit her. I believe that the girls, having realised what they had done and that they would be in trouble, quickly decided to make out that Garry had hit them so that it justified their own actions. One of the doormen, being a fierce believer in not hitting women, pounced on Garry, and four others joined in, dragging him to the floor. In the course of the fight, Garry's leg was broken.

I screamed at my friend whose birthday it was to call the police, and he ran off down the road. I stood and screamed hysterically at the men on top of Garry. Amid the chaos and with five huge men fighting in the foyer, a police car rolled up and suddenly everything was quiet again. Garry was helped up from the floor and taken to hospital in an ambulance while I stood and shouted at the police to do something. The girls had beaten me up once before; now they had thrown drinks over us and tried to harm me again, and, for that, Garry had been hurt. The police vowed to look into it and tried to calm me down as I was by now so angry that I was shouting obscenities through the tears.

I climbed into a car with my mate to follow Garry to the hospital. Once there, the wait to be seen was around six hours and Garry, being absolutely covered in blood, just wanted to get home and clean himself up. He didn't even know at that point that his leg was broken – he just thought he had twisted it in the fight. My friend and I helped him to limp out of the hospital, where we were confronted by two policemen who arrested Garry on suspicion of attacking some girls in the club. He then spent another few hours in the police station while my friend and I sat on the floor with our heads in our hands. When he was finally released, I took him home and helped to clean him up. We had a few hours of restless sleep and in the morning we drove to another hospital in Essex where we waited another five hours to be seen before being told that his leg was badly broken. He needed an operation and would be in a cast for a number of weeks.

As a result of that hideous night, Garry was taken to court for his supposed attacks on the girls and we went through weeks of agony; I spoke as a witness and had to face the evil bitches in the courtroom. Our 'friend' whose birthday it was refused to give evidence because his mum didn't want him to be involved. The thought of Garry being locked up terrified me, so the day the jury announced their verdict of not guilty, I cried loud tears of joy from the gallery, and hugged my parents who were with me for moral support. We went out that night to celebrate, and Garry wore a T-shirt with 'Not Guilty' printed on the front in huge letters. The doormen who battered Garry and ruined his boxing career for a whole year got away scot-free.

CHAPTER FIVE

Ministry of Madness

After the whole hideous affair was over, we set about rebuilding his career and our lives. During the trial, I had taken a job with my parents in the office, as Garry was out of action and unable to box. I had to support the pair of us financially. He spent all day watching TV and had daily visits from a nurse to clean up his leg wound, as it had become infected.

Garry gradually started to train again with me behind him, spurring him on. I took a job at the Ministry of Sound. Gareth Cooke, a DJ I had known from Hollywood, was now promoting the Friday nights there and wanted someone glamorous to do the door for him. He already had a gorgeous-looking guy, but he needed a girl to work alongside him.

I turned up and met my door partner, Kyle Kaine. Kyle was the loveliest, warmest person I had ever met, and I fell in love at first sight. Unfortunately, he was also gay. His opening line to me was 'Is that 01 Beech?' – he was referring to the lipliner I was using. We bonded there and then over a Body Shop lip colour. I spent the next year trying to turn him straight, but, having realised it wasn't going to happen, I accepted it and, after eight years, we're still best friends and soul mates.

It was while working at Ministry that I met Dave Courtney, the infamous celebrity gangster, and Ricardo who would later find fame in *The Salon*. Dave became a firm friend. I was attracted to his reputation of being a hard man, and to his power within the underworld. Dave and I had our moments of flirting outrageously and getting drunk together in Ministry, and I discovered that he's actually a big softie who loves the ladies. Ricardo was just as outrageous then as he is now, and provided me and Kyle with much entertainment. He turned up every week in skimpier outfits than I've ever worn, if that's possible, and got ridiculously drunk. Occasionally we found him at the end of the night, lying on the floor of the toilets wearing just a silver sparkly bikini! Oh, yes, he knows how to party, that one!

Ministry was good for me. There wasn't any bitchiness, I loved my role there and Kyle was one in a million. It was the most popular club in London, where we partied until dawn and dressed outrageously. Loads of celebs passed through the doors and it was our job to look after them. Kyle and I were like a double act. We complemented each other perfectly and were more than polite to everyone, even if we were turning people away. One night a guy at the front of the queue had jeans on, which were against the dress policy. He was alone and told us he had come all the way from Liverpool to celebrate a friend's birthday. He begged us to let him in. There wasn't anything we could do. It was more than our jobs were worth to let him in wearing jeans, so we explained that, if he could get a pair of trousers from somewhere, he could come in – but it was hardly possible for him to go home and come back again. Not knowing what to do and with us not being able to help him, he stood chatting for a few minutes. Suddenly, the local tramp who slept under the arches beside the club staggered past. Kyle and I used to chat to him on a nightly basis and give him hot drinks from the vending machine in the office. We said hello and the guy from Liverpool turned to see who we were talking to. Without a second's hesitation, he ran after the tramp – who had been wearing the same piss-soaked corduroy trousers for the last six months – and offered him a deal he couldn't refuse. The guy swapped his brand new Levi 501s *and* 50 quid for the tramp's cords. They stripped in the street to exchange trousers. The tramp danced off down the street in what looked like a scene from a musical, jumping and clicking his heels together in mid-air; we walked the guy from Liverpool into the club at arm's length, holding our noses. Kyle and I had many an entertaining night like this one. Through the cold winter months, we stood on the door wearing thick duffel coats and drinking hot tomato soup to keep warm. We nicknamed ourselves the 'market traders', as that's what we looked like. Ministry was great fun too. On one special occasion, they set up a big wheel fairground ride in the courtyard entrance and another time they drove a tank full of clubbers through the streets of London. I felt proud to be a part of clubbing history and to mingle with the likes of Judge Jules and Pete Tong. DJs at that time were more popular than celebs and thousands turned up and queued for half-a-mile down the road to get into the club.

Working three jobs, I was very busy and Garry recovered fully. His career took off again and he started to do really well. He had a few warm-up fights against journeymen – guys who aren't that good but just fight for the sake of it – before fighting for the Southern Area title. When I met him, he was already holding the WBO Penta-Continental and the WBO Intercontinental. The Southern Area, however, was a real grudge match fight against the reigning champion Dominic Negus, another big face in boxing around London and Essex. The night of the fight was so exciting: the atmosphere in the boxing hall was electric and, to make things even better, Garry and I were flying to Barbados two days later. It was his treat to me for sticking by him through the whole horrible trial and for nursing him better. Over the years I had been to Barbados loads of times with my family, and we always stayed at the same hotel. It had become almost like a second home to me. I knew all the local people and all the staff in the hotels, restaurants, bars and shops out there. This, however, was the first time I would be going without my mum, dad and brother – and I couldn't wait!

It felt like everything was going our way. Even though Garry still lost his cool occasionally when he was drunk, every other aspect of my life seemed good. I was prepared to turn a blind eye to his moods for the sake of an otherwise perfect relationship with a successful and respected boxer who kept me safe from others and treated me well. Garry won the fight while I was outside being sick with nerves for him, and we partied hard afterwards. A local pub threw a party for him and we invited all our friends to join us. It was the night before we were due to fly to Barbados and everyone got very drunk. As usual we had an amazing night; however, Garry changed when he got home. A girlfriend of mine called Jess had pulled a mate of Garry's at the party and had gone home with him, having only just met him that night. Garry decided from this that he didn't like her, and was angry with me for being friends with her.

I tried to play on his conscience by telling him that we were going to have an amazing time away together. I even pretended that I agreed with him about Jess. It seemed to work. He spent the next few hours on the sofa while I cried quietly in the bedroom and wondered to myself when the time would come that I would be strong enough to face the world alone. Stupidly, in my weakness, I boarded the plane that morning, slightly nervous about being so far away, but also happy at the thought that I was going 'home'.

We spent the first week in absolute bliss while I revelled in showing Garry the whole island. Our balcony looked over a beautiful, pure white, empty beach, and every night we sat together and watched the sun set. I actually thought for a while that things might change one day and that it could be lovely like this forever.

I was wrong.

On the third night of our second week, we went out for dinner with a couple we had met. We had a lovely time and, as we were chatting, the conversation turned to how violent the world was becoming. A few weeks earlier, a friend of mine who worked on the door of a pub in Brentwood had been hit on the head with a lump of metal. I had been in the pub that night and happened to be carrying a small bottle of liquid Savlon around with me as I had just had my belly button pierced. Before my friend was taken away to have stitches, I cleaned the blood up and applied some Savlon to the gash, which was very deep. The conversation was purely about the nastiness that goes on in pubs and clubs around the country and, after the meal, we said our goodnights. Garry and I walked back to our room hand in hand. 'I didn't know you cleaned his head up,' he said quietly.

'Yes,' I replied. 'I thought you knew.' He certainly knew I had been there that night as I was out with my brother, and we told him all about the awful fight that had kicked off. He started to get quite ratty, stating again that I hadn't told him that I was the one to clean the blood away.

'It doesn't matter, Garry,' I argued back softly. 'All I did was wipe the blood away with some tissue soaked in Savlon.'

Instantly Garry was in a foul temper. Once inside the room, we didn't speak as I got into my little nightdress and took out my contact lenses. When I tried to slip into bed next to him where he was lying on top of the covers, still fully clothed, he shouted at me. I tried to reason with him again softly, but in the end I left the apartment. I was just in my nightie and bare feet. I was in floods of tears and I knew it was the end of our relationship. Barbados was my favourite place in the world: I had always dreamed of getting married and eventually retiring there. Garry had destroyed that for me. He had ruined my perfect vision of the place. I wouldn't be able to bring myself to go back there for the next four years.

The hotel owner was amazing and offered me another room, but the couple we had been to dinner with were still up and they offered the spare bed in their suite, which I took. They gave me a T-shirt and shorts to wear until, two days later, I needed to go back into the room to get some things. We didn't really connect again properly for the rest of the holiday, although I made peace with him on the surface and accepted his pathetic apologies. We spent the last couple of days together, but I couldn't afford another flight home and it was better being a 'loving' girlfriend to Garry. Moreover, I still didn't want my mum and dad to find out that it was almost over, so it would be easier to pretend everything was good and then split up with him somehow when we got home.

I spent the week after we returned home working out how to end it with Garry.

I needed to twist things to make it look as though he had walked out on me. The opportunity came one night when we were out in our local nightclub. A girl I knew called Jane was with us, and she looked particularly sexy. Garry spent most of the night looking at her, and I clocked this. Knowing that he wouldn't get too angry in such a public place, I confronted him about Jane, asking if he fancied her. Sure enough, it started a row, and we stood and had a slanging match in the club until Garry got to boiling point. He did the right thing and turned and walked straight out of the door. It was exactly what I had hoped for.

For three days I ignored his calls, hoping he would get the message and leave me in peace, but one day I came home to find him kicking at the door to my flat. My parents were out, but my brother was with me and between the pair of us we tried to reason with him, without any luck. Eventually we had to threaten to call the police if he didn't go away.

That day was the first time I told my parents a little of what our relationship was like, and from then on they received calls from him too. The calls would keep coming throughout the night until the early hours and he wouldn't be making sense as he shouted down the phone. My parents took to leaving the phone off the hook and I switched my mobile off. This only irritated him more: he would relax a bit when he heard my voice. For this reason I didn't change my mobile number. I put up with the calls for a number of weeks until they began to get less frequent, and my life gradually started to calm down. My dad and I informed the police of his behaviour and they made a note of the messages he left and the texts he sent. We just wanted to have it on record. Life then started to calm down and I resumed a proper job. Ministry had begun to bore me, and the cold nights of standing on the door until the small hours had become painful. I left there to concentrate on getting my life straight.

One night I was moping around the house when my brother insisted I go out with him. Not feeling up to it but saying yes anyway, to keep him happy, we went to our local nightclub where I sat at the bar by myself while my brother and his mates went off to chat up some girls. I didn't move off the stool for a good hour, until a girl approached me and introduced herself. I recognised her from being out and about in Brentwood. Her name was Rachael, and she was by herself too. Her other friends had gone home early and, not ready to leave, she had decided to befriend me. Her first words to me after introducing herself were 'Want a shot?'

She flagged down the barman, ordered four sambucas and handed me two of them with a large grin. I returned the favour, and before we knew it we had sunk about ten each and were gyrating on the dance floor like a couple of lesbians. I fell into bed that night happy that I had made a new friend and that she was as mad as me!

Rachael introduced me to her other mates: Kim, Tasha, Becky, Lauren and Jo. I got on well with all of them and they accepted me into their group immediately. I still had other friends, such as Kyle and my London clubbing crew, but for the first time in my life I now had friends who lived in Brentwood. I loved Rachael to bits and got on with all the girls but Kim was the most like me. She had a hyper energy that matched mine and was the only one willing to party every single night of the week. She spent all her spare time at mine or she would come and pick me up to go to the pub. She reminded me of myself and of the days I used to go clubbing without drinking. By now I had begun to enjoy the dizziness and confidence that alcohol brought, but Kim still managed to dance all night on orange juice. We had exactly the same taste in men – big, hard blokes – and we were as attention-seeking (in the nicest possible way!) as each other.

My brother Jordan, who had performed as a solo act in local pubs since he was sixteen, now had a band and was gigging all over Essex. I went to every gig with my parents and had always supported him. Now the girls started coming too. Five of us, all single, would spend hours at my house, pampering ourselves and singing and dancing, and at weekends we would support my brother in pubs. Jordan occasionally asked us to get up and sing backing for him to songs like 'Mustang Sally' and 'Gimme Some Lovin''. We loved it – Kim and I especially would jump to get behind the microphone. As a result, five of us – myself, Kim, Rachael, Jo and Tasha – decided that we should form a girl band. None of us could sing particularly well, but we thought that it didn't matter. Jordan had nicknamed us The Chickens, as he said that was what we sounded like when we were all together. None of us ever shut up and he said our constant babbling and high-pitched giggling reminded him of a group of chickens clucking. The Chickens became the temporary name of our band. We decided on a few songs and got the words off the Internet while my brother learned them on piano. Three nights a week we met at my house to 'practise' our songs – 'Never Ever' by All Saints and 'Build Me Up Buttercup' by The Foundations. I don't know if we really thought we were going to get anywhere, but it provided much amusement and laughter anyway. Jordan despaired of the fact that none of us could sing in tune, but he humoured us with our new project and sat for hours playing along to our warbling. We soon got bored of the whole thing, but Kim, Rachael and I continued to sing with his band at gigs.

I got back with Garry after a few months and everyone else soon had boyfriends, including Kim, but that didn't stop me seeing the girls. Kim and her boyfriend John, in particular, spent lots of time with us as a couple. We would still go to Jordan's gigs but also went out to dinner together or had pool parties at mine. Kim was the bubbliest girl I'd ever known. She bounced her way through life, singing and dancing and making people laugh. I loved her energy and always called her if I needed cheering up. We were like partners in crime.

Kim and I both had a weakness for men and, after I finally split with Garry for good, but before she started seeing John, we spent all our summer days staking out fit blokes in pubs. Like me, she had a wild and dangerous side to her and loved doing things spontaneously. I fondly recall one hot summer's afternoon when, on pulling into the car park in my open-top jeep, we attracted the attention of two fit blokes with their tops off. One look at their muscle-bound torsos encouraged us to invite them to join us at our table. Kim kept forgetting their names, so she nicknamed them Harry and Jarry and it stuck. The four of us sat there drinking for a few hours and I got in trouble with my mum because I was late showing up for a barbecue they were hosting. As Kim and I hurriedly left, we swapped numbers and told them we would see them later.

As we dressed for our 'date' after dinner, we giggled to ourselves. Harry and Jarry were *very* fit, and we couldn't wait to see them again. We met them in another local pub, where we sat in the warm air of the summer evening and drank. Suddenly, though, the weather took a turn for the worse: the heavens opened and it started to pelt it down. We darted to Kim's car and sat inside with our drinks – hardly the exciting date we had imagined! Realising we couldn't sit in the car all night, we drove off in the direction of my house, thinking we could go back and watch a film. On the way back, however, I decided that I really fancied the one we called Jarry. Kim had come to the decision that she didn't fancy either, but snogged Harry anyway while I snogged Jarry to keep things balanced. When they had gone, she pretended to be sick and told me that his breath was 'rancid' and that he had yellow teeth. We fell about laughing as she gagged and jokingly moaned that she always got the rough one. That's how Kim was: hilariously funny, supportive of her mates and the best friend a girl could ever have.

I was now working full time for my parents. Their bookkeeper had decided she wanted to give up work, so I took a six-week crash course in bookkeeping and took over the whole accounts system for their building company. It wasn't something I wanted to do forever: the job gave me permanent headaches from sitting at a computer all day, and I was surrounded by what I considered to be 'old' people. The youngest person apart from me was 48. Even so, the money was OK and I felt like I had a proper job for the first time ever. I'd only ever worked with people, nightclubs and boxers before, so to hold down a nine-to-five job was different and interesting for a while. I also felt good that I played an important part in the company and wasn't just an office junior, and I enjoyed the fact that the job was taxing my brain. My parents were very happy with the way I worked, and probably secretly hoped that I might actually start running the company myself one day – something they had wanted my brother and me to do since we were born. It was never going to happen, though. The thrill of having a responsible job soon wore off and I hated the fact that I was stuck at a desk all day with 50-year-olds for company. I craved attention from men and also the sort of attention I had got years earlier when I was paid to dance on Tuesday nights in a cage suspended from the ceiling at a place called the O Bar in Soho.

I set to work finding a part-time dancing job in a club. I thought I could still work throughout the week for my parents and dance at weekends. It paid good money, I loved the limelight and it kept me fit. Through a friend, I met the owner of Café de Paris in the West End. He was a really nice guy called Jamie and he offered me a test run as a dancer one night on a podium. When I had finished, Jamie told me I danced very sexily, almost like a lap dancer. 'Have you ever been to a strip club?' he asked.

'I went to Stringfellows once,' I told him. Jamie offered to take me back, saying that they went regularly and would be well looked after. Not one to miss an opportunity, I got my stuff together and left with him and his mates to go to Stringfellows.

Once inside, we were escorted to a table and Jamie ordered a bottle of vodka and a bottle of champagne. Girls were coming over every five minutes and trying to get all of us to have dances. Jamie expertly declined and grinned at me suggestively as I sat in awe of the beautiful girls. After a while – and half a bottle of vodka – Jamie accepted a dance from a stunning blonde and I sat in a state of excitement as she stripped for him. She started off slowly, gyrating in front of him and standing just between his legs. Within 30 seconds, her top was off. She had fake but lovely boobs, and was running her hands all over them as she bent down over Jamie's grinning face to hold her nipples just centimetres from his nose. I was squirming in my chair by now – I felt very turned on and couldn't take my eyes off her body. A minute went by and she was down to just her thong, which came off quite quickly to reveal her shaven pussy. In the subdued lighting and with pumping music, she looked amazing, and I felt the need to have someone dance for me – pronto!

After the dance was over, the girl chatted to Jamie casually as she put her clothes back on and he gave her £20. She kissed him on the cheek and walked away. Jamie turned to me. 'Your turn,' he said.

I couldn't wait. Jamie told me to pick a girl I wanted to dance for me, and I began to scan the club. Being the perfectionist I am, I wanted the best-looking girl I could find. Inside the club, there were TV screens everywhere showing live images from the stage downstairs where the girls were taking it in turns to pole dance. After watching that for a while, I suddenly saw the most beautiful-looking girl and pointed her out to Jamie. 'I want her!' I said in his ear.

By now, all Jamie's mates were having dances; I was surrounded by naked girls and couldn't wait to have one of my own.

'How do we get her?' I asked.

'Leave it to me,' he said, and disappeared downstairs.

Five minutes later he was back with the babe in tow. She walked over to my chair, smiled and shook my hand. 'Hello,' she said. 'My name's Holly.' She looked even better than she did on the screen, and I was confident that I had picked the sexiest girl in the club. I was eagerly sitting upright on my chair, leaning forwards in anticipation; she began her dance by pushing me back into the chair in a sexy dominatrix style. As I sat back to enjoy the dance, I just caught the smug look on Jamie's face as he too sat back to have a perv. Starting in the same way as Jamie's dancer, Holly opened my legs, stood between them and began gyrating her hips. Her knees rubbed against mine as she danced slowly and sexily. I could barely contain myself as she peeled off her top. Her breasts were full and pert – obviously fake but perfect nevertheless, and I desperately wanted to touch them. She stroked herself and played with her nipples before bending down to me.

Her head was now over my shoulder and her boobs were nearly touching my face. It was all I could do to sit on my hands and lick my lips as her nipple 'accidentally' brushed my cheek. I could feel her breath on my neck; I could smell her, and my God she smelled so good. It wasn't a strong, overbearing perfume, but a smell more like some kind of body lotion. She smelled good enough to eat and her skin glistened in the lights, which got me even more excited. By now she was down to her thong. She stood up and turned so that her peachy arse was in my face. I snapped back to reality for a second and, looking at Jamie sitting opposite, mouthed in mock frustration, 'I want to touch her!' He laughed and I averted my eyes back to the beautiful smooth bum just inches from my face. She had turned her head to look at me and smouldered like she was about to climax. By now, my knickers were well and truly wet, and I felt like I was on fire. I'd always been very sexual and always had good sex, but this was a new kind of turn-on. She turned to face me one last time and slowly rolled her knickers down to her thighs, before she then let them fall to the floor. Her pussy was shaven into a little landing strip. It was beautiful. She had curves in all the right places and a long mane of honey-coloured hair which brushed against me every time she got close.

My senses were incredibly heightened by now, and her smell was driving me wild. I craved to touch her or lick her perfect skin. She looked me in the eye as she touched her breasts, slowly running her hands down over her stomach to her thighs, just brushing past the smooth sides of her tight little minge. It was as if nobody else existed – it was just the two of us. I was so aroused that for a moment I considered whether I might be a lesbian. Naked in front of me, she was turning me on as much as – if not more than –any fit man, and flashing through my head were thoughts of joining her in stripping off and making love to her there and then. She knew that I was excited, and I could see that she was enjoying it. She kept eye contact at all times, apart from when she looked down at her body as she touched herself and looked back at me to get a reaction. I sat the whole time, biting my bottom lip, as I imagined what I wanted to do to her and tried to stop myself from touching her. I was very hot and could feel sweat forming underneath the rubber top I had on. My own nipples were erect with excitement and grazing against the rubber. If she had touched me at that moment, I think I would have come on the spot.

Suddenly the song she was dancing to came to an end and she leaned over, kissed me on the cheek and bent down to pick up her discarded clothes, including the thong. As she sat down beside me, I grinned at Jamie and breathed out. 'Wow!'

'Was that OK for you?' she asked.

'It was incredible,' I told her. I said that she smelled

amazing and that it had been difficult to avoid touching her.

'Thank you,' she laughed, as Jamie slipped her some money. She kissed me again and told me to enjoy my night. It was only then that I turned to see all Jamie's mates staring open-mouthed at me. They had watched the whole dance and had clearly been as turned on as I was. One by one they started talking and soon I couldn't hear any of them as they talked over one another, saying how gorgeous she was and that she gave me a better dance than the dances they had had.

Jamie asked me what I thought. I grinned sheepishly. 'Amazing,' I said quietly. I was buzzing and my face was flushed with excitement.

'Welcome to the club,' replied Jamie, as I lit a cigarette and sat back to compose myself.

I couldn't stop thinking about Holly for the rest of the night, although I didn't see her again – she must have gone downstairs. She had totally blown me away. I had never felt so in awe of a woman or wanted to touch one so badly before. I had dabbled in playing with girls before on occasion, like the time I had the fivesome, but I had never felt so strongly turned on by a woman or wanted to start eating her there and then. At the end of the night, Jamie said he would take me there again next week. I wasn't going to say no.

CHAPTER SIX

Peter's Angels

The following week, I made my way to Café de Paris, did an hour's dancing on a podium and then took off with Jamie and a few friends to Stringfellows. I told Jamie on the way that I wanted to have another dance from Holly and he agreed that she was stunning and extremely sexy. 'But you're just as sexy,' he said. 'It turned me on to see you dance tonight. Would you ever consider lap dancing?'

'Yes, probably,' I replied, although to be honest it was not something I had ever considered. I suppose I didn't think I would ever have the confidence to dance naked in front of someone. I could do it at home, perhaps, but not in a nightclub.

When we reached the club, we soon discovered that Holly wasn't working, so I had a dance from another girl. It was still very erotic and I thoroughly enjoyed it, but she wasn't quite as sexy as Holly. Still, we had a great night and got quite merry on the vodka at our table. Towards the end of the night I had another dance from a girl called Amy. She was a very petite girl with real boobs and shoulder-length blonde hair. She seemed different to all the other glamorous women in there, more real somehow. She actually reminded me of myself. She was cute and girly, but a little bit tomboyish – nothing like the tall, elegant, if slightly plastic-looking strippers that all the others seemed to be. After my dance, she sat down next to me for the usual routine of getting dressed. 'Why do you come in here?' she asked.

'I like it.'

'What I mean is, you should be working here instead of paying for dances.'

I laughed nervously. 'I don't think I'd be much good,' I told her.

'Rubbish,' she said. 'You'd make a lot of money. You're a really pretty girl with big boobs – the men would love you. I make £500 a night, sometimes more. You'd easily make that.'

Suddenly it was a serious proposition. Although deep down I still didn't think I could do it, the money if nothing else had got my interest. If one of the other girls had told me all this, I think I would have just laughed it off and thought nothing more of it – I was so far removed from these Californian-looking Barbie Doll women. They all wore long sparkly dresses and were dripping in jewels, their hair was big and bouffed and their nails were perfectly manicured. There was no way I could compete. I was happier in tiny hot pants and biker boots, I hadn't had my nails done in years, preferring to keep them short and square, and I hated long dresses. Their heroes were themselves – mine were Pamela Anderson and Angelina Jolie. Amy, very real and similar to me, put a whole new slant on it. 'If I can do it, then so can you,' she told me. Coming from her, it seemed almost realistic.

She told me to wait there. I told Jamie in disbelief that she thought I should come and work there. Five minutes later she was back with an older guy in tow whom she introduced as her boss, Roger. Roger kissed my hand to greet me and asked if I was enjoying myself. I told him I was and that it was my second time at the club. Amy then said, 'See, Roger, wouldn't she be great? Tell her she could work here!' Roger smiled and agreed, telling me that I'd go down a storm. He said that normally they held auditions, but I wouldn't need to attend – the job was mine if I wanted it and he would happily let me start work tomorrow night.

'I'm flattered,' I told him, 'but I'm not sure I'm up to it. I'll have to have a think.' After our little chat, Amy hung around for a while and told me the ins and outs of the job. When we were ready to leave, she wrote her number down and told me to call her if I wanted to know anything else. I left the club grinning from ear to ear and chatting away excitedly to Jamie, who thought that I should definitely work there. My head was spinning. On the one hand I was gobsmacked that Roger had thought me good enough to work there without even seeing me audition, and the money *was* fantastic; on the other hand I didn't want to bring shame upon my parents, and I didn't know if I really had the guts to dance naked for a living.

I went home in a daze, my head whirling with thoughts of how I would spend that sort of money and how exciting it would be to say, 'I am a lap dancer.' I kept thinking how all my bullies from school would react to the news that I had become a stripper – not just any old stripper, but one at the best lap-dancing club in the world. Doing a job like that would finally prove to myself, and to them, that I wasn't ugly.

I decided to speak to my parents first. I knew that, when it came down to it, if they didn't want me to do it, then I wouldn't. The next day, when they were home from work, I said to them, 'I need to talk to you.' Immediately they looked worried, as any parent would when their kids say that. I asked them to sit down and I came straight out with it. 'I've been offered a job as a lap dancer.' My mum gasped and my dad's eyes widened in surprise. Before they could say anything, I added, 'Hear me out, though.' I told them all about the club, about how much money I could make and how nice Amy had been. I assured them that it was very strictly run, that no touching was allowed and that many of the girls were just like me. The only thing I failed to bring myself to tell them was that it was fully nude. I said that it was topless dancing and reasoned that blokes saw me on the beach topless for nothing so why shouldn't I make some money from them looking at me in a club?

I think my parents were quite relieved that I hadn't said 'I'm pregnant'. They sat quietly for a minute, before bombarding me with a torrent of questions. What exactly did I have to do? Was it honestly just topless? Were the blokes definitely not allowed to touch? I assured them that it was all above board and asked for their blessing in taking the job. I also assured them that it wouldn't be a permanent thing and that I just wanted to do it for a little while to make some money; in the meantime, I would figure out what I was going to do with my life.

My dad was the first to agree that it might be good for me. The first thing to have crossed his mind was that taking the job might boost my confidence. It's not that I was exactly shy and retiring, but my parents had been on at me for years to pursue my dreams of modelling. Having sent pictures to the *Sun* years before, only to be rejected, had knocked my confidence and I had been on a large number of auditions and castings for modelling work and failed repeatedly. I had all but given up on ever getting anywhere. My dad thought that working at Stringfellows might give me the boost I needed to try again. My mum wasn't as readily agreeable. She didn't really like the idea, and stressed to me that she would be worried what people would think if they found out that their daughter was a lap dancer. My dad hurriedly put her straight on that: firstly, we didn't have to broadcast it; secondly, so what? If I was making good money and enjoying myself then it wouldn't matter what other people thought. After much discussion, my mum came round to the idea and said that she would give me her blessing as long as I promised that it wasn't going to be a permanent thing. I agreed that I would only do it for as long as it took to boost my confidence and find something else.

Later that day I phoned Roger. 'I'm probably going to take the job,' I told him.

'Great,' he said. 'When do you want to start?'

I suddenly felt terrified. 'When are the auditions?' I asked, trying to stall the starting date.

'Tomorrow,' he replied. 'But, like I said, you don't have to audition.'

'I know,' I told him, 'but I'd rather not be thrown in at the deep end, and I don't want any special treatment.' In a way that was true – I had learned from working at Hollywood that special treatment just leads to jealousy. I wanted to start the same way as all the other girls. 'Do you mind if I come and audition with everybody else?'

'OK,' he said, 'if that's what you want. Auditions are at seven o'clock. Bring a dress and a thong.'

I spoke to my parents again and told them that I had booked an audition slot for the following night, and they offered to drive me there. I accepted straight away, as I thought I'd be too nervous to drive anyway and I felt comforted by the thought of them waiting outside for me. The next night came far too quickly. All day I panicked over what to wear, and physically shook with nerves while I was getting ready. Just before we were about to leave, I said I'd forgotten something and ran back into the house. I took a small empty Evian bottle and went to the bar. I filled it up with half vodka and half lemonade. It still looked like water but I knew it would relax me on the way there. I sat in the back of the car and chatted away about anything and everything to try and calm my nerves, sipping constantly on the vodka. By the time we got to the club, I was feeling very merry but still extremely nervous.

As I walked in, I was confronted by dozens of half-naked girls getting ready for their night's work. I went downstairs, where girls lay all over the sofas eating and applying make-up. It reminded me of being backstage in a theatre – it was as if they were getting ready to put on a big performance as they chattered away loudly, not paying me a blind bit of notice. I scanned the crowd for Roger but couldn't see him, so I approached a girl instead. 'Excuse me,' I asked, 'do you know where I go to audition?'

She pointed me in the direction of the dressing room. 'Go and see the house-mum,' she said. Nervously I opened the big, gold-framed door and stepped inside to find a frenzy of naked women. Two hairdressers were blow-drying and straightening in a corner, a make-up artist was trying to get a girl to sit still and a queue of girls waited to see a glamorous woman at the far side of the room whom I immediately presumed was the house-mum. She must have been in her fifties, and sat talking soothingly to a girl who was obviously upset. I joined the queue and stood nervously, trying not to make eye contact with anyone while I soaked up what was going on inside the room. Never before had I seen so many naked girls in one place. One whole wall of the room was mirrored and two girls with fake boobs stood looking at themselves, comparing scars. Next to me a stark-naked girl was rubbing moisturiser into her legs; on the other side, another stark-naked girl was sitting on the floor wrapping Sellotape around a broken shoe.

I found the whole situation fascinating and tried to take in as much as I could about my surroundings. I had taken my bottle of vodka and lemonade in with me, so I continued to sip on that as I waited. Eventually I came to the front of the queue and the woman smiled warmly and asked how she could help. I told her I was here to audition and she said that I would need to go to the office, which was at the far end of the club. I thanked her and left the carnage of the dressing room to find the office. Once there, another woman gave me a form to fill out, and then I sat with the other auditioning girls watching the antics in the club. I was just wondering if Amy was in that night when, lo and behold, she appeared. She came over to say hello and I told her that I was auditioning. 'You're mad,' she laughed, 'but good luck anyway.'

'What will I have to do,' I asked.

'Perform a pole dance on the show stage,' she said. 'You won't have to go naked, but you will have to go down to a thong.' It sounded absolutely terrifying.

Roger appeared minutes later and told our group of six

to make our way to the show stage. Then he winked at me. 'Here goes,' I said to Amy, and she promised to watch as I danced.

I had never danced on a pole before, but luckily the vodka had really kicked in by then. I knew that my dancing skills were good enough, but I was more worried about the stripping off. I had chosen a long turquoise dress to wear – the only sophisticated thing I owned – with an American stars-and-stripes bikini thong underneath. We took it in turns to audition and, when my turn came, I was physically shaking and felt sick with nerves. Knowing that Amy was watching and Roger liked me made me feel better, though, and I gave the performance my best shot. Facing the show stage was a wall of mirrors, and there was another one behind the stage. The mirrors made it easier to dance because you could actually see what you were doing. I started off slowly, walking sexily round the centre pole. When it came to taking the top of my dress down, I faced the back, peeled it down slowly and spun round the pole one-handed to reveal my boobs to Roger and the huge group of girls that had gathered to watch the auditions. Roger smiled and Amy wolf-whistled. It gave me confidence and I finished the dance with a number of sexy moves round the pole until I was just in my thong. Roger held his hands up to signal 'enough', and Amy started clapping. I nervously stood rooted to the stage, still undressed and looking at Roger for some reassurance that I was good enough. There was an unnerving silence before he shouted, 'Will you marry me?'

The girls who were watching seemed delighted that their boss had loosened up for a moment. They whooped and cheered as he followed it with, 'I think I'm in love!' I grinned ecstatically and gathered my dress from the floor.

Once dressed, I went over to see Roger. 'You're extremely good,' he told me. 'Are your boobs your own?'

'Yes.'

'You're going to do very well here. Make sure you're here at seven o'clock tomorrow.'

I practically ran out of the club to my parents' car. I jumped in and told them that I had done really well. The buzz of Roger's reaction was incredible. I couldn't believe that he honestly thought I was so good, especially when there were so many perfect-looking girls in the club! Horrible, scary audition over, I buzzed the whole way home and went to sleep smiling.

The next day, although I was still buzzing from the night before, I realised I had actually only practised the easy bit. Pole dancing on stage hadn't been that different to dancing on a podium in a normal nightclub, but the thought of stripping totally naked for someone privately still sent shivers through my body. Somehow, now that the reality of what I was going to have to do had sunk in, I wasn't sure if I could go through with it. I needed time to psych myself up, so I called Roger and said that I wouldn't be able to make it in that night. I made up some lame excuse about having to go somewhere else, but I told him I would be in the following night.

The next day came and I tried desperately to think of another excuse not to go in. I didn't even have anything to wear! Eventually, as the day wore on, I realised that I would either have to go in or forget it for good. I looked in my wardrobe and found a red skirt that I normally wore as a dress. As I put it into a carrier bag, along with another Evian bottle of vodka, I wondered what on earth I was doing. I took the same thong, now washed, that I had worn the other night, and set off in my car.

Once at the club, I had to sign in with the house-mum. I also had to choose a name for myself. None of the girls used their real names, I had found out on the day of the audition, so the previous night my friend Rachael had come over and we had made a list of names. The first on the list was Ginger – after the Sharon Stone character in the film *Casino*. It was one of my favourite films, and I thought the name sounded glamorous without being too girly. Someone was already called Ginger, however, so I went to the next name on the list. The first five names I asked for were already gone. I had a laugh with the house-mum over silly names I could have. Most girls typically used names like Chardonnay and Crystal, but I didn't want anything like that. I eventually settled on the name Red as it was unusual and the closest thing I was going to get to Ginger.

I then got changed into my dress. It was bright red and crocheted with a tie at the top. As a skirt it was knee-length, but as a dress it was very short. I went into the toilets downstairs to apply my make-up, preferring to have some privacy from the madness in the dressing room. I still wasn't confident enough to start up conversations with any of the girls, and I wanted to drink some of the vodka in my bag before I started work. By the time I was ready, I was well on the way to being merry. I walked slowly back to the dressing room to put my things away and to speak to the house-mum. She then explained how the club worked. All girls had to pay £100 a night to the house-mum, and everything you made after that was your own. A topless dance was £10 and a nude dance was £20. So basically, you did five nude dances to cover the money you owed and then kept the rest. She explained that £85 of the money we paid her went to the club for the privilege of working there; the remaining £15 was split between the make-up artist, the hairdressers and the house-mum. She also told me all about the 'Heavenly Money'. This was fake money that looked like monopoly money with a naked girl on the front. Customers could buy it from the club on credit cards and use it to pay the girls. The only drawback was that, when we handed it in to exchange it for real money, we lost 20 per cent of it in commission. The customer also had to pay 20 per cent on what they bought. If they bought £100 worth, they paid £120 and we only got back £80. The club made £40 on every £100 purchased!

I warmed to the house-mum straight away. Her job was to keep control of the girls and look after them. She dealt with everything from periods to injuries. She was the person the girls talked to when they were upset, and was the only one in the club who appeared to know everybody's name – with 250 girls on the books, only a few stood out to most. She had a very kind face and twinkly eyes. I knew that the time I spent there was going to be made better with her for company.

The night's work came all too quickly. Before I knew it, the dressing room was empty and the music outside in the club was pumping. As I loitered around, not really sure what to do, a girl came flying back into the dressing room squealing that she needed a tampon. Once her crisis was over, she turned to me. 'Come on, girl,' she said, 'time to work!' With that, she strode back out the door. Taking it as a cue to follow, I chased after her and asked her name, which she told me was Levi.

'It's my first night,' I explained to her. 'I don't really know what to do.'

She gave me a kind look. 'Stay with me and I'll show you the ropes.' We went upstairs to the bar, which consisted of about five male customers and thirty girls. The girls swooned over the men. Some chatted; others stood nearby fluttering their eyelashes. 'No point even trying yet,' Levi told me bluntly. 'Let's get a drink.'

We went to the bar, where we had to buy our own drinks at £6 a time – not that I cared, as vodka was needed in large amounts to get me through this horror. What once seemed so glamorous and exciting was now the scariest and most nerve-wracking thing I had ever known.

Why on earth did I decide to do this? I thought to myself, wondering about making a run for it. I could easily pack up my things and leave through the back door, never to return. I certainly wanted to do that. Somehow, however, my curiosity and strength got the better of me. I wanted to prove to myself that I could do this. I stayed silently rooted to the spot as Levi chatted away to another girl about her new boob job. Half an hour went by and the club began to fill up. Levi said that we should do some work. Too terrified to move I said that I wanted to wait for a while. I still didn't have a clue what I was supposed to do. I knew that I had to get dances to make money but I didn't know where to begin, and I definitely didn't feel ready to take my clothes off. 'Don't worry,' Levi said sweetly. 'I'll stay with you until we have to do the free dance.'

'Free what?' I asked her in horror. She explained that every hour, on the hour, we had to give a free dance to the nearest customer. If we were caught not giving the dance, we would either be fined or sacked. A certain song was played to signify the dance. She looked at her watch and told me we had fifteen minutes to go. The panic that set in that moment remains unmatched to this day. Levi told me that there was no way out of doing it and that I might as well get it over and done with. My head was banging. I honestly didn't think I could do it. I would have cried had I not been in total shock. My hands shook so much that I couldn't even hold my drink and had to put it down. I had honestly never felt so scared in my life.

The fifteen minutes were up in no time. I stood trembling and mute while Levi got two guys over for the dance. She sat them down next to each other and stood over one, telling me to dance for the other. I managed a quiet 'Hi' to my bloke and, watching Levi, I started to wiggle my hips stiffly in front of the customer. I couldn't bring myself to make eye contact with the guy; instead, I tried to copy what Levi was doing. After a minute, Levi's top was off and I knew I had to follow suit. I struggled inelegantly with the tie at the top of my dress and finally got it undone, letting it fall to the floor. I shook all the way through the dance. I kept thinking that the guy was studying my body. I had never been shy during sex, but this was different. Here I was, in just a thong, trying to look sexy just inches from a total stranger. I had never felt so conscious of my movements or of my body before. I turned around when Levi did to give him a look at my arse. Or so he thought. I took it as a much-need breather from making eye contact.

The dance seemed to go on forever. I wobbled on my high heels and prayed for it to end. I had started to sweat with nerves and I could feel the drops forming at the base of my spine. When it finally came to an end, the two guys got up and Levi managed to persuade them to give us a tip, even though it was supposed to be a free dance. She winked at me and placed a tenner in my hand. 'Wasn't that bad, was it?' she asked.

'No,' I said. 'Thank you.' What I was thinking was, Hell yes! Worse than bad! Horrific! With that I made an excuse to go downstairs and ran towards the dressing room. Once inside the door, I breathed a huge sigh of relief and slumped against the worktop in front of the mirrors. On the one hand I was thinking, I've done it! I've actually given a lap dance! On the other hand I was thinking, I can't do that ever again! I decided to hide in the dressing room for as long as I could.

While I stood and tried to regain my composure, it suddenly entered my head that I hadn't seen Amy, so I asked the house-mum where she was. She told me that she had gone to work at the Paris Stringfellows for a while and it was while chatting to her that a beautiful black girl entered the room. She took one look at me and gasped in horror. 'You can't possibly wear that dress,' she told me. 'Are you new?'

'Is it that obvious?' I asked.

'Don't worry,' she smiled. 'I've got a dress you can borrow until you've made enough money to buy your own. I'm Sweet-pea, by the way.'

Sweet-pea threw a dress at me from her locker. I was still not really sure what was wrong with my own dress but, not wanting to offend her, I took hers and went back to the toilet to change. It was the shortest, tightest, black Lycra. Once on, it only came halfway down my backside, leaving my butt cheeks in full view. It crossed over at the front and two strips of material just covered my nipples while tying in a bow at my neck. I have to say that it did look fabulous. Immediately I felt much sexier. It made my boobs look great and my legs look really long. I thanked her massively, and just at that moment Levi appeared in the dressing room. 'I've been looking for you,' she said. 'I've got us a dance!'

I followed her back out of the dressing room and up the

stairs while she explained that a guy she had been chatting to wanted a dance and he had told her to find someone to dance for his friend at the same time. Nervously I thanked her for getting me, and she introduced me to the guys. Without even any small talk, she led the guys straight to a row of chairs and began dancing, shouting across to my one that it was my first night and to be gentle with me. I smiled sheepishly at him and started dancing too. Still scared stiff, I did the same as before and it was over fairly quickly. I took the money he offered, thanked him and turned to talk to Levi as I pulled my dress on.

The club had been open an hour and a half and I had only made £20. I hadn't even done a nude dance yet. I really wasn't sure if I was cut out for this.

A little while later, I was standing with Levi chatting to some guys when I heard the DJ call 'Red' over the microphone. I turned to Levi in horror and asked what it meant. She pushed me towards the stage upstairs known as the 'cocktail stage'. 'Go,' she hissed, 'it means you've got to dance on there.' There were two poles on the stage and a small flight of stairs at either end. I reached the bottom of the steps nearest me and followed another girl on to the stage. Confusion arose as I realised you weren't meant to board the stage from the same side as the other girl. Luckily she must have known I was new and moved across the stage to the other pole. I grinned and mouthed 'Sorry!', then followed her lead in dancing. We had to stay up there for three songs, and each song was perfectly timed to last three minutes. For the first song we remained fully clothed; for the second song we had to take our tops off; and for the third song we had to dance in just our thongs. Levi watched me out of the corner of her eye and I looked to her for reassurance every now and then, which she gave in the form of a smile. It actually wasn't that bad. I certainly found it a damn sight easier than dancing for a guy. Up on the stage, I felt like no one else existed and that I could be as sexy as I wanted to be. I felt powerful and in control and I loved the men looking at me. As with the free dance, we didn't get paid to dance on the stages, but it was something we had to do. If we didn't show up, we would be fined or sacked, depending on how the DJ or the managers were feeling.

The rest of the night went very quickly. I only did a few more dances with Levi, all topless, but found out that on your first night you didn't have to pay the house fee so I walked away with about £50. It wasn't tons, but I was happy that I had made anything at all.

It took me about a week to get really into the swing of things. On my second night I bought a dress from the shop in the downstairs toilet that sold thongs and what all the girls called stripper outfits. Hence, the woman who ran it was known as the lady in the toilet. I bought exactly the same dress as the one I had borrowed from Sweet-pea, but in red, and I bought a new red thong. I was told I wasn't allowed to wear the stars and stripes one, as it wasn't see-through. Thongs had to be see-through, but not lacy or patterned.

Once the fear of removing my clothes had worn off, I had to overcome my fear of approaching the men in the first place. For the first few nights I relied on Levi or another girl I had become friendly with, Summer, to get me dances. I preferred working with Summer because Levi didn't go fully nude. Summer did, which meant we earned £20 a dance. I got the impression that Levi found working with me to be a bit of a burden anyway. She did all the talking as I was too shy to speak, and I followed her round like a puppy dog. Summer, on the other hand, always worked with a partner, but hers had gone away to work in the Paris Stringfellows for a while so it worked out nicely.

After a week or so, my confidence was through the roof. I didn't even find the nudity a big problem. The lighting in the club was very subdued anyway and it wasn't that much different to dancing topless. Its not like the men could see everything, because you weren't allowed to open your legs while naked. I never tried to be sexy or put on an act. I found that, if I was just myself, nine times out of ten the men liked me. A lot of the girls, I noticed, would put on husky voices and approach men with 'Hello, big boy!' I had never been one to pretend to be something I wasn't, so instead I started with a cheeky smile and an 'All right, mate, fancy a dance?' Most of the time it worked. Certain men were harder to crack, but I enjoyed the challenge.

After a week passed, I bought another outfit from the lady in the toilet. It was a camouflage-print two-piece consisting of tiny hipster knickers and two strips of material held together with a bit of string for the top. I bought a see-through black thong to wear underneath. That boosted my confidence again. Finally I felt like me. It was extremely sexy but not too girly, and it made me stand out from all the other girls in their long sparkly dresses. As the weeks passed, I began to get to grips with the job. Summer – real name Gina – had taught me that you could charge men for your time. For example, instead of paying you for dances, they could buy you at a rate of your choice by the hour. That meant you would sit and keep them company for however long they wished *and* give them as many dances as they wanted throughout that time. Summer and I charged £200 an hour. The pair of us were dynamite, and we complemented each other perfectly. She had a similar frame to me, very petite but with a big full bust. Her boobs were real too, which was rare in Strings. We got on really well and earned a lot of money. Two weeks into the job, I was earning at least £500 a night and loving it. Even when Summer's partner came back from Paris, I wasn't bothered. I just worked alone, and it was rare that a guy refused a dance from me. I seemed to have the touch when it came to selling myself. Even Peter Stringfellow himself noticed my charms. He would come in two or three nights a week. His table was big enough to seat ten people and he would always fill it with various friends. He took a shine to me and passed work my way. He would always ask me to dance for his friends and slip me some money (although it was always in Heavenly bills). I once heard him say, 'Red is one of our best girls,' which pleased me no end.

I got to know all the tricks: there was no money to be made on Saturday nights – the big spenders came in during the week; the men liked to be made to feel special, so flirting and eye contact went a long way; keeping a £50 note on the outside of your garter made you look more expensive and would therefore make the rich guys pay you attention; obtaining regular customers would mean a regular income; making eye contact with men while dancing on stage would pretty much guarantee you a dance afterwards; and I always remembered the thing I had loved about Holly – her smell. Every night before work I would moisturise all over with a perfumed lotion, and I would spray a light scent over my neck, wrists, bust, bum and fanny. It meant that men would get a faint whiff of pleasure each time I stripped. I quickly became one of the highest earners in the club, and notched up several regulars, one of whom was a very big spender who gave me £500 every time he saw me, even if he only had one dance.

All was good. My confidence continued to soar and my parents noticed the difference. They couldn't believe the change in me. Working for them I had become sulky, tired and bored. Suddenly I was full of life, jumping around and chattering excitedly to them every day. When they were coming *in* from work, I was getting ready to *go* to work, and I didn't get in until five in the morning. I slept until midday and then went for lunch with my brother or did some shopping. The hours suited me to a tee, as I have never needed much sleep and have always been a bit of a night owl. Earning such good money, I was able to treat us all every now and then: I took them out for dinner and bought them little gifts, I treated my brother to clothes and shoes he wanted and I bought myself a new car. I loved every minute of my new lifestyle. For the first time ever, I felt settled, content and independent.

Coming from a small town like Brentwood, it was unheard of to be a stripper and the attention was overwhelming. Everywhere I went, people asked if it was true that I worked at Stringfellows. I loved being able to say yes, as I knew it was a big deal in this small town. As soon as word spread, I had lots of boys coming to the club who knew me. Whether they had gone to my school or just knew me from the pubs, they all wanted a dance from Jodie Marsh. I hated getting naked for them, but I secretly enjoyed taking their money. Once I was the ugly duckling of my school; now they were paying to see me dance, and boy were they paying! One guy spent about £500 on me one night. He went to my school but was a few years older than me. He was quite good looking and all the younger girls fancied him. I myself had really looked up to him as this gorgeous, untouchable stud, like young girls do. To see him drunk and swaying in his chair, demanding another dance and eagerly throwing money at me, made me realise that sometimes things aren't the way they seem. He wasn't an untouchable hunk who could have his pick of any girl; he was a sad, drunk twenty-something who couldn't pull and needed to pay to look at me to get his kick for the night. The real low point for him came when he begged me to go home with him. I said a flat 'No'.

I soon made two new friends in the club, who remain two of my closest friends to this day. One was a girl called Lauren – stage name Tatiana – who, like me, didn't know anyone when she started; the other was a girl called Chloe who, ironically, came to the club like me on a night out and found herself talked into coming to work there – by me! Chloe came three or four times with her boyfriend and a group of friends and they all took a shine to me, paying me over and over for dances. From this I got to know the whole group pretty well and I often sat chatting to them if I couldn't be bothered to do any work. After accepting the job, she called herself Wish – we still laugh about that now. Nice one, babe! Lauren, Chloe and I had a real giggle working together.

However, it wasn't always fun, as Lauren and I found out the hard way. One night we sat with a couple of blokes who agreed to the £200-an-hour fee. The guys were real geeks and perverts, but we made the most of it and kept the strained conversation going as best we could, giving them dances every fifteen minutes or so. When the hour was up, we told them that they could buy us for another hour if they liked, to which they said yes. They were boring the hell out of us, but we both just kept thinking of the money. They ordered drink after drink for us and we got quite drunk sitting there, which was just as well considering how tedious it was keeping them entertained. Nevertheless, another hour passed and they asked for yet another. 'Are you sure?' I asked one of them. 'That'll be £600.'

'No problem,' he told me, 'I'll go get it from that booth with my credit card.' Even though that kind of money sounds amazing for such a small amount of time, sometimes you felt like you had really earned it, and this was one of those nights – we had made two boring, middle-aged men feel attractive and funny for three hours. We had laughed at their unfunny jokes, fluttered our eyelashes at their not-so-handsome faces and struggled to keep the conversation going. It drained us completely and, when the third hour was up, we were both feeling like we wanted to go home.

One of the guys got up to go to the toilet and said he would get the money out on his credit card from one of the booths on the way back. Ten minutes went by and he hadn't come back, so the other guy said he would go and look for him. Alarm bells immediately went off in my head and I watched him walk to the toilet. After a few minutes he emerged from the gents and carried on walking towards the stairs. Quick as a flash, I was out of my seat and running after him up the stairs. As he got to the door of the club, where his mate was putting his coat on, I confronted the pair of them and asked about our money. Lauren was two seconds behind me and an argument ensued. The shouts attracted the attention of the doormen, who rushed over to see what the fuss was about. 'These guys have taken three hours of our time and not paid us,' I explained.

'Is this true?' one of the doormen asked.

'We didn't realise we had to pay for their time,' the guys mumbled unconvincingly. Fucking liars! Lauren and I begged the doormen to do something, but they told us they couldn't hold the blokes there against their will – that was called kidnapping – so the two guys headed towards the door. Lauren started screaming and made a dash at the men, now in the foyer. The two doormen lunged at her and pinned her against a wall to restrain her. With her arms and legs flying all over the place, they had enough on their hands trying to control her and they obviously weren't thinking about me. In a fit of rage, I ran through the foyer doors and kicked one of the guys as hard as I could up the arse with my six-inch (stripper shoe) stilettos. He went crashing down and I turned on my heel and ran back to the doormen, who were now propping up a crying Lauren. We were escorted down to the dressing room where we were told we could go home if we wanted. The best part of the night was over and we weren't likely to make any money now. We had repeatedly got naked and drained ourselves mentally for a couple of wankers, and all for nothing. We were gutted. Times like those made the job feel as degrading and low as it probably was.

The few girls who were in the dressing room came to see what was going on and sympathised with us about the pricks we had just encountered. It seemed everybody had been through the same thing at one time or another. Most girls' advice to us was always to get the money up front, but that was easier said than done. To get the guy to buy you for an hour, you have to charm him into thinking you fancy him and that you *want* to spend your time with him. Then you casually slip in that, much as you would prefer to sit here with him all night, you need to make money – unless he wants to buy your time and then you can stay and chat as long as he wants. Insisting on the money immediately is too businesslike and the men don't like it: it destroys the fantasy you've created of fancying them because it becomes too obvious that it's all about the money. I had always worked on a trust basis before that and – apart from my regulars – difficult as it was, I didn't trust in there again.

Two or three months went by during which time I was happy working at Stringfellows. I had a new boyfriend called Darren who was probably the best-looking bloke I had ever been out with, and he didn't mind the fact that I was a stripper. He came to the club regularly to watch me dance and it suited me fine. In fact, I asked him to come as much as possible because I gave him all the free dances we had to do on the hour. It turned him on and meant that some sleazy bloke didn't get to see me naked unless he was paying.

Working at Stringfellows certainly made me see men in a different light. For a start, most of my customers were married. My highest-paying regulars even had kids. Sometimes I felt sorry for them that they had to come to the club every week for a kick, but mostly I felt sorry for their wives. It gutted me to think that they probably didn't even know their husband, the father of their children, was spending so much money on getting girls to strip for them. All my customers asked me to go home with them at some point, which I found horrifying. It takes a good actress to smile sweetly and say, 'Baby, you know it's against the rules!' Really I wanted to kick them in the balls and scream, 'What the hell in a million years makes you think I'd be one bit interested in you? Go home to your wife!' They made me feel sick. One time a girlfriend told me her bloke wanted to go there and asked my thoughts on letting him. I told her honestly: any bloke wanting to go to a strip club on his own was not worth staying with.

The offers of outside work were high. One time, a guy offered me ten grand to go back to his hotel with him. I wasn't tempted, not even in the slightest. Other girls were more easily swayed. Night after night, I'd see girls in the street at four in the morning getting into cars with guys I'd seen in the club. It disgusted me, but then I didn't fraternise with those girls. Lauren and Chloe were all the mates I needed in there.

It was very bitchy – I discovered that almost immediately. Girls fought over high-paying customers and slagged each other off constantly. I never got involved. My routine was the same each night. Drive myself in, drink my cheap vodka from my Evian bottle, do as many dances as I could, pray that a regular came in and bought me for a few hours, and then drive home over the limit (not big or clever, I know, but I didn't feel I had a choice).

I had a few music-biz clients. One of my regulars was from a well-known rock band. He used to come in and drink neat whisky and, from the first time I danced for him, he decided that I was 'his' girl. He would buy me for a few hours each time he came and we would sit and chat. Mostly he just wanted company, with a few nude dances thrown in for good measure. Our little arrangement came to an end the night he asked how much I wanted to go back to his hotel with him. I made my excuses and avoided him every time he came in after that.

A gorgeous, long-haired, married rock star from America came in one night. I had been a big fan of his for years and had even seen him at Wembley. I wasn't going to pass up the chance to meet him. As I approached him with another stripper who also wanted to meet him, his eyes lit up and, charmingly, he took one of her hands and one of mine to kiss us. As he took mine, his hand 'accidentally' brushed my breast, half-exposed in my tiny Lycra dress. I flinched and took a step back in shock. World-famous rock star or not, he wasn't allowed to touch and I wasn't going to let him. I continued to chat to him anyway, but within a few minutes he was offering the pair of us money to kiss and play with each other.

I politely told him that, just as customers weren't allowed to touch the girls, we weren't allowed to touch each other. He persisted, saying that, as he was a 'special guest' of Peter's, he was sure rules could be ignored. By this stage, I was fairly annoyed and vehemently repeated that it *really* wasn't allowed. Eventually he realised he was wasting his time and gave up – by which time my adoration for him had been completely destroyed.

Another guest was a fun-loving front man from a punk rock band, also American, who came to Strings with someone I guess was his girlfriend. They took a shine to me and paid me for the entire night to dance repeatedly for them. They didn't even let me get dressed between dances – they just kept throwing money at me to continue. If I'm honest, I was quite chuffed – the whole club was in a state of excitement that they were in and all eyes were on us for the duration of the night.

When Stringfellows was good, it was really good, but when it was bad, it was diabolical. If you were having an off night and couldn't seem to make any money, you tended to drink more, thinking it would help. Wrong. One night, after not making a penny in the first two hours, Chloe and I sat and drank with two guys who weren't paying for our time but were happy to provide alcohol. We must have got through a good few bottles of champagne before I started to feel very drunk. The room span and felt very hot as I tried not to sway too much on my chair. Knowing that I was going to be sick, or pass out, or both, I mumbled some incoherent excuse and tottered off in the direction of the dressing room. I don't remember anything after that. Chloe tells me she found me slumped on the floor against the lockers. I couldn't talk and wouldn't sit up. It was the night of the weekly meeting, which happened at half-past four in the morning after the club closed, and Peter insisted that *everybody* attend. Chloe and Lauren had managed to drag me out of the dressing room and lay me on the floor in the main club, and Peter conducted the whole meeting without so much as looking at the heap on the floor that was me. At the very end, throwing a disapproving if slightly amused glance in my direction, he simply said, 'Oh, and, girls, don't drink so much that you pass out!' It was not my finest moment.

CHAPTER SEVEN

Essex Wives

After about four months of working at Stringfellows, the novelty was definitely starting to wear thin. I split with Darren after three months, having found out that he also had a long-term girlfriend of three years. Once I had lost the buzz for doing the job, it became very hard to approach men for dances. If you have a few dodgy nights where you don't make much money, you spend the rest of the week trying to catch up with what you owe to the club, or you just give up. I gave up. Instead of worrying about how I would pay the house fee, I bunked off early and went clubbing with Lauren and Chloe. A new club had opened in Soho called Click, and I fancied the guy whom I thought was the owner, Fran Cosgrave. Fran was going out with Natasha Hamilton from Atomic Kitten, so I admired him from a distance for a while until he made a beeline for me one night. We got chatting and hit it off instantly.

Even though I fancied Fran madly, it never entered my

head that anything would ever come of it as he was attached and had recently become a father. Still, it was fun to be mates, and he looked after me in the club. Every time I took my friends there, he gave us the VIP treatment and free drinks. We went out regularly and became quite well known on the London club scene. My girlfriends and I mingled with celebrities and VIPs all the time, and never paid for a single thing. The club owners liked having us there, probably because we were attractive young girls – oh, and also strippers! Something about saying we worked at Stringfellows always got us looked after.

I began to make contacts and use them to my advantage. Through them I found someone who wanted to be my manager. One night in Chinawhite, I was introduced to the potential candidate, on the same night I met actor Gary Lucy. Gary and I hit it off straight away, both of us being from Essex, and I ended up pulling him that night and driving him home. This manager also showed a great deal of interest in me and asked lots of questions – while plying me with vodka. After swapping phone numbers with everyone, Gary and I left the club to be greeted by about ten paparazzi snapping away at us. Knowing that simply holding his hand would have landed us in the newspapers, I purposefully kept my distance. It's true that I wanted fame more than anything, but I wanted to do it my way. I wasn't going to get famous for being somebody's girl. Gary and I didn't sleep together that first night, but he gave me great oral and made me come, quite noisily I have to say, in his parents' house in Chigwell. I never wanted to go out with Gary, and he felt the same, but it was the start of a fuck-buddy friendship that continued for quite a few months.

The would-be manager, however, was on my case big

time. He told me one day that he had been looking for someone who could be the 'new' Jordan, and he thought I was it. He said that she had reigned alone for some time now and that the market was ready for someone to rival her. He thought I had the looks, the personality and the outrageous dress sense to carry it off. I jumped for joy. He said that he would need to see what I looked like in pictures first, and arranged for me to do a photo shoot with the famous glamour photographer Jeff Kaine. I had actually approached Jeff years earlier with a cheap set of topless pictures to see if he could help me, and he had turned me down flat. I had seen him on TV loads of times in documentaries about photography and glamour modelling, and I couldn't believe he was actually going to be taking my picture.

The day of the shoot I was incredibly nervous, but also the most excited I had ever been. It was the first time I'd ever been in a studio, let alone posed for proper pictures. I took a selection of my stripper knickers and shoes, and had my hair and make-up done by a professional. Even so, I felt a bit like a silly little girl playing at dressing up. I was confident enough in my body, but I still didn't feel like a real model. I felt like an intruder. Deep down inside I was still the ugly duckling from school that got picked on. Surely I couldn't compete with the likes of Jordan? I thought. Still, I was professional about it and did everything that was asked of me. I couldn't believe how long the shoot went on for. We started at about nine in the morning and didn't finish until eight o'clock that night. The guy who wanted to be my manager told me he thought it had gone well and we arranged a meeting for a few days later to have a look at the finished pictures. I was bubbling with excitement.

The day of the meeting, I drove up to London, my tummy jumping with nerves. My brother sent me a text which read, 'GOOD LUCK FOR TODAY, TELL HIM THAT IF HE DOESN'T MAKE YOU FAMOUS, I'M GOING TO POO IN HIS EYE.' It made me laugh lots and I could feel that this was the start of something big. Once in the management office, I was talked through all the photos on the computer. He was completely honest, telling me where I had gone wrong, but also pointing out what I had done well. Some of the pictures were minging and I hated them; but some I loved – I looked very glamorous and pretty – and I couldn't have been happier. I asked him where we went from there. 'Leave it to me,' he said. 'I can get you into all the papers. You're going to be a star.'

Before we knew it, it was six o'clock and we were both starving. He had a room booked at a hotel down the road, so he invited me there to get some food. After eating, he said that he had to get ready to go out and asked if I would join him at Chinawhite with the usual mob. I was wearing jeans, but I had a little denim skirt in my car left over from the photo shoot, so I put that on and made a top out of a white bandana. With the white furry boots I was already wearing, it looked OK.

Chinas was heaving and Gary and Dean Gaffney, who I'd met when I was doing work experience with the paparazzi photographer, joined us at our table after a while. The alcohol was flowing and everyone had a good time. Towards the end of the night, the manager patted his knee and gestured at me to sit on it. I obliged and he put his arm round my waist. He started telling me how big I was going to be, how all the papers were going to love me and how he was going to make me a lot of money. I didn't even care about the money by then, I just wanted the fame. I thought that once and for all I would be completely happy. Stringfellows was becoming a chore and I wanted more than anything to feel attractive and special. I thought that by finally making it big my insecurities would be gone forever and I would, at last, be satisfied in life. He raved to me about how great it was going to be, and I lapped it up. What came next completely threw me. To say he took the wind out of my sails is an understatement.

'All you have to do is come back to my hotel tonight,' he said. I mumbled some excuse and pushed my way through the crowds to the toilet. Inside a cubicle, I slumped to the floor and cried. I had honestly thought this guy was genuine. Why had he gone to the trouble of arranging a photo shoot for me if he hadn't thought I had potential? Was it all just his way of conning girls into bed? Surely he didn't need to go that far in his ploys. I couldn't understand anything. Numb and confused, I sat on the floor trying to get my head around the whole messy situation. This was the closest I had come to getting somewhere. He had appealed to everything I had felt and craved since I was a kid. I thought he believed in me and I was devastated to learn that it was all possibly a lie to get me into bed.

After a while I patched up my tear-stained face and went back out to join everyone at the table. 'I'm sorry,' I said, 'I don't feel well.' I told him I would call him the following day, and left alone. Why was life so difficult? Just when you thought everything was going your way, something always ruined it! It was just such a shame that the something that ruined my good fortune was also the something that had made it.

I now had some serious thinking to do. It was obvious I

couldn't put any faith in the manager to pull through with his promises of stardom and I didn't want to work at Stringfellows for ever. God, however, must have been smiling down on me that week: help came in the form of one of my best friends.

About a year before I started lap dancing, I was out one night in my local nightclub in Brentwood, and I met Michelle who would become one of my best friends. My parents had gone away at the time, and my brother and I were looking after the house for them. We randomly decided to throw a party, but only had about ten mates with us. Deciding we needed more people, or rather my brother stating that we needed more 'fit' girls, it became my job to recruit people in the club to come back to ours. Michelle was the first good-looking girl I approached. She couldn't come as she was staying at a friend's house, but she asked for my number and told me she would be in touch. I thought nothing more of her until I got a phone call the following week from her asking me to go to a celebrity party. It turned out she worked for Granada Media. Not one to turn down any party, let alone a celebrity one, I went, and we've been best friends ever since.

Over the last few years, we have dabbled in organising celebrity parties together, the best of which being the after-party we held for ITV's *Record of the Year*. We had Westlife, Ant and Dec, Sonique, DJ Pied Piper, Atomic Kitten, Blue and S Club Seven, to name a few. It worked for us because she had the contacts in TV and I had the contacts in clubs and knew how to throw a party. Anyway, Michelle and I were firm friends and she would come to all my brother's gigs with me. We often went out in Essex and got drunk and, at the same time, whenever she fancied joining me on one of my trips to a London club, I'd sort her out a guest list and get her free drinks. So it was with the trust and loyalty of a best mate that I agreed to a favour she needed. They had been in a meeting at work and a new programme had been commissioned for which they needed a family. The show was to be called *Essex Wives* and needed to be centred around three families from Essex. The catch was this: they didn't just want any old families, they wanted larger-than-life, Osbourne-style families. Since we were already nicknamed the Osbournes of Essex by our friends due to our madness and millions of animals (at the time we had four dogs, two cats, a snake, two horses and five tortoises), Michelle had already put my name forward and given the researcher, a girl called Zoe, my number.

I didn't mind in the slightest. I thought it sounded like a laugh, and they were prepared to feature one of my brother's gigs heavily in the hope of him being spotted. The only problem was persuading my mum. I knew my dad would be fine, but I had been approached a few years earlier to do a TV show about cooking which would feature the whole family and my mum was so nervous she wouldn't step into view of the camera. We ended up having to push her from behind so she suddenly flew into view looking terrified. I called Zoe to get the low-down on the programme and spent the next two days, along with my dad and brother, convincing my mum to say yes. I can honestly say that at that point I really didn't think the programme was going to be very big. I had done bits of TV work in the past that had amounted to nothing, so I didn't expect this to be any different. The most we hoped to gain from it was some recognition for my brother's band.

We had an initial meeting with Chris Carey the

producer, and he assured us he wasn't out to stitch us up. All he wanted was an insight into the 'wacky world of the Marshes', and again he promised us that my brother Jordan's band would feature heavily. He told us that filming would take place over a period of four months, from September to December, and that we were to act like the cameras weren't there. Somehow my mum found herself saying yes, even though she didn't want to, and contracts were signed. I took an instant liking to Chris and, even though I hardly knew him, I trusted him implicitly.

We gave the film crew access all areas – there was nothing we were ashamed of letting people see. We let them into our home and our lives. They filmed a bit of every single thing we did: our home life and our social lives, one of Jordan's gigs, as promised, and of course our different jobs. Chris loved the fact that I was a stripper and that my parents had never been to a strip club, so it was his idea for me to take them to Stringfellows for a night out, not to see me dance but just to watch the other girls. It turned out to be a very funny night. My parents didn't know where to look and my brother got so drunk he forgot he was in a strip club and tried to pull all the girls. All the way through filming, we still thought the show would go unnoticed, but we really enjoyed having the crew around – they began to feel like part of the family. We always had a full house and we enjoyed the banter. We had a laugh with the filming as well and there was stuff that we knew would never be used, but we filmed it for amusement anyway. There was the time we made Chris film Jordan running into my mum's bedroom dangling his pet snake, Shithead, in front of her. She was terrified of the thing and her screams must have been heard for miles! We all had a laugh and in fact we were sad when filming came to an end. We promised to keep in touch and the crew said they wanted to come over and sample one of my dad's amazing roast dinners which they had had the discomfort of filming, starving hungry, one Sunday. True to our word, we had them all over recently and we reminisced about the filming of *Essex Wives* and they marvelled over how well I'd done since.

During filming I was going to Click a lot. I still fancied Fran like mad and loved being near him. We had become good friends, and spent quite a bit of time talking on the phone. Although I never seriously thought about pulling him, I dreamed of the day that he would be mine. One night, a girlfriend of mine called Claire and I went out to Chinawhite, where we bumped into the usual crowd, including the manager who'd tried it on with me. I was nervous of being around him, but I was still good mates with Gary and Dean so I didn't think it would be a problem. Dean had met Claire a few months previously at a lap-dancing club we had all been to and they had got it on at my house afterwards. They had been texting each other ever since, so were happy to see each other. We drank until the club closed and Dean and the manager invited us back to their hotel.

We were all keen to carry on partying. I pulled Claire to one side and said that I was happy to go but that she was to promise me that she wouldn't go off with Dean and leave me alone with that manager. She promised she wouldn't and we jumped into cabs back to the hotel. The manager ordered vast amounts of champagne and we all sat on the huge king-sized bed in the middle of the room. Claire and Dean were flirting and getting touchy-feely and I began to feel uncomfortable. Although I trusted her not to leave me alone with the other guy, I could still see an awkward situation arising. Sure enough, after a while Dean and Claire had begun kissing on the bed and I had gone to the toilet in embarrassment. While in there, I called Fran. He had wanted to come to Chinawhite with us earlier as he couldn't get in on his own and he needed me to get him in. I had forgotten all about him in the fun we were having, so I wanted to apologise. I pretended that he hadn't missed anything anyway.

I could only have been on the phone for five minutes when I stuck my head out of the bathroom door to see Claire, naked from the waist down, her legs spread, taking a good old shafting from Dean, while the manager lay next to them watching. As soon as he saw me, he beckoned for me to join them. Horrified, I stuck my head back inside and whispered to Fran that he wouldn't believe what just happened. I told him Claire was shagging Dean openly on the bed for all to see and he laughed. I explained that I didn't want to get left with the manager, so Fran told me to get into a cab to his house. Not wanting to be anywhere near that other guy, but also not wanting to leave Claire on her own at the hotel with two blokes, I told Fran I would ring him back in a minute and hung up. My heart was thumping. Fran was very much attached, and I knew I shouldn't even be considering going to see him, but it was two in the morning by now and Claire was mid-shag. She had put me in a very awkward position and I wanted to escape the hotel more than anything. I ventured slowly into the bedroom, where by now the other guy had his cock in his hand.

'Come here, babe, have a feel of this,' he said.

'Hang on a minute,' I said, before turning to Claire. 'Something's come up,' I told her. 'I'm going to have to go soon.'

Giggling, she pushed Dean off and turned to me, adjusting her skirt and knickers. 'Are you all right?' she asked, turning serious for a second before mouthing, 'Sorry!'

'Fine,' I told her, 'but you're going to have to finish up in a bit. We've got to get going.' Dean had her knickers down again in two seconds flat and she was back on the bed again, legs spread. I couldn't resist the opportunity and quickly took a couple of pictures on my camera phone of the pair of them shagging and went back into the toilet, telling the other guy (who still had his knob in his hand) that a problem had come up. Half laughing about the pictures I had just taken and half desperate to get out of there, I called Fran back. He urged me to hurry up and leave, but I told him that I was wary of leaving Claire on her own – I'd be as quick as I could. Fran made me promise not to tell anyone where I was going – he had always been cagey about our friendship and whenever Natasha and I were in Click at the same time he practically pretended not to know me.

I sat in the toilet for another half-hour or so until Claire knocked on the door to use the loo. I told her again that I wanted to go and she said she would finish up. I went back into the bedroom with her where she spent another five minutes kissing Dean, while sadly the manager was still drunkenly trying to wank off his only half-hard knob. Once we finally got out of the door and into the lift, Claire begged forgiveness. I told her it was revenge time and that we were going to Fran's. The revenge part was that she wasn't allowed in. We hailed a cab to my car and I drove us across London to Fran and Natasha's house. Once outside, I told Claire I wouldn't be long and she put her seat back to lie down. I nervously knocked on the door; Fran opened it, grabbed me by the arm and pulled me inside quickly, like he was scared of being seen.

We went into the living room, which was decorated with a huge Christmas tree. I remember feeling very guilty at this point and wondering to myself why I had come. Natasha was away with Atomic Kitten and had taken their son Josh with them. Fran was alone and wanted company, I reasoned to myself. Hesitantly I sat on the sofa. MTV was playing on the television and Fran offered me a drink. I accepted a glass of water and we sat and chatted.

What followed was quite frankly the weirdest night of my life. I fancied the arse off Fran and ached to touch him, but had more morals than to do anything with him. He had a tiny baby and a girlfriend and there was no way I was going to mess with that. I had always enjoyed his company until now, but I wondered if Natasha knew. I saw him in a different light and I wasn't sure if I actually liked him. The only problem was, just looking at him made me go weak at the knees. I ended up sitting for more than three hours with him, chatting and watching MTV.

At seven o'clock, I told him it was about time I made a move as I had to 'get Claire from the hotel'. He didn't know she was asleep outside in the car. He would have shit himself if he did.

As he walked me to the door, it was almost like that awkward first-date scenario. It felt like we were supposed to kiss, but deep down I knew it wasn't right. Instead I gave him a peck on the cheek, then turned and opened the door. As the door opened a few inches, Fran's arm came from over my head and pushed it shut. I turned to face him and he leaned down and kissed me on the mouth. Not a full-on snog, just a lush, lingering kiss. It was like that first kiss with a bloke when fireworks go off in your head. My whole body tingled with excitement as I looked up at him. 'Fran,' I said, 'it's not right that we do anything.'

(Although I was really wishing we could have done more.)

I'll never forget what he said next. 'Don't tell me you're leaving here without shagging me.' Stunned, I stared at him open-mouthed. 'You can't spend all this time with me and then not shag me.'

His rudeness brought me back down to earth and I mustered all the courage I could. 'Yes I can,' I told him, 'and I will.' I turned on my heels and opened the door to the daylight that now felt so hideous.

Once back at the car, I saw that Claire was awake. Turned out she'd been awake for hours and had been trying to call me. We laughed all the way home. I thought her punishment had been fair considering the horrid position she had put me in back at the hotel, and she agreed. She swore never to tell anyone that I had been to Fran's house and I blushed as I recounted what had happened. On the one hand, I thought he was the most gorgeous-looking man I had ever seen and it was obvious he fancied me too, but, on the other, he was taken. By the time we got home, I had made sense of everything in my head and had started to feel guilty. Claire agreed that nothing could ever happen between Fran and me, but I worried that things were going to be awkward between us.

Claire thought the best way to deal with it was to go back to Click that very night. She said that, if I left it, it might become worse, but if I just faced the music and told him straight away that I wasn't interested, hopefully we might be able to salvage the friendship. I agreed and, later on that night, got dolled up and took off in my car with my other mate Jess, who by now also knew of the situation. I drove to Click with a feeling of dread in my stomach. I hoped desperately that things would be normal between us. I suppose that really a part of me was hoping he wouldn't accept my friendship and would want more; but the truth of it was that I couldn't have lived with myself if I was to blame for him splitting with Natasha, and I wasn't prepared to have a sordid affair. I had to do the right thing.

On arriving at the club, I walked in feeling like everyone would somehow know what had happened, but everything was as normal. When I entered the plush VIP room, I saw Fran straight away, champagne glass in hand, standing by the bar. He wasn't alone: a girl stood with him and, as I approached, I saw to my horror that it was Natasha. My heart sank. When I think about it, it was probably for the best that she was there that night. It hit home even more to me how wrong it would have been to have let anything further happen between us. Fran kept his distance, only speaking to me once when Natasha had gone to the toilet. 'Have you told anybody?' he asked.

'No,' I said, a lie as two of my best mates knew, but he seemed satisfied. Somehow, even though I had gone there to put a stop to any developments between us, seeing him with Natasha made me feel a little stupid and, if I'm honest, slightly used. Even though all we had done was kiss on the lips, I felt like it had meant more than that. We had been friends for a while now and he had often turned to me when he had a problem, as I had to him. Even though I wanted nothing further to happen, I did wonder whether I was just one in a long line of girls Fran associated with while Natasha was away.

Jess was great. As we danced the night away, I did my best to forget all about him. I wasn't going to be anybody's bit on the side and I wasn't going to break up relationships. I felt sorry for Natasha that she obviously didn't have a clue what Fran was capable of, but I felt glad that things weren't too awkward with him.

I continued to go to Click regularly as I still got VIP treatment and free drinks, but for a while I avoided too much contact with Fran. I found myself visiting other clubs like Chinawhite more. It was here one night that I bumped into Westlife for the second time. It was just before Christmas, my filming was coming to an end, everyone was in high spirits and my mate Becky and I were ready to party. The club looked absolutely beautiful: the whole floor was covered with fake snow and it looked like a fabulous Christmas grotto. There was a French film crew in the lobby of the club interviewing people as they came in, and it was while I was desperately trying to remember some French from school that Mark Feehily spotted me and recognised me from the ITV *Record of the Year* party I had thrown with Michelle. He waited until I had finished talking to camera and then came up to say hello. Becky was impressed. He invited us to join them at their table, which was a result because we didn't particularly want to pay £500 for a table for the two of us.

Once at the table, Kian Egan vaguely remembered me too and ordered a load more vodka. The boys were quite drunk and we indulged to catch up. The rest of the night was carnage. The drunker we all got, the funnier the snow everywhere seemed and we ended up having a huge snow fight. Kian and Mark were rolling around the floor in the snow and throwing handfuls of it at me and Becky. We all acted like kids and spent half the night dancing on our table. When the bill came, we offered some money but the boys were having none of it and, once it was paid, asked if we wanted to go back to their hotel to carry on. Their minder Paul had been sitting quietly at the side of the table all night and he told us all to wait there while he went outside and got a car for us. He was back within five minutes and a conversation occurred whereby Paul told the boys there were lots of paparazzi waiting outside. I don't think he got a word of sense in reply – they were too drunk to comprehend what he was saying and all they wanted to do was leave. Not wanting to cause any trouble, I told Paul that, if he got the boys in a car, Becky and I would follow on in a cab, and Paul agreed that it was a good idea.

The boys left a few minutes before us so we avoided being pictured together. The outside of the club was madness as photographers surrounded the exit and people milled around trying to get a glimpse of any celebrities. Becky and I looked around for a cab. As we fought our way through the crowds, a hand suddenly grabbed my arm and within seconds flash bulbs were popping from every direction. The hand on my arm was Kian's. He had obviously decided not to leave us to make our own way, and was trying to get me to go to the waiting car with him. I shook him off, turned round and grabbed Becky's hand. In the chaos, I pulled her towards the direction Kian was headed. The paparazzi were going nuts. We crossed Regents Street with at least ten photographers in front of us logging on film our every move. Kian was a few feet ahead and pointed to me to get into the car parked at the side of the road. I could see that Paul was visibly stressed. He hadn't banked on Kian running back to get us, or on the paps following him back.

Mark was waiting in the car and beckoned for me to get in, but Paul was by now groaning aloud and asking if this was really wise. Kian ignored him completely, jumped into the car and shouted to me to get in. I clambered in quick as a flash with Becky following close behind. Becky covered her face with her hands and I bent my head down. Kian put his hand over the top of my head to push me down further but all that did was make it look like I was giving him a blow job. The paps chased the car down the road as we pulled away.

After a few minutes we were all laughing raucously, but back at the Conrad Hotel, the 'party' that we were going to have was more like afternoon tea. The TV was on in their suite and Kian was so drunk that he just slumped on the sofa. We chatted for a while but, realising how late it was and that not a lot was actually happening, Becky and I made our excuses and left. Mark was a complete gent: he phoned a cab for us, walked us to the lift and kissed us both on the cheek. It had been an eventful night and we didn't get home until about 6am. Before we left the house in the evening, Becky had made me promise that we'd be home in bed by 2am as she was leaving for Scotland at 7am. She left, having had no sleep, but she said it had been worth it as she'd partied with Westlife.

Pictures appeared in a magazine the following week asking who Westlife's mystery girlfriends were. I was shopping when I got a phone call from a friend. She screeched down the phone that I was in a magazine being called Kian's girlfriend. I went into WHSmith and laughed – the fake snow from the club made it look like we all had terrible dandruff. Still, the magazine called me 'a Britney Spears lookalike', which was all good in my eyes. Luckily they didn't know who I was or what I did – I don't think Westlife really wanted it to be known that they had been hanging around with a stripper!

Fran, who frequently scanned newspapers and magazines for pictures of himself with Natasha, saw the article that same day. He called me up sounding annoyed. 'How come you were out with the boys?' he asked.

'Because we bumped into them.' I wondered if he might have been jealous – not that he had any right to be, considering he was still very much engaged. He then invited me out that night. He had barely spoken to me since the incident at his house, and I couldn't help wondering if my new friendship with Westlife had sparked his interest in me again. Deciding it didn't matter what his reasons were, I said that I'd see him later and went home to start getting ready.

Once at Click, Fran was extremely attentive. He hardly left my side all night and, by the end of the evening, I knew he wanted to say something. In a darkened corner of the VIP room, he told me that the kiss we had shared at his house had been amazing and that he couldn't stop thinking about it. I told him that I felt the same but that it had to end there. I wasn't prepared to be the sort of person who broke up relationships. He confided in me that his relationship was on the verge of ending anyway. 'I'm still not interested,' I told him.

He was clearly stung. 'Well,' he hit back, 'I couldn't be seen with a lap dancer anyway.' It hurt, but I didn't let him know that. Instead, I just smiled sweetly and thought to myself, One day, Fran Cosgrave, you *will* want me. We had a love–hate thing going on: we wanted to be near each other and fought for each other's attention, but we also annoyed each other. He resented how much attention I got from blokes, and I played on that; I hated liking him so much when he was obviously a player who loved himself more than anybody else.

Chris, the producer of *Essex Wives*, had taken me to one side and said that I should try to milk the programme and get out if it what I could. I didn't understand what he meant at the time. I thought it would be shown, my mates would watch it and laugh and that would be it. Two weeks before it was aired in January 2003, I realised what he meant. I'll be eternally grateful to him for that and for his brilliance in directing and editing and the advice he gave me about milking the show.

I was sitting in the Slug and Lettuce in Brentwood High Street with my brother and Jess. By this time I had left Stringfellows; I had grown to hate it and was pondering what to do with my life when I got a text from a friend saying that I was in the *Daily Star*. Lo and behold, on page 37 there was a full-page picture of me, accompanied by a small article about the forthcoming TV show. I was over the moon and immediately craved more of this attention. It was only one of the publicity shots I had done for *Essex Wives*: I was wearing white combat trousers and a white vest – it was very low cut and made my boobs looked huge. It struck me that, if they deemed me good enough for a whole-page feature, maybe they would want to see more of me?

I asked Jordan and Jess if they thought I should phone them. Jordan shrugged – he has always been completely uninterested in fame – and Jess told me not to, saying I would just make myself look silly. I ignored both of them and phoned the *Star*. I said I wanted to speak to someone about the article on page 37 of today's paper. The guy asked me who I was and, excitedly, I told him I was the girl in the paper. (Like they cared. Stop press – there's some random girl from Essex on the phone!)

The next person I spoke to was very friendly, and asked if they could help. I told them who I was and said that I wanted to do Page 3. He took my number and said that someone would call me back.

Within five minutes the picture editor himself, a guy called Ernie, phoned me and told me that they would love to have me on Page 3. How would I like to do a daily strip show in the paper, starting off fully clothed and ending up topless? I told him I'd love to. Not quite believing it, I put the phone down and announced to the whole pub that I was going to be on Page 3!

That very afternoon a photographer met me at my house. I posed for her in the garden and in a bedroom. These were just the teaser shots of me with clothes on, because I had told Ernie about the topless shots I had already done with Jeff Kaine a few months before that and he decided to use those because we were short on time and he wanted me to start the strip show in the following day's paper.

And so began my quick rise to fame. I used the quote, 'I want to be as big as Jordan, not in boob size but name-wise!' as my quote for my Page 3 debut. Jordan, bless her, didn't seem to believe it was meant as a compliment. I'm big enough to admit it helped my new career, I laughed about her silicone boobs and became a front runner for women with real ones and the 90 per cent of men who prefer them.

Life had never been better. I knew that I wasn't going to disappear as quickly as I had appeared, I had too much ambition for that. I was finally doing the job I'd always wanted to do and I had great friends and family around me who were very supportive. I had honestly never felt happier. Finally, I felt an inner peace. Peace that I wasn't ugly any more (I couldn't be, if Page 3 wanted me), peace that my family were just as happy about it as I was and peace that I was going to be earning decent money from doing something I enjoyed. Then the single most painful moment of my life came, followed closely by the second. Tragedy struck and ripped that peace away from me. Life was never going to be the same again.

CHAPTER EIGHT

RIP

12 January 2003. Two friends and I were getting ready for a night out. As we were getting into the car, my phone rang and it was a friend of mine, Jon. 'Jodie,' he said, 'I'm so sorry.'

'Sorry for what?' I asked him.

'Oh, my God,' he gasped, sounding shaky, and quietly continued, 'You don't know.'

Something was badly wrong and my heart started thumping. 'Know what, Jon?' I asked him, trying to remain calm, when already I could feel an anger burning up inside me, even though I didn't know what I was angry at.

'I don't know how to tell you this, babe,' he stuttered, 'but Kim's dead.'

There and then my world collapsed.

I yelled at him to tell me he was joking or that it wasn't true. I called him every name under the sun and effed and blinded until I couldn't shout any more. Then I broke down and begged him to tell me what had happened. All I remember is listening to him in silence, a shaking hand covering my mouth as I thought I was going to be sick. I didn't take in all of what he said, but I managed to hear something about a car crash and the word accident. The truth that later emerged was far more horrifying and made me wish it had been a car crash. That sounds awful, but losing someone to murder was not only devastating, but was to leave me with a feeling of bitterness and anger that, even now, doesn't seem to be easing.

I can't remember what I said to Jon at that point but, when I hung up, the first thing I did was try to call Kim's mobile. It makes no sense now, looking back, but it was the only thing I wanted to do – talk to her. The next thing I knew I was back in my flat with a friend comforting me on either side. I felt completely numb. It was like a bad dream: nothing felt real and I couldn't understand anything. My head, that had been so clear a few hours earlier, was now fuzzy and dream-like as I tried to take in what I had just been told. I wanted to know more, but I didn't dare call her parents as I knew it was the last thing they needed. Instead, I called Rachael, one of the other Chickens and broke the news to her. Together we sobbed over the phone.

About an hour after I came off the phone to Rachael, my brother came knocking at the door of my flat. He had just finished band practice and was coming to see what I was up to. One of my friends let him in and he knew instantly that something was wrong. He sat on the end of my bed and asked me what was the matter. I could hardly find the words to tell him, as I knew it was going to hurt him badly too. He had also loved Kim and got on extremely well with her. They had the kind of bond that I shared with him, a brother–sister love. They constantly ribbed one another and even play-fought, but always with affection and laughter. He didn't cry when I told him. I think he was in shock and couldn't really take it in. He later told me that he didn't cry for her properly until the night before her funeral, where his band had the honour of playing. It was when he was setting up his equipment that it hit him and, when it hit him, it hit him hard. I didn't cry again that night, just sat quietly with my friends who piled into my big double bed and stayed the night with me.

Rachael came over to mine the next morning, followed sharply by a detective. I can't remember who broke the next piece of horrific news to me, but I do remember that it came as a body blow.

Kim had been murdered.

The detective wanted a statement from me as I was one of the last people to have seen her alive. She had called me up out of the blue the day before New Year's Eve and asked to come over with her little boy. I thought it was a little out of character for her: since she had had him, she hadn't really left the house other than to see family. Moreover, since becoming pregnant she had been incredibly organised. She no longer did anything on the spur of the moment. I had planned to go to Dukes, a nightclub in Chelmsford, with my brother and a friend from Stringfellows called Sara who was already at my house, but I told Kim it was fine for her to come over, thinking that, if it came to it, I could spend a couple of hours with her and meet the others at Dukes later on. When she arrived, Jordan and Sara were just leaving, and I promised I would be along soon. As it happened, I never made it to the club: I loved seeing Kim and her child and she ended up staying for about five hours. We sat and chatted with my mum and dad; Mum and I fought over who got to hold the baby; and Kim had a cheeky fag with me – she hadn't smoked throughout her pregnancy, but before that had been as heavy a smoker as me.

I still try to remember as much as I can of what we talked about that night. We discussed her baby a lot, and my mum had a stack of presents for him. I also know that we told her about the filming of *Essex Wives*. The only other thing I remember her telling me was that she wasn't getting on very well with John at the time; that was why she wanted to come round. She said that his family were annoying her because they were interfering with how she brought up her child. She told me how she only wanted him to drink water or milk because sugary drinks would be bad for him and that, although she had told John's family this, she kept catching them giving him orange squash. To be honest, I just took these to be normal family issues, and I wasn't too worried for her. She was a brilliant, natural mother and very outspoken, so I sort of found the orange squash incident amusing because I knew she would probably get her own way in the end or she'd be swearing under her breath about them, an image which made me laugh.

When she decided it was time to go, I helped her get the child into his baby seat in the car, then stood on my drive waving her off. If only I had known it was to be the last time I would see her, I would have hung on to her for dear life and begged her not to go; I would have told her I loved her and that she was an amazing person; I would have done all the things you wish you could do or say after you lose someone and it's too late.

The detective questioned me fully about her state of mind, and asked me if she was wearing her jewellery when I saw her. I told him that she was. I knew this because she and my mum had had a conversation about it – they both had the same bracelet, which somehow they had only noticed that night. He then told me how Kim had died: he didn't want to go into too much detail but he told me that it had been brutal. By this point I already knew she had been murdered. I also knew who had done it: John Dore, her boyfriend, the man she loved, the man she owned a house with and the father of her baby.

I had never liked John, and I never thought he was good enough for my best friend. He was from Canning Town, the same place that my ex Garry came from. John really looked up to Garry, who thought he was a prick. John was a wannabe gangster, what people who were real gangsters called a 'plastic gangster'. Someone who tried to be hard and scary but somehow it just didn't quite suit him. He always seemed to me to be the type of bloke who got bullied at school over his pretty-boy looks and was now trying to prove to the world that he was tough. He always talked about fights he had been involved in, but we had never even seen him argue with anyone, let alone knock a bloke out, as he claimed he'd done every week. Despite all this, however, I never thought him capable of anything more sinister, nor did I think he would ever hurt Kim. I just disliked him, as a best mate does when you know they can do better. I didn't hate John, just found him massively annoying and grew tired of listening to his bragging. He was a stupid little boy, trying to be a man in the only way he knew.

At this point, although he still wouldn't tell me all the facts, the detective did tell me how they had discovered Kim. Two police officers had been driving through wasteland in Bromley by Bow the previous night and had seen two men lifting something out of the boot of a car. When the men saw the headlights, they dropped whatever it was they were holding and ran. The officers acted swiftly and chased after them, eventually catching them. After they had handcuffed them, they made their way back to the car and found that the package, which at this point they thought was simply stolen goods, was actually Kim's body wrapped in tarpaulin. Beside the car were tools used for digging and a shallow grave. One of the men they arrested was John and the other who had been helping him was his father Steven, her baby's granddad.

I still hadn't been told how Kim had died and I didn't know that John had actually killed her three days earlier, on her 22nd birthday. He had kept her body in the bath for three days. Looking back on it, I think I'm glad I wasn't told these gruesome facts immediately, as I don't think I would have been able to cope.

The fact that she was gone and I was never going to see her again or the news that it was John who had stamped out her short life would have been enough to deal with in one go. Combined, they were the most difficult things I've ever had to try and understand. I realised I was never going to see Kim again but it took me ages to come to terms with the fact that John had murdered her. All I kept saying was that the last time I had seen him was a few weeks before, when he and Kim had brought the baby over to my flat and my brother had gone out to get us all a takeaway McDonald's which I paid for. I had let a murderer into my home and bought him dinner. It may sound strange, but I couldn't deal with that. Kim and John had been to my house so many times before, during and after her pregnancy. Each time, even though I didn't particularly like him, I had welcomed John with open arms. They had been to parties with me, they had come over to go swimming, we had gone out clubbing, they came to all my brother's gigs and we used to go out as a foursome when I was with Garry. I could not understand why the fuck he had done this.

After the detective had taken my statement and gone, a few more friends turned up and we sat numbly together, talking quietly and crying lots. Everybody around me had gone to pieces and I still hadn't even told my mum and dad. From that day on, I knew that I was going to have to be strong. Because I was slightly older than the rest of The Chickens, I think they looked to me for comfort and understanding, neither of which I had, but I pretended I did. My pain became something I learned not to show.

I didn't tell my mum and dad until the following evening. Dad had collapsed while cooking dinner on the day I heard the news and had been rushed to hospital where he was diagnosed with high blood pressure. Everyone was very worried about him, but he came home after a few hours and seemed to be fine. Even so, I didn't want to upset them – I think that deep down I just wanted to spare them from the pain for as long as I could. They had loved Kim as much as I had. All my friends get on with my parents because they're so cool and such nice people, but my parents had an extra-soft spot for Kim. Whenever she was at the house, she would spend just as long chatting with them as she would me. She was so bubbly that often she'd come over to see me and spend two hours telling my mum funny stories and keeping her company while she ironed. I knew they were going to be devastated.

When I told them, they were both frozen to the spot until the silence was broken by howls from my mum. We all hugged and they cried lots. All my life my parents had been emotionally strong for me and I had rarely seen either of them cry. The only time I had seen my dad cry was when his brother died of a heart attack aged 48 and it made me feel even more like I needed to be strong. I knew my dad had been ill and they were both stressed over that. For the previous year or so they had been worried about their business, as the building trade had taken a nosedive and things hadn't been looking good. They'd had to make cutbacks on staff and were therefore working ten times as hard as normal. At a time in their life, at the age of 53, when they should have been starting to think about an early retirement after how hard they had worked all their lives, they were now working harder than ever. I'm sure this had contributed to my dad's high blood pressure or at least to him feeling as ill as he had recently. They were up at six every morning and didn't get in until six in the evening, when they continued to work until eleven at night on the books.

Added to that was the pressure of both my nans being ill. My mum's mum had not really been capable of doing much since my granddad passed away a few years before and my mum spent every Wednesday evening at her house until nearly midnight, doing all her banking for her. My dad's mum had suffered a stroke and had been moved into a home. She had been stone-deaf for most of her life but always coped very well through lip-reading and been very fit and strong. After the stroke she began to lose her eyesight, her only means of communication with the world and could no longer go out or do much for herself. Consequently, they spent a lot of time with her too. Neither my mum nor my dad needed any more stress. It seems awful now that I was thinking all of these things at a time when I had just lost somebody so close to me but, as I said before, I'm a deep thinker and I was worried for my parents.

From that minute on I subconsciously made a decision to be strong and in control, not just for their sake but for everyone who needed me – and that included Kim's parents. I met with them and Kim's sister at my mate's pub, the White Hart in Brentwood High Street. Although I could feel their pain and I was ripped and twisted up inside, I needed to say and do the right thing. I hugged all three of them for ages, but I hugged Kim's sister just that little bit tighter and for longer. I knew how easy it would be for people to show their sympathy to the parents, but I felt that Kim's sister, being younger, needed it more than anyone. I told her funny stories about Kim, and even made her laugh. I joked that Kim would be looking down on us now, laughing and saying something like, 'Don't bloody cry over me, you silly cows.' She appreciated that, I think. It certainly made us both smile to think of Kim's cheekiness. I offered my help in any way they needed, and they said that they wanted me to help organise the funeral – I knew who most of Kim's friends were, and they wanted to make sure everybody was there. I said they should leave it to me and we all hugged again and went our separate ways.

The next few days passed in a blur of numbness. On the morning of Wednesday, 15 January, the day that *Essex Wives* was due to be shown, me and my mum had been booked to appear on *GMTV* to promote the show. I really didn't want to do it – I hadn't washed or changed my clothes since Sunday night, and all I could think about was Kim. The girl from the press office at ITV was great, though. She made me see that it was just a job and that sometimes we have to carry on. I showered and changed, and looked surprisingly well, all things considered. When friends of mine saw the show, their only comment was that I looked extremely relaxed and that my mum looked as tense as hell. I think it was because deep down I didn't care about being on a stupid programme – it was more a case of not wanting to be there and having no enthusiasm than actually being relaxed. My mum, on the other hand, who hated being on camera anyway, was liable to burst into tears at any point, as was everybody who knew Kim.

When we arrived home from the studio, my dad and brother were waiting to greet us at the house, looking whiter than white. 'I'm afraid there's been an accident,' my dad said nervously. 'It's Pixie.' I felt my knees buckle. If anything had happened to my little dog on top of everything else, I wouldn't be able to cope. My dad continued, 'It wasn't anybody's fault, but Pixie was out in the garden and a fox grabbed her. When Jordan went out, the fox dropped her and ran off. She was cut a bit, but still alive so we rushed her to the animal hospital down the road. They've decided to keep her overnight to be on the safe side, but they think she's going to be fine.'

We piled into the car – I needed to see my baby girl and make sure she was all right. When we got there, we were ushered into a room where Pixie was in a small cage attached to a drip. They got her out and passed her to me, saying that she was a little high on the drugs they had given her to keep her calm; she would be disorientated, but she would still knew who we were. I spoke soothingly to her and kissed her again and again. We all took turns stroking her head, kissing her and talking to her. She seemed fine for ages when, all of a sudden, she freaked out. She started yelping and crying and flailing about. I immediately freaked out myself and burst into tears, so the vet rushed to our side and took Pixie off me. She said that it was nothing to worry about, and that Pixie would be completely fine. She promised that it was just a side-effect of the drugs they had given her, put her back into the cage and told us to come back tomorrow morning to pick her up. She also said I could phone them again later to check up on her, which I did – she was fine but tired.

We were very subdued for the rest of the day, but knew we had to put on brave faces as the previous week we had invited about fifteen people over to our house that night to watch *Essex Wives*. A lot of our friends had been filmed with us for the show and so were very excited about seeing it; they did call and ask if we still wanted them to come after what had happened to Kim, but we told them we would be glad of the company. People started arriving at about eight o'clock and, although since Sunday I hadn't given the show a second thought, I did feel a tiny twinge of excitement as ten o'clock neared. None of us had a clue what had actually made it into the programme as we had filmed about 60 hours of footage and we were only one of three families in the hour-long documentary. They had only finished editing the show a few days previously, so we never got to see a preview of it. My mum and dad decided to watch it upstairs in their bedroom – I think they were slightly nervous about how they were going to come across so they wanted to watch it alone. Other friends were texting me throughout the programme about things I said and they were making me laugh. Everyone loved it. So, as it turned out, my parents had nothing to worry about. The show was great, it was very true to life and showed us exactly how we were. No flashy displays for the cameras, just us as the loving and close family that we were – with a bit of our madness thrown in, such as the stripping and drunken nights out.

For weeks after that, people approached all of us in all sorts of places and praised us, saying we had a wonderful family. Even one of the other women who starred in the show, who had two very young children, said to my mum at the party for the end of the series a few weeks later that she hoped she could have a bond with her kids when they were older like Mum did with us. We were all proud of each other.

The following morning, we were up early to go and collect Pixie. We were about to leave to get her when the phone rang and my dad answered it in the study. When he walked back into the dining room, he was as white as a sheet. He nearly choked on his words. 'Pixie's dead,' he said. For the second time that week as a family, we were all in floods of tears.

My legs went from under me as I shouted, 'Why me?' and 'Please God, no!' until I collapsed on the floor in pain. Jordan, who rarely ever cried, was sobbing; and my mum was sitting down with her head in her lap, crying loudly. My dad just stood there, tears rolling down his cheeks, stroking my mum's back. Life was not fucking fair.

Once we had all calmed down a bit, my mum and dad went to collect Pixie. Jordan and I sat numbly in the lounge until they got back. When they walked in, my mum was carrying Pixie wrapped up in a soft blanket. Crying, she sat next to me with Pixie on her lap and was just about to peel back the blanket to let me see Pixie when our other dog Teddy bounded into the room towards her. He stood up at her lap and sniffed at the blanket, which made my mum panic. She shouted at Dad to take Teddy away as she didn't want to distress him, but my dad came over, put his arm round me and said that it was probably for the best that Teddy saw her as it might help him understand that she was dead. Then my mum told me not to worry: Pixie looked beautiful, just like she was asleep. She pulled back the blanket slowly and I reached out with a shaking hand to stroke her. I couldn't even really see properly as I was blinded with tears. Kim was gone, and now my little girl was gone too. Teddy was obviously distressed, so I swept him up into a cuddle and curled up on the sofa. For the second time in my life, I wanted to die.

CHAPTER NINE

The Aftermath

Even thinking about it as I write, it is very difficult for me to understand Kim's death and explain why women stay with abusive men for so long. It's one of the reasons I do a lot of charity work for Refuge in aid of domestic violence to women, now that I'm known publicly. I am certain of two things, though, that I would never tolerate a man raising even one finger to me and that it's not always openly weak women who get battered.

The week after Kim's death, and four days after Pixie's, I was offered another photo shoot with the *Daily Star*. Ernie wanted me in a studio for a professional shoot with one of his top glamour photographers, Jeanny Savage. It sounded very exciting and would have been all my dreams come true had I not just lost a best friend and, with Pixie, what felt like my right arm; now, though, doing a photo shoot was the last thing on my mind, and what had once been my dream seemed so shallow and pointless. How could I possibly think about myself and my career at a time like this?

However, after letting slip to a couple of friends that I had been offered the chance, they begged me to do it. They drummed it into me that it was what Kim would have wanted. If Kim could speak to me from above, she would be screaming at me to go for it. I knew they were right. Kim was the least selfish friend I had ever had, and I know she would have been proud of me. The *Daily Star* had been running pictures of me every day since my Page 3 debut, as I had gone down well with the readers. Most of my friends were pleased for me and I knew that Kim, if she had still been with us, would have been buying it every day. But one friend, Jess, refused to buy it even though I texted her to say I was in it. It upset me at the time because she was a close friend and I wanted her to be proud of me. Events that followed made me see that she was jealous of my newfound fame and that's why she wouldn't buy it. I knew Kim, though, would have been telling everyone she knew that I was her best mate. My other friends were right and I began to feel like I owed it to myself and to Kim to go ahead with the shoot. I also knew that this was probably my last stab at getting somewhere in life, as opportunities like that don't come along every day. It was listening to lyrics from an Eminem song in the film *8 Mile* one day that finally made up my mind: 'You only get one shot, do not miss this chance to blow, this opportunity comes once in a lifetime...' I called Ernie and said yes.

My mum and dad drove me to the shoot on the day. They were probably still worried about my state of mind, but they were also keen to see what went on behind the scenes at a glamour shoot. When we arrived, the studio impressed all of us. It was huge, airy and exactly how I imagined a top photographer's place to be. I had been warned by a few friends in the business that Jeanny was a difficult woman and could be quite harsh, so I was prepared not to like her – and also to tell her exactly where to go if she was horrible to me. Although being there might have been everything I had always dreamed of, having had Kim and Pixie taken from me so horribly, I was also in a place where I knew what was important and what wasn't in the grand scheme of things. If she's horrid, I thought, I'll just walk out.

As it turned out, Jeanny was really nice. She welcomed me like I was an old friend and made my mum and dad feel comfortable. Immediately I felt I could talk to her, so while I was having my make-up done, I thought I would be honest with her and explain that I wasn't on top form at the moment and that she might have to bear with me. I told her all about Kim and Pixie and cried all the way through the story. Although Gary the make-up artist had to keep retouching my face through the tears, Jeanny sympathised and let me talk, touching my hands reassuringly every now and then and generally making me feel like she understood the pain I was in. I told her that I still wanted the pictures to look great, and that I was doing it for Kim. We worked well together and, although to this day I hate the pictures, everyone else loved them; and when anybody asked how I found it working with Jeanny, I told them she was lovely and that I really liked her.

I began to force myself to go out a lot. I wanted to be around people who didn't know Kim as a way of blocking out the pain. I felt like I couldn't talk to anyone who knew her – they were feeling as much pain as I was, and I felt like I didn't deserve their sympathy and didn't want to upset them. I know now that I was running away from the problem, but I didn't feel like I had any other choice. I was spending more and more time at Click with Fran and other random friends I had made in London. I felt more comfortable being around him now: he had just split with Natasha and was on a partying bender.

I didn't want to sit at home and I wasn't sleeping anyway so I thought I might as well surround myself with things to keep me occupied. The girl spy in the *News of the World*'s *Sunday* magazine reported seeing me out in Click and said I looked awful. My hair was greasy, my make-up looked like it had been on for three days, she said. It was a real nasty piece saying that she couldn't understand what people saw in me. Well, bitch, I can tell you that you were right; my hair *was* greasy and my make-up probably *had* been on for three days. That's because my best friend and soul mate had just been brutally murdered and my baby girl Pixie, who had been the love of my life for six years, had been killed too. Do you think I gave a shit about what I looked like? Have some fucking compassion. Talk about knocking a person when they're down! She might say that she didn't know what had happened – well, if she's a journalist, she should have found out. I wonder how she would have looked if the same had just happened to her? On second thought, she's probably so fucking cold and pretentious that all she'd care about *is* her lip-gloss looking perfect.

It was at Click in the weeks following Kim's death that I met Fenton. He was a friend of Gary Lucy's and I had met him once before at Gary's birthday party a few months previously. He had seemed nice enough at the party, and was even friendlier when I met him again in Click. He had watched *Essex Wives* and loved it, and we ended up chatting for a number of hours. Eventually I found myself telling him all about Kim and Pixie and how terrible I was feeling. As I sat there numbly explaining the tragedies, he became obviously concerned and gave me lots of sympathy. He was from Essex too, but went out in London a lot so by the end of the night we had swapped numbers and I thought that, if nothing else, he was somebody to go out with and somebody to whom I felt I *could* talk about Kim.

Things happened very quickly between us. Within a week, he was calling himself my boyfriend, which I liked, and we were spending every day together. I enjoyed being with him because I could unload on him. Looking back now, I know I was completely unfair towards him and I used him as an emotional crutch. Don't get me wrong, Fenton was and still is a lovely bloke, but my heart wasn't in it. I was just looking for somebody to lean on and cry with. I still felt like I had to be strong in front of anybody who knew Kim and my partying friends in London were too shallow to care. Fenton fitted the bill perfectly and we dated for a hazy two months while I continued to bury myself in clubbing and working. My relationship with Fenton wasn't real, however – not to me anyway. I still had feelings for Fran and my head was consumed by thoughts of Kim and Pixie. Fenton was like a comfort blanket that I cuddled up to at night. He made me feel like I wasn't alone and gave me someone to talk to. The whole time I was with Fenton and still going to Click, I didn't even tell Fran I was seeing him. It wasn't because I was ashamed of Fenton, more that I was ashamed of myself because I knew that it wasn't going to last. I *needed* Fenton; I didn't *want* him.

I had a tattoo done on the back of my neck in the form of a cross, with 'Pixie' written vertically inside the cross and 'Kim' written horizontally. Underneath it has the letters

'R.I.P.' I designed it myself at Fenton's house one day and had it done a few days later. The pain of it, and the fact that I had scarred my body for life with their names, brought me some comfort.

Because Kim's death had been by murder, nobody knew when the funeral was going to take place. All we were told was that it would be 'a while'. That 'while' ended up being nearly two months, and for those two months I thought of nothing but Kim and how much I missed her. I decided to make a 'memory box' for her son which would include letters, photographs and newspaper and magazine cuttings about her for him to see when he was older. I spent many hours writing a letter to him detailing every single thing I could remember about her so that he might understand how wonderful she was and at least know a little bit about his mum.

It was about three weeks into my relationship with Fenton that we were told that Kim's body would be released in a few weeks' time, and the date for the funeral was set for 4 March 2003, my brother's 21st birthday. I felt a huge sense of relief that finally we would be able to lay her to rest; but I was gutted for my brother that it would be on his birthday, and not just any birthday but the big one. I clung to Fenton even more. Anybody who has experienced a death, and even more so a murder, will understand that waiting for a funeral to happen is like having a huge black cloud hanging over you. You can't function normally at all. I was completely disturbed by my grief, which I still didn't show to anyone but Fenton, and tried to control it by helping to organise the funeral. I ended up being the person that told most of Kim's friends where and when it was going to be held and where to get the flowers from. I spent hours on the phone to people, and I chatted with the vicar at length, as he wanted to talk to her closest friends to gain an insight into what she was like as a person. I gave him a copy of the letter I had written for Kim's child so that he could read it and maybe take something from it for the service.

Then I was asked the biggest, scariest question of my life. 'Will you read at the funeral?' It was a decision unanimously made by Kim's immediate family and her three other closest friends and it had to be one of the four of us as we were her best friends. None of the others felt strong enough to do it; so, with the deepest sadness and greatest honour I have ever felt in my life, I said yes and started to prepare my speech. There were two parts to it. The first part was a summing up of the Kim that we knew and loved which included funny stories and moving words and detailed how amazing she was and how gutted we all were; the second part was a poem written by my dad. He wrote it in the week after Kim and Pixie's death as a way of dealing with his own grief. It was written for Pixie, his 'grandchild', but it was beautiful and perfectly fitting.

> You were here for such a short time, you touched so many lives, including mine.
> Were you an angel, we just don't know. We only wish you hadn't had to go.
> Now there's a void, an empty place. All I see before me is your sweet face.
> Life seems so cruel and so unfair. I only wish that you were still here.
> Although I know our loss is your gain, for where you are there is no pain,
> I tell you now, of this I'm certain. When life here ends, it's no final curtain.

Just a door to a bright new place, full of joy, light
and space.
You will be remembered always as someone who
brightened all our days.
I say farewell, but not goodbye, for I know that we
will meet again on high.

On the day of the funeral I was an absolute wreck. I didn't want to wear all black as Kim's parents had specifically requested that the funeral and wake be more a celebration of her life rather than a mourning, so I wore my black trousers and black shirt with a pair of cow-skin-patterned stiletto boots as I knew Kim would have liked that. More than 400 people turned up at the church, which was amazing and brought a tiny bit of comfort, but, from the minute the service began, all hell broke loose. I had only ever been to funerals of really old people before, like my great-grandma's, where the congregation contained their grief and cried quietly or you just heard a few sniffs from the row behind. This was completely different and nothing could have prepared me for it. Seeing the coffin as it approached my aisle, I felt the strongest mix of anger and sadness I have ever known. Knowing that I would never see her smiley face or hear her raucous laughter again made me feel like I could have killed somebody. It hurt so much to think that I never got to tell her how much I loved her, how happy she had made me, how honoured I was to have even known her, or how much of an impact she had had on my life.

Everybody around me was sobbing, not just a little bit and not at all quietly: they were literally howling. It was the most horrible sound I have ever heard. I too was crying, but not wanting to lose it in front of all The

Chickens and my family, I tried to hold it together. I still had a reading to get through and I didn't want to let Kim or her family and friends down (for the rest of my life, though, I'll never forget the noise of the people's pain in the church that day).

Everybody stood united in their grief over the loss of such a young, beautiful, amazing person. Their wails will haunt me forever. I held Fenton's hand on one side and my mum's on the other, and after what seemed like only a minute I was standing alone in front of hundreds of people. I don't know how I got through the reading. My legs turned to jelly beneath me, I couldn't feel them at all and my head was spinning.

Before the reading I received about twenty texts from various friends wishing me luck with it; afterwards I received another twenty saying well done. I remember all of them, and the one that especially stood out was my brother's: 'I CAN'T SAY IT 2 UR FACE COS IT'S 2 PAINFUL BUT WELL DONE ON UR SPEECH. U DID HER PROUD AND I WANT U 2 KNOW THAT WE'RE ALL PROUD OF U 2.' Being the lad that he is, he very rarely shows any emotion and normally deals with things in a cocky, boyish way, so I knew how hard it had been for him to write that message. I've still got all the texts to this day. I don't ever want to forget them.

Before I knew it, I was back at the White Hart. The wake was held there and Jordan's band were playing. A group of us sat quietly and spent the next few hours reminiscing over times we had spent with Kim. Fenton didn't let go of my hand. He was a rock that day, soaking up my grief with cuddles and affection. At some point later in the night, when everybody had a few drinks inside them and were not so tearful, I felt it the right time to show Kim's dad my tattoo. I wanted him to see how much Kim had meant to me and I knew he would appreciate it, but I didn't want to get the timing wrong and cause upset. As it was, it did make him cry – but in a good way. He thought it was lovely, hugged me lots and we cried together. He told me that I had done Kim proud and that my reading was beautiful. It meant a lot to hear it from them because I was so nervous about it and so wanted to get it right. We spent the rest of the night in a hazy, puffy-eyed state, singing and dancing until we all left feeling totally drained.

Everybody had told me that I would find some sort of peace after the funeral, so I expected to wake up the next day a different person. That didn't happen. I woke up the next day feeling like nothing had changed and that Kim still wasn't coming back. Even so, I knew it was time to try and move on and at least try and find some happiness.

CHAPTER TEN

From Bullshit to Jeff

Around the time I did the shoot with Jeanny, the *Star* was still running pictures of me daily and getting lots of good feedback. One day they ran a front page and a huge double-page centre spread of me versus Jordan. It asked readers to vote for whom they preferred. Although nothing seemed important any more with what I was going through, secretly I wanted to win – not just for myself but for Kim, as she would have found it so amusing. My phone was red hot all day with journalists trying to get an interview and friends telling me they had seen it and voted. That night I got a call from the *Star* to tell me I had won hands down with a massive 70 per cent of the vote. I thanked them for their support and whispered towards the skies, 'That was for you, Kim.'

The next day I took a call from a girl called Sara at the *Sun* newspaper asking me to meet with her. They wanted to offer me a deal to be their new girl. She offered me a large sum of money to be exclusively theirs for six months as a Page 3 girl. I haggled with her over the amount of money and managed to up it by a large chunk, then shakily signed on the dotted line. I didn't want to turn my back on the *Star* who had supported me from day one, but also I still hadn't been paid (or offered!) a penny from them and I knew it was about making business decisions from now on. The *Sun* had a much bigger circulation, which meant more people would see me, and they were offering an amount of money I didn't want to turn down. Out of courtesy I called Ernie from the *Star* to tell him and, although he was disappointed, he understood and said that he hoped we could work together again soon. I promised him we would.

An hour after I signed the contract with the *Sun*, I received a phone call from the manager I'd kept at arm's length since the incident in Chinawhite. I had been on the phone to him countless times over the two weeks leading up to *Essex Wives*, saying, 'I think it's going to be huge, get me work!' He hadn't been able to come up with anything. This was the first time he had ever had a proper job to offer me – a photo shoot and interview with the *Daily Sport* for £1,000. I had to go topless and he would take 20 per cent of that money. I had just signed a deal worth a lot more than that, and I now couldn't pose topless for anybody else, so I politely declined. I didn't tell him why, I just said I wasn't interested. Two days later the photographer I had done work experience with, who now worked for the manager doing 'paparazzi'-style set-up pictures of his clients, was on the phone. He told me that they had found out how much money I was getting from the *Sun* and felt entitled to a share for his services as a manager. I felt I hadn't signed with him, he hadn't got me any work – with the exception of the offer from the *Daily Sport* – and I did the deal with the *Sun* completely on my own.

The photographer told me that this guy was huge in the business and could make or break a person. If I didn't pay up, he'd be sure to see to it I never worked again. I broke down in tears and asked him why he was doing this to me. We had been friends – or so I thought – for eight or nine years and he knew that I was still reeling from Kim's death. He told me that he was very sorry and tried to make out he was doing me a favour by warning me what the manager was going to do if I didn't pay up. He said I was nothing in the eyes of the *Sun* and that they would drop me the next day if this guy told them to do so. Devastated and in tears, I told him that I would have to think about it and hung up.

I didn't tell my parents straight away because I was in complete shock that a guy I thought was my friend could be so horrible at such a terrible time in my life. I couldn't believe that he had threatened me the way he had, and I was terrified that the thing I had dreamed of for years was going to be taken away from me. Naively, I thought that this manager really could break me. I sobbed for ages before going to tell my parents. They too were horrified and their first reaction was that they wanted to call the photographer and tell him where to go; luckily I talked them out of that. Instead, we came to a decision that I definitely didn't owe them a penny and that I should ignore the phone call and hope for the best. For the next week I walked around, still dazed about Kim and now scared that at any moment I was going to get a call from the *Sun* to say it was over.

I knew that I was going to need an agent as work was flying in for me. I had a list of agents already calling me, trying to sign me up, so I had a long chat with Michelle and asked her who she thought I should go with from my list. She told me none of them. Then she told me about a guy named Jeff Weston from a company called SEM. She said that, as my aim was eventually to get into TV, he would be a better bet as he had turned Ian Wright from a footballer to a media and TV star and didn't look after too many other media personalities. It would mean that he would have more time to devote just to me. She got me his number and I called him up and asked for a meeting.

Jeff hadn't watched *Essex Wives* or seen my daily appearances in the newspapers, so he didn't have a clue who I was. He granted me a meeting anyway because I was persistent, and I arranged to see him a few days later after a day's shooting for the *Sun*. We met at his office along with a girl called Emma. The pair of them looked quite scary, and if I hadn't been so weary of everything I would have been very nervous; but I plonked myself down and relayed to them exactly what I had already done and what I wanted out of life. I finished up by saying, 'And my best friend's just been killed, so my head's not right at the moment.' Jeff and Emma said I blew them away. As a company, SEM don't usually take on glamour models, and now they have me they won't take any more. They take people purely on the basis of their talent and personality. Jeff and Emma both said that, although I could certainly rival others in the glamour stakes, they saw my personality and a definite X factor. The rest, as they say, is history. He signed me up there and then for three years. I mentioned to him my concerns about the previous manager, and he told me not to worry, which was a weight off my shoulders. I went home feeling tired but happy.

The first job I got from Jeff was to be the reserve for *I'm*

A Celebrity Get Me Out of Here!. I was paid to be flown first class to Australia for two weeks to stay in a penthouse suite in the six-star Palazzo Versace hotel on the Gold Coast. Not bad! Although I missed home terribly and couldn't stop thinking about Kim, I enjoyed the break and I even made the Australian papers as I did a few photo shoots on the beach while I was out there. Daniella Westbrook was having her breakdown at the time and everyone thought she was going to walk out, so I was fitted up with all the clothes and told to be prepared. Luckily she stayed and I didn't have to go into the jungle – not that I wouldn't have done it, but my head wasn't right at the time anyway and, looking back at it now, I *definitely* wouldn't have coped with all the spiders and animal-eating antics. I'm perfectly happy doing a bungee jump, a 1,000-foot aerial slide or learning to ride a 600cc motorbike – in fact, I've done all of these – but try and make me go near a spider or eat a worm and I'll be screaming from here to Timbuktu.

Life was, although not happy (I still had a bitter sadness inside of me), definitely looking up, and my career went from strength to strength. Modelling jobs flew in, as did TV work – bit parts here and there, interviews and appearances. I made the most of it. Looking back now, I'm very happy with the way my career took off. The only thing that makes me sad is when I see pictures of myself fake-smiling in the first eight months or so of my career. Deep down I was thoroughly depressed about Kim and looking for a love I felt I was never going to find. The press occasionally gave me a hard time, calling me a slapper and ugly and I found it difficult to be cheerful.

My friends and family were very proud, though, and spurred me on and there were some definite perks. One of those perks was being asked to be the Formula 1 Jordan Grand Prix team mascot. By then I had done a few men's magazine covers and was loving the fact that, somewhere out there, men found me sexy. So it was with great pride that I donned the famous yellow race suit and became the girl of PlayStation Formula 1. The night before my first photo call as their girl, I went out clubbing with a group of friends and was photographed leaving the club at half-past five in the morning. I was fully made up and posing on the bonnet of a car by half-past eight. The papers loved it and ran stories about my wild nights of clubbing, followed by looking fresh as a daisy just three hours later. For some reason I always work better when I've had little or no sleep, and it has become a running joke with people I've worked with that I always turn up hungover to shoots or interviews with last night's make-up still on.

The Grand Prix itself was amazing, and I took along my dad who has been a fan of Formula 1 for years. We were given the royal treatment all day and met lots of lovely people, including Rick Parfitt Junior, son of Rick Parfitt, guitarist from Status Quo. Status Quo were playing a concert in the evening to 70,000 people; I somehow managed to get dragged on stage with them (with a little encouragement from Rick Junior, I'm sure) and played air guitar to 'Rocking All Over the World' with them. Hilarious! My dad was on the phone to my mum saying, 'You won't believe what I'm watching right now!' A very good day was had by all, and there was lots of good press coverage – just what the doctor ordered!

Before long I split with Fenton, as I couldn't continue something that wasn't real on my part. I felt bad for being with him anyway, as I realised by now that he had just been a shoulder to cry on. I also forced myself to go out as much as possible because when I stayed in I just wallowed in my grief. It was on one of these nights out that Westlife came to Click and I met Kian once more. He told me how the pictures of our last evening together had got him in trouble with his record company – they didn't like the boys to be seen with girls as they thought it would put their young fans off them. He wasn't any different with me now that I was famous; he just congratulated me on my success and we spent the night getting pissed. It ended in a lock-in with Westlife singing songs to me and my friends and playing imaginary golf with pretend clubs in the VIP room. By about six in the morning I was tired so my mates and I said our goodbyes and left.

Kian came to Click again the following week. I had told him it was my regular haunt and I couldn't help wondering if this time he had come to see me, as he only had his minder Paul with him. It soon became apparent that if he hadn't come specifically for that reason, he was at least very pleased to see me. He asked me to sit and get pissed with him and, again, we spent all night drinking. I was still reeling over Fran at this point and glad of the attention. Fran had told me the previous week that Westlife were 'real stars', so I knew he would be shocked that one of them was so interested in me, so I let Kian flirt with me all night, even sneaking in a cheeky snog when no one was looking. If I'm completely honest, I didn't even fancy Kian. The only thing he had going for him (apart from his money, which had never interested me – I make my own) was the Irish accent which always goes down well with me. At the end of the night Fran offered Kian and Paul a lift home with Marco, a driver we sometimes used, and both Kian and Fran told me to come with them. I didn't want to go back to Kian's, but I was certainly up for being alone with Fran, so I went.

When we got to Kian's, he begged me to get out of the car, which I did because he was starting to sound desperate and I didn't want to be rude and blatantly fuck him off. He spent twenty minutes trying to persuade me to come into his house, but I refused. Fran was waiting in the car and both he and Paul were starting to get annoyed. It was about six in the morning by then and starting to get light – they just wanted to go home to bed. I was trying to reason with Kian and reject his offer without being rude or offending him. Twice Marco tried to drive off and leave me there on Fran's orders; twice I chased after the car and begged him to wait. If he wasn't fussed about seeing a very drunk Kian safely inside the door, I was and he wouldn't go inside. Eventually Paul got out of the car and told Kian to stop being a idiot and to go to bed; he could see me again next week if he wanted. He finally went indoors and I got back into the car. Fran was in a foul mood by now. I couldn't work out if it was because Kian was on my case or because he was just tired and wanted to go to bed, but I didn't question him and we all got dropped home to our separate houses.

After that incident, I thought that, if Fran had been moody about Kian liking me, at least now he should be ready to make his move. After all, he knew that I liked him, and we were both single. No such luck. Fran continued to watch my every move when I was in Click; he even put blokes off talking to me and told them he was my boyfriend, but still he didn't come on to me. The following week, Kian turned up on his own again and was even more all over me than the last time. By now I was thinking to myself, What do I have to do to make this guy interested in me? As it happened, Fran took that question totally out of my hands: at the end of the night, Fran didn't ask but *told* me we were going back to Kian's because he liked me. Obviously, I thought, Fran doesn't have feelings for me at all. Perhaps he just saw me as a best mate. After all, if he had feelings for me, he wouldn't be telling me to go back to Kian's. I later found out that it had been a test to see if I would go, which Fran would later hold against me for the duration of our relationship.

Since Fran seemed so keen for me to go, I decided I would. Not only that, but I would shag Kian within earshot of Fran and make him listen to the screams so he would know how good I was in bed: it might make him realise what he was missing. Stupid, I know, but, after Kim, I don't think my brain was functioning normally. And when I think I'm in love, I'll play any trick in the book to get the guy.

When we left the club that night after a good few hours' late drinking, we decided to play up to the paps who had been waiting outside for ages. Or should I say, Fran decided to play up to the paps. Kian wasn't bothered about being seen with me, we were all drunk and having a good time. I suppose that, guessing Kian and I were going to step out in public for the first time, Fran wanted in on the publicity. Standing at the bottom of the stairs, about to leave the club, he noticed that Kian and I were holding hands and suggested that we do something 'really funny'. He said that we should leave all holding hands, with me in the middle of the two of them so that the press wouldn't know who I was going out with. He thought it would be hilarious and that they would have a field day with it. Too drunk to care, or realise that Fran was muscling in on the limelight, we agreed. As the three of us staggered up the stairs giggling, we threw the doors open to find an empty street. The paps must have got bored waiting and gone home. Blimey, it *was* five in the morning by then! Kian and I didn't care but Fran chirped on for ages that he 'couldn't believe' that they had gone. Rather, he probably couldn't believe that the one time we had been drunk enough to go along with his attention-seeking suggestion, there had been no paps to capture it.

We got to Kian's house and all sat on the brown leather sofas in the living room. He had a very nice house and I thought to myself that it wasn't what I had expected at all – very tasteful for a member of a boy band! Kian sat next to me and paid me lots of attention. I could see that Fran was annoyed, but I thought it was just because he was a gooseberry, not because he cared. Eventually Kian whispered in my ear, 'Shall we go upstairs?'

'Yes,' I replied, without hesitation. I was happy to get away from Fran – he was giving me the impression that he didn't care, and his moody face was annoying me.

Once upstairs, I gave Kian probably the best sex he has ever had. I really turned it on for him because I knew Fran could hear us – I had left the door open to make sure. I did things to him that I know he'd never had done before, and he loved every minute of it. He turned out to be dirtier than I imagined him to be, which was a bonus. Our first session lasted about two hours and we fell asleep in each other's arms (another bonus – nothing worse than a guy who rolls over after sex, eh, girls?). We woke up in the morning and went at it again. This must have woken Fran because before long he was knocking at our door, which was now closed. Fran wanted to go and get breakfast and wouldn't give us any peace until we got up and went. Kian drove us down to the Fulham Road to a place he liked that did a good fry-up. I was surprised because, with all the money he earns, he drove what looked like a very old BMW. It certainly wasn't a flash new one. After breakfast we all went our separate ways and I told Kian I'd see him at the weekend in Click.

Our relationship, if you can call it that, lasted about eight weeks. It soon made the papers and I'm sure that it came from Fran as he desperately needed the press for Click. He was also unusually good mates with Rav from the *News of the World*, who broke the story first. Rav himself told me he had got it from Kian's own PR as the lads were about to embark on a tour and needed some press. I denied that I was seeing Kian and tried to carry on normally; we would meet in Click and stay at his house afterwards. Sometimes I'd have a few girls with me and would bring them back to Kian's where they would sleep on sofas or in the spare room.

One time was especially funny. Becky and a friend of mine called Carlee came back to Kian's, where he was drunk and telling jokes, but talking too quickly in his thick Irish accent. We couldn't understand a word he was saying and so the way he told jokes was funnier than the joke itself. Whenever he told Englishmen, Irishmen and Scotsman jokes (which, surprisingly, were his favourite) he said 'Paddy Englishman, Paddy Irishman and Paddy Scotsman' every time, which we found utterly hysterical. There was no reasoning behind adding the word Paddy, all it did was make the joke even longer, but we found it highly amusing. I don't think he ever realised that we were laughing at him rather than with him. The next morning was Mother's Day and we all got up early in a state of panic because we weren't at home and hadn't got our mums a present. We stopped at a beautiful flower stall on the way home and I had a huge bouquet of flowers made up because I felt extra guilty for not being there. I'd never missed a Mother's Day before! Becky had them on her knee the whole way home. She joked that if I crashed she would die by suffocating in flowers and then we all imagined the funeral – no flowers please. We laughed all the way home.

Other times I stayed at Kian's on my own and he would play guitar and sing songs to me – something I found sweet but, because there were no feelings involved, a little bit boring. If he had been the love of my life, I would have adored the romantic touch, but because all I was after was dirty sex, which was what we were having, I didn't care for his drunken warbling and badly played guitar.

One day I opened the papers to find stories splashed across them that I had dumped Kian because he was a bad kisser and had bad breath. To this day I don't know for definite where these stories came from. But, even though there was not much emotion involved, I certainly didn't want Kian to think that these horrible made-up stories had come from me. I know it might sound strange, but I didn't even have Kian's number as we always arranged to see each other in Click on a certain night and we never let each other down. So I asked Fran to call Paul, Kian's minder, and to pass on my number and tell him to call me. I wanted to tell him that it wasn't me and to see if he wanted me to speak out to set it straight. Naively, I thought that he would be devastated by these nasty lies – I knew I would have been if I thought someone had been so horrible about me. I didn't realise that people in this business got nasty and untrue press all the time and that after a while it was like water off a duck's back! Anyway, I never heard from Kian. Looking back on it now, I'm sure Fran never passed on the message, but, even if he had, it's not like we were a serious couple so he probably still wouldn't have called.

I, on the other hand, was very upset by the stories at the time and didn't want Kian thinking that I would say something so nasty. I started getting harassed left, right and centre by journalists wanting to know if it was true; I just kept hanging up on them. I knew it was time to change my number again but I also thought I needed to set the record straight that Kian was *not* a bad kisser and *didn't* have bad breath. I agreed to do an interview with a guy called Jules Stenson, a reporter I got on with from the *News of the World*. With no word from Kian, I went ahead and told the truth to Jules: that we had been seeing each other but it wasn't serious. I explained that I hadn't dumped him and that he was actually a great kisser and didn't have bad breath. I said that he was good in bed, but didn't reveal too much detail; and I went on to say that he was extremely talented, as he often used to play the guitar and had written his own songs away from Westlife. You couldn't have read a nicer story about someone! Of course, the paper focused more on the sexual side, but it made him out to be an absolute sex god and they included all the nice bits as well about the guitar playing and such like.

The next thing I remember was waking up on Sunday morning to a torrent of abuse from Fran on the mobile. He was still out drunk from the night before and had seen the day's papers. He called me a story-selling slag and said that our friendship was over. I was in tears and couldn't understand why he didn't see I was just trying to set the facts straight and counteract the bad-kisser stories. He called me later on to apologise and said that he knew my intentions were all good as he knew I had a heart of gold. He'd calmed down and asked my forgiveness for his outburst. He told me that he was prepared to lose his 'friendship' with Westlife for me. 'What do you mean?' I asked him.

He explained that as a group they had come to him to ask if I was trustworthy. 'I totally backed you up,' he said. Now he was prepared to stand by me when they turned on me for selling stories. He made me feel like I needed him and he was there for me when it mattered. As it turned out, Kian never spoke to me again; but the other boys did, which I thank them for, and to this day I have the utmost respect for them as professionals and as people. Bryan and Mark especially are very genuine and down to earth and I love them for that.

The following week, stories of Kian denying our sexual relationship appeared in various papers and magazines, along with nasty quotes from him that hurt me – not because I cared about him, but because I didn't feel like I had done anything to deserve that. I was only trying to restore his dignity in giving an interview, and I felt hard done by. I learned from that it was never a good idea to speak to the press about anyone without their consent, unless you didn't care about them. It just wasn't worth the aggro and I didn't want to be labelled a story-seller, which I knew I wasn't. Fuck Kian, I thought. He may be denying sleeping with me now, but I have ambitions and when he's 70 he'll be bragging about the times he shagged me!

CHAPTER ELEVEN

Simply The Best

Monday night was Ten Rooms, Tuesday was Funky Buddha, Wednesday was Chinawhite, Thursday was Click and Friday and Saturday were either rest days or Click for those who didn't want to stay at home. My group of friends and I were taking over the London club scene and everyone wanted to hang around with us because we were the loudest and maddest group of people. It was on one of these nights out that I met Calum Best for the second time.

The first time was during my Stringfellows days, but I don't suppose he would remember that meeting! Lauren, Chloe and I had started to hate taking our clothes off for lecherous men and were finding any excuse we could to leave early and go out clubbing. If we left before twelve it meant we didn't have to pay the house fee, but the manager had cottoned on to girls doing this, so we had to come up with pretty good excuses to leave. That night,

Lauren pretended to be ill with severe stomach cramps, and Chloe pretended that her grandmother had been rushed to hospital and that, since I had driven her in, we both had to leave immediately. We had to time our excuses so that they wouldn't get suspicious. Lauren went first and doubled up in mock pain; the house-mum, being the lovely woman she was, took pity and signed her off. Chloe went five minutes later and put on such a good act she nearly cried. Definitely worthy of an Oscar, babe!

We gathered our things and quietly walked out of the building until we were in the car park where Lauren was waiting. Once there, we screamed in delight that our plan had worked. We all stopped for a minute to say a prayer for Chloe's grandmother – we felt bad that she had had to use a perfectly healthy nan as an excuse – but really, that's how strict it was. Then we stopped to consider the dilemma of what to wear and where to go. As we all just used to wear tracksuits into work, that's all we had with us except for our stripper outfits. Lauren's stripper outfit consisted of a pair of completely see-through black trousers and matching top which she was happy to wear out with a black G-string underneath. Mine was the shortest black rubber dress you have ever seen – it showed my whole bum – and Chloe's was the same dress but in pink. We decided that we couldn't go out in those as they were – it was too obvious that we were strippers – so we both wore our dresses as tops with our tracksuit bottoms and trainers. To top off my ridiculous ensemble I wore a *Rainbow* zip-up jumper with Bungle, George and Zippy on the front. If I'm going to look stupid, I thought, then I may as well look *really* stupid. We headed down towards Emporium because we had been there a few times and liked it, but there was a private party on and they wouldn't let us in. (More likely they took one look at our weirdly dressed combo arriving on a rickshaw and said, 'No way!') We had already paid the guy who dropped us off so were left with nowhere to go. As we started to walk down Kingly Street, a black guy came up to us and asked us where we were going. We told him that we couldn't get into Emporium, and asked if he knew of anywhere good. He told us he could take us into Attica if we liked, which is in the same street. Having been to Attica before and been treated like a piece of dirt by the door staff – if you're not famous they make you stand the other side of the street to decide who looks good enough to come in – I didn't really want to go there, but I felt like we didn't have much choice as the night was getting on and we really wanted to get a drink down our necks. (It was to be the last time I went to Attica. Out of principle I've never been there since I've been known. Take heed, club owners. You never know who somebody might become. Don't be rude to people!) As we approached the door, we were ushered straight through by the same guy who had refused me entrance a few weeks before that. The prick even kissed me on the cheek and called me darling as he led us to a table in the VIP.

I didn't recognise the black guy, who was obviously of some importance to get treatment like that; he had told me that he was in the building game, which I believed. When we got to the table a couple more black guys were sitting around with a white, long-haired, greasy-looking guy. They had the biggest bottle of champagne I had ever seen, a bottle of vodka and a bottle of Jack Daniel's on the table. Even though this was all very impressive, I still had no reason to think that he wasn't a builder – after all, my mum and dad owned a building company so I knew how much money you could make. We had a scream, anyway, partly because it was so random to end up with a load of strangers getting VIP treatment in Attica, and partly because we were dressed so ridiculously. The other girls in there were so sophisticated and we must have looked like tramps, not that we cared – we weren't there to impress anyone.

After a little while Chloe's boyfriend Ram called to see what we were doing as he was out in the West End. We told him to come to Attica and sent the black guy we had met in the street (we still didn't know his name) to get him in. When he joined us, he was grinning from ear to ear. It turned out that our host was Celestine Babayaro, a Chelsea football player. The other black guys were also high-profile footballers – although I can't for the life of me remember their names – and the white greasy guy was Calum Best, son of the legendary George. Immediately we all felt like idiots. What were we doing in such a pretentious club, wearing stripper outfits with tracksuit bottoms and trainers? We felt like groupies, which we definitely weren't, although I suppose we also felt a little bit cool because at least we hadn't tried it on with any of them and we certainly weren't dressed to impress – unlike all the other girls in the club who were glammed up to the nines and desperately trying to get near our little group. The end of the night came and I thanked Celestine for his hospitality (I didn't let on that I knew he wasn't a builder), kissed Calum on the cheek and we all left. We walked back to my car, which was miles away and Lauren whinged the whole way that everyone could see her bum in her see-through trousers. Me and Chloe took the piss out of her, calling her a hooker, and we still cringe when we think of how we must have looked that night.

The second time I met Calum it was a different story. It was a Tuesday night – Funky Buddha night. I had been at a party thrown by Damon Albarn from Blur earlier in the evening. He had hired out Click, but we left because I was getting abuse from all the indie crowd in there. I wasn't even dressed that outrageously that night – I was wearing a black and red Adidas jumpsuit. All right, so I did have a very impressive cleavage on show as I had it unzipped all the way down the front, but I was pretty covered up for me! For the record, I do actually love 'real' music and I accept people as I find them, regardless of their dress sense or taste in music. Shame others can't be the same. Anyway, Funky Buddha was heaving and we were soon dancing on the tables. Suddenly I noticed that Fran had latched on to a bloke at the side of our table. It was Calum. He was a lot better looking than I remembered; he also couldn't take his eyes off me. I teased him for ages by dancing with my mates knowing that he was watching me, and kept making eye contact until finally I walked straight up to him. 'Aren't you going to introduce us?' I asked Fran, pretending not to know who Calum was.

As we took each other's hand and he leaned over to kiss me on the cheek, I sneaked a look at Fran's face and it was like thunder. I later found out from Calum that he had asked Fran about me and had been told to stay away. Calum cheekily kissed me full on the lips, which I liked, and we spent the rest of the night chatting. He was all over me which I enjoyed because, although he didn't realise it, we had met before and he hadn't shown me any interest then. Funny how things change when you get famous! I played with him that night and took his number at the end; I wouldn't give him mine and I had no intention of calling him in any case.

I carried on bumping into Calum about three times a week after that second meeting, and every time we saw each other we chatted some more. I started to realise that he was actually a really nice guy who had had a difficult time living up to having such a famous father. And, of course, I fancied him. Who wouldn't? He's a successful male model with a beautiful face and amazing eyes. He looks just like George did when he was younger, and my mum used to fancy George, as did the rest of the nation's women. Like mother, like daughter, I suppose. I began to fall for Calum's beauty and it wasn't long, maybe a few weeks, before we ended up in bed together, although we did go out on a few dates first. He took me for a Chinese and we had a regular routine of going for breakfast when we came out of a club at six in the morning. He liked Balan's in Soho which is open 24 hours.

Calum had only moved over to England a couple of years previously from Los Angeles where he had lived since he was young, so the first thing he loved about me were my real boobs – and he made that very obvious. He was always playing with them and, whenever he talked dirty to me during sex, he would always say how much he loved 'my tits'. Calum was a good lover, but that's all he was. I could have fallen for him in a big way but he doesn't let people close to him very easily: he didn't open up to me, so I didn't open up to him. We continued to see each other for a month or so, and our liaisons would always follow the same pattern: clubbing, breakfast, then back to his mate Tim's flat where he was crashing on the floor. Sometimes Tim would be there and we would have to use the bathroom for sex (there was only one bedroom), while Tim would pretend to be asleep. Once I rode him for a whole hour until my knees were cut and bruised on that sodding bathroom floor – but Calum still tells me now it was really great riding and that he often thinks of it! Calum had a fetish about using lubricant. He couldn't have sex without using it and each session we would get through a whole bottle. I had never come across that before – I have never had any problem in getting wet, so I had never tried it – but it was still enjoyable sex and we had many a steamy night at Tim's flat and in nightclub toilets. We shagged in the men's toilets in Click one night during one of the famous lock-ins, which annoyed Fran no end. Good. I wanted to make him suffer, and why shouldn't I enjoy myself?

Calum was gorgeous, on my level and I was a single girl having fun. Even though we were never a proper couple, I remained faithful throughout the time I was seeing him. I have been known to have more than one guy at the same time, but after Kim's death I was looking for love more than I was looking for sex. So, although the sex was good, Calum was more a time-filler because I was lonely and deep down I still wanted Fran and wanted him to see what other blokes saw in me. I could tell that Fran was madly jealous, but he still never came on to me.

Once I had driven into London with a friend called Drew. At the end of a night sitting on Calum's lap in Click, he wanted me to go back to Tim's for a session. I had Drew with me and couldn't just leave him to make his own way home, so I drove us all back to Calum's with the intention of asking Drew to wait in the car for five minutes so we could have a quickie. On the way back, though, we got lost, so we stopped to ask a road-sweeper for directions. Calum was in the passenger seat and Drew was in the back. Just before we pulled away, Calum, being a bit drunk and his normal cocky self, said to the road-sweeper in his slow American drawl, 'Excuse me, sir, who is the greatest footballer of all time?'

Before he could answer, Drew shouted at the top of his

voice from the back, 'Ryan Giggs!' It was a classic comedy moment, and Calum was speechless.

Back at Tim's, I asked Drew to stay in the car as I was only popping in for five minutes, but Drew, knowing me better than that, said I would be hours and refused to wait quietly. We ended up having a joke row in the street before I left him in order to have a quickie with Calum. I emerged three hours later, after Drew had run his and my mobile batteries flat calling me, which I ignored. He'd been going nuts in the car. It was daylight by then and I was in my hot pants and leg warmers from the night before. Calum had given me one of his army-style shirts to wear to cover me slightly. I apologised profusely to Drew, who fortunately saw the funny side.

The papers the next day screamed that Calum and I had had a massive row in the street and woken up all the neighbours. It was actually me and Drew, and we hadn't even been arguing seriously, so Drew had the last laugh. Damn you people with your twitching curtains!

What ended the shag matches between Calum and I was completely and utterly his fault. I had arranged to meet him at Funky Buddha one Tuesday and I hadn't even bothered to dress up. I was in green combats and a white vest – Calum had told me that he preferred me like that anyway. We spent the evening as usual – having fun, drinking, dancing and snogging in corners – until, towards the end of the night, a girl who looked a bit like a prostitute in a tight, short skirt with stockings and suspenders was hanging around Calum. I didn't think anything of it until she approached me. 'Are you Calum's girlfriend?' she asked.

'Sort of,' I replied as I didn't want to say 'Yes' or 'No'. She grinned smugly at me before walking away and whispering in Calum's ear. I don't know what was said, but

Calum came over and told me to go, the car and that he would meet me outside in five minutes. I did so, as I was ready to leave anyway, and two minutes later I got a call from a male friend who told me Calum had got into a taxi with a 'cheap-looking girl'. He described her and it was the girl who had approached me before. He told me how sorry he was; I drove home alone.

I never shed any tears over Calum as I hadn't connected with him emotionally, but I did feel angry and disappointed that he had treated me this way. I knew that he had blown it and would never stand a chance with me again. From that day on I let him flirt with me at every opportunity, but I never spent the night with him again. Calum and I are now good friends and I can laugh about what a male slag he is. We even still go out to dinner every now and then, and I have nothing but good things to say about him. He is a wonderful person, and I told Alex Best as much when I met her on a programme we did about smoking for the BBC. Sometimes, between relationships, I even snog him when I'm drunk. You know what it's like when you don't want sex but a snog is enough to make your night better! He's a very good kisser, and no doubt I'll snog him again soon if we're both single. Passes the time, eh, girls?

CHAPTER TWELVE

To the Max

About a year previously, when I was still a lap dancer, I was having a mad night out in Chinawhite when Dean Gaffney tried to set me up with a scruffy-looking friend of his called Max. Max was sitting at our table and, although I was drunk and seeing double, he didn't look like my type of guy at all (not that I have a type, I've come to realise): he was wearing jeans and a T-shirt and those hideous Converse trainers. Sorry if anyone likes those, but I don't, especially on a man! His hair was a long, gingery mess and all I could think was that he must be a bit of a loser if he needed Dean to try and pull for him. In any case, I didn't have much faith in Dean's judgement. Five minutes earlier he had tried to set me up with another 'friend' of his, a guy called Jonathan Barnham. 'He's a really genuine bloke,' Dean told me. I recognised him as being Martine McCutcheon's ex. I politely declined getting to know either bloke and finished the night dancing with my girlfriends on a table. I thought nothing more of Max until the following March.

My friends Becky, Ade and I were all on a night out one Saturday. We had started in Click and moved on to Browns because we wanted a late drink. We didn't arrive there until about five in the morning, and we quickly made our way to the VIP area to get a drink. By this time Becky was drunkenly snogging Ade and I was left feeling like a bit of a gooseberry – Calum was there, but he was alternating between flirting with some girl and grabbing my arse, which on that particular night was annoying me. I was scanning the crowds for any other familiar faces and secretly wanting Fran to walk through the door when I spotted him. With his eyes locked on me and a face that looked like he wanted to shag me there and then, there was the gorgeous actor, musician and all-round charmer Max Beesley. I cheekily smiled at him and turned away, heart thumping. Wow, I thought.

Within a minute he was at my side, phone in hand, and his first words to me were 'So, what's your number then?' A combination of his amazing looks, his outright cockiness and his broad Mancunian accent made me laugh and give it to him without hesitation. He then insisted that I take his number so that when he called me, I would know it was him and answer it. As I put it into my phone, he looked down at what I was doing and saw the name 'Max Weirdo' on the screen. 'Eh, love, that's fucking great, that is. I'm a fucking freak now, am I?' I laughed for a full five minutes before I could finally tell him that it was a different Max. Often random people get hold of my number and call me 'to see if it's the real Jodie Marsh'; others just pester me at different times of the day or night. If their number shows up – and you'd be surprised at how many don't even withhold it – I save it as a weirdo so that I know not to answer it. It certainly made us both laugh, though, and that's how our relationship started.

Within a day he was on the phone and we had arranged a date for a couple of days later. Coincidentally, one of his favourite places was Wellington and I loved it in there. We arranged to meet in there quite early, have a few drinks and go on to Click (my choice, of course). I definitely had a great feeling about Max, but I also thought it was time to show Fran once again that other men were interested in me. On the day of the date, Max called me and said that he was really sorry but could I bring a friend because one of his friends was in town and wanted to go out. He couldn't really say no to the friend.

'No problem,' I said, and invited my friend Nikki.

I got ready very carefully with Kyle as my stylist. I chose a pure white miniskirt, a white vest and furry white boots, and Kyle did my make-up a lot lighter than usual. For years he's wanted me to stop piling on the black eyeshadow, and for once I listened to him.

Nikki and I arrived at Wellington before Max so we got a drink at the bar. I was facing the stairs by the entrance because I wanted to be able to see when Max arrived. Sure enough, five minutes later, I spotted him coming down the stairs, followed closely by none other than Robbie Williams. I quickly put two and two together in my head – Shit, I thought, I knew they were friends but surely this wasn't the mate he wanted to bring to our date. As they were heading towards us, I figured it was and did what any girl would in that situation. I grabbed Nikki, who was still unaware of the superstar getting ever closer, and pleaded quietly in her ear, 'Please, please stay calm. Don't react at all, but the other bloke out with us tonight is Robbie Williams.' By the time I had said this, they were at our side so she just had time to turn and smile. As I greeted Max, she was left to say hello to Rob.

You have to understand at this point that I have always been, and still am, just a normal girl from Essex with normal friends, so having Robbie Williams on a double date with us was exciting to say the least. Rob's first words to me were 'Hello, babe, you look great in the paper today.' It was the day that I was on the front page of three newspapers wearing the army belts. The night went smoothly after that: we had a few drinks and danced a lot – at one point Nikki and I had Rob sandwiched between us and were grinding up against him. Jealous? I'd have been jealous of myself! I have to say, however, that even though Rob is more gorgeous in the flesh, and has the twinkliest eyes I've ever seen, my affections really did lie with Max, and I spent all night getting up close and personal with him on the dance floor.

When Wellington closed at one o'clock we were keen to get along to Click. Unfortunately Rob had decided he was tired and wanted to go home, so it was just me, Max and Nikki – a good move on Rob's part because when we got to Click it was packed to the rafters and I'm sure he would have just got harassed. Nikki and I went in a separate car to Max as there were paparazzi waiting outside, and we both agreed it was too early to be seen together.

I had been bragging to Fran all week that I had a date with Max Beesley, partly to make him jealous and partly because I was excited, so when I showed up at Click with him, Fran was ever the gentleman to him, even if he was a bit off with me. Whatever he thought of me going out with him, he was over the moon to have Max in his club. Fran had always been a bit of a lick-arse to celebrities. I noticed from early on in our friendship that he pandered to them and it bugged me but I reasoned to myself that it didn't make him a bad person. Max was by far the biggest celebrity Fran had seen in Click, and he didn't hold back in showing his excitement. Nothing more eventful happened except that Calum was there and spent all night staring at me until, at the end of the night when Max was in the toilet, he came up and asked if I wanted to go home with him. Typical, eh? They always want you when they can't have you!

When we were leaving Click, Max and I kissed downstairs because we couldn't be seen leaving together, and went our separate ways. Nikki and I walked to the car accompanied by ten paparazzi, and we giggled the whole way. The paps did their usual trick of trying to get a shot up my skirt. By then Max had already called me to see if I'd got to the car safely and the shots that appeared in the newspaper two days later were only of me on my phone in the car. The papers were calling me 'the new Pammie', which still makes me proud because I've loved her ever since I knew who she was. Only one paper printed that they thought something was going on with me and Max, and that was the *Sport*; the others focused on my outfit, so we kind of got away with it.

Max and I continued our relationship by phone for a few days and had some of those three-hour-long conversations where you really get to know someone, and that Sunday night he invited me out for dinner. I had paparazzi and journalists waiting outside my house a lot of the time because I had recently done the army-belt outfit and wasn't giving interviews. It made them all the more desperate to get shots of me or a comment, so we decided it was best that I go to Max's house. He gave directions to my dad over the phone, who then drew me a route of how to get there.

I agonised over what to wear for ages. I had already

discovered in one of our many conversations that Max has a thing about short skirts and killer boots, so I originally planned to wear a tiny mini and stiletto boots; but, as we were going out to a restaurant and then back to his, I knew I would feel uncomfortable and overdressed, so I changed into combats, a vest and Timberlands on the advice of my mum: 'You look beautiful whatever you wear, darling. Just go in whatever you feel comfortable.' I also reasoned that if he didn't like the real me – a bit of a tomboy who does wear combats – then he wasn't worth it anyway.

I needn't have worried. When I pulled up at his house he came out to greet me and told me I looked fantastic. He said he was surprised to see me looking so casual – do men honestly think I sit at home on the sofa in two belts? – but that it looked great. He drove us to an Indian restaurant close by in his brand new Porsche (with the number plate MB) and we chatted for a good few hours over the meal. At one point his dad rang on his mobile and Max made me speak to him. He'd already told his dad about me and his dad was impressed. I got on well with him straight away, as he's just like an older version of Max – lots of fun and a real lad. Max was sitting smiling at me as I chatted away to his dad in a joke flirty way. It was obvious he was pleased with my confidence and the ease of my conversation with his dad. This, I thought, could be the start of something beautiful.

After dinner, we went to a Blockbuster down the road and picked out some DVDs to watch back at his house. Max took me round the shop pointing out all the films he had been in, mostly with him on the cover. It impressed me – I only really knew him as being Mel B's ex, and didn't realise he had done so well for himself. We spent a good hour in there chatting about films, and then rented *Catch*

Me If You Can. We put the film on when we got back, but didn't end up watching it as we couldn't stop talking. Already I felt like I had known him for years. Max was the first bloke in ages I felt like I could talk to about anything, and that's just what we did. Max even let me smoke in his house, although he doesn't smoke himself and hates the smell of it.

I stayed at his that night and, although we did share a kiss and a cuddle, which was lovely, I didn't sleep with him as I didn't want him to think I was easy. He gave me a T-shirt to wear in bed and we lay there chatting until the early hours. The next morning, he made me breakfast. His brother Jason, who lived with him at the time, was there, and we all had a laugh in the kitchen for an hour or so. Max, who hates the tabloids, went out to get me the papers because I knew I was going to be in them from Saturday night and I wanted to see what they were saying. I left after a kiss on the lips and a promise that we would see each other soon, and drove the whole way home smiling to myself.

We continued our long phone calls, which were getting more and more frequent. By this time, Max was in rehearsals with Robbie Williams for his famous Knebworth gigs, but he was calling me three or four times a day. Our conversations were half serious and half hysterical laughter. I told Max all about Kim and how much pain I was in over her; he completely understood because he had lost his mother not so long ago. I really opened up to him about her and felt like I didn't have to be strong in front of him. Max didn't care if I cried, and I didn't care if he saw me crying. One time I texted him while he was away on tour with Rob. The text just said, 'BABE, I'M FEELING REALLY DOWN TODAY, JUST HEARD A SONG THAT REMINDED ME OF

KIM, SAY SOMETHING TO MAKE ME FEEL BETTER.' He called ten seconds later and I was in tears. 'Hello,' I sniffed at him.

'So,' he shouted, 'there was an Englishman, an Irishman and a Scotsman…' He launched into this joke with such passion that I was laughing again within a minute. Max always knew exactly what to say or do. Here was a guy who, at 32, had his head screwed on and was deeper than most of the guys I had met since Kim's death. We shared the same sense of humour and discovered we had a few mutual friends, including Dave Courtney, who I had met when I was working at the Ministry of Sound. Max knew how to make me laugh and I him. We knew what made each other tick and we both loved our conversations.

The next time I saw him was about a week later. Again I drove to his and he took me out for dinner, this time to a beautiful little Italian that he visited regularly. He knew all the staff and they treated me like a princess when Max introduced me. All night they teased him about how lucky he was to have such a beautiful girl out to dinner with him, and he ribbed them back saying that I actually fancied one of the chefs! We went back to his again afterwards, and this time I wanted him so badly. Not only had we connected on a deep level, but I found him incredibly attractive. Being with him had even banished all thoughts of Fran from my head. Suddenly I felt like I never wanted to lose this man.

As we got into bed that night, him completely naked and me in a black thong and one of his black vests, we practically jumped on each other. It was full-on passion. We both wanted each other so much, there wasn't any question of whether or not we were going to have sex. He was insistent about using a condom, which was a first for me because any guy I had been with before had tried to make me not use one, but he explained that he was one of the ambassadors for the Terence Higgins Trust which promoted safe sex. He made me feel wanted and special – not just for my body and looks, but for my mind. I already knew we stimulated each other mentally, but boy did we stimulate each other physically. I suppose his age had a bit to do with his experience and for the first time in ages I was with a real man who knew how to please me.

From that night on, the deal was sealed. Max and I were a proper couple and saw each other as often as we could. Our conversations got longer and deeper and I felt like I had not only made the best friend I was ever going to have, I had also met the man of my dreams. Our sex got wilder, too. One night, on coming home from a restaurant where Max had asked them to wrap up our leftover food for later, we walked through the door of his top-floor flat only for me to put the doggy bag on the floor and shag him there and then on the stairs. We still laugh about that now. Chicken in hand, knickers down – classy! Another time, he took me from behind while I was leaning out of his bedroom window watching the builders working down below. He loved that. One day I was due to do a photo shoot and interview for *New* magazine. I was in bed with Max that morning and didn't want to tear myself away. I ended up being late for the shoot. When they ran the piece, it started, 'The chain-smoking Miss Marsh arrives an hour late for our shoot in her lime-green convertible.'

We laughed about that for ages, because we both knew why I was late. 'If only they knew,' we giggled. When I was with Max, he made me go weak at the knees; when I wasn't and I thought of him, I had butterflies in my stomach. I was head over heels in love.

We had both agreed that it was much better to keep our relationship secret because the press were still hounding me at every opportunity and he didn't like them, full stop. He had had a bad experience with Mel B once when one of the horrible 3am Girls from the *Mirror* had been unpleasant to her at the Brits and he had defended her. They wrote nasty things about him for about six months after that, so he stayed well away from it all. At first the secrecy was fun and I loved the fact that at his house we could just be ourselves with no one else watching or gossiping, but after a while it did start to become a problem. I was invited to a party by Jonathan Wilkes to celebrate his appearance in *The Rocky Horror Show*. Max was already going with Robbie. I mulled it over for ages before deciding not to go. I didn't see how I could stand in a room all night long with the man I loved and not be able to touch him or speak to him properly. No big loss, but it began to annoy me. It wasn't even that I wanted everyone to know about us, more that I just wanted a normal relationship, and sneaking around isn't normal.

During the European leg of the Robbie Williams tour, Max I and spoke three or four times every day. He was the first person I spoke to in the morning and the last person I spoke to before I went to bed. I was working hard too, so I wasn't bothered that we didn't see each other that much – plus I knew that he would be coming home soon for Knebworth and he had got me tickets to that. Whenever he was back in this country, even if it was only for a day, we met up, cuddled lots and had great sex.

Suddenly, a week before Knebworth, he called me with bad news. As soon as the tour finished, he was going to Los Angeles to film a movie for six months. We had to make a decision whether it was worth trying to have a long-distance relationship. My first reaction was that of course we could make it work. I was utterly in love with him by then and definitely prepared to wait for him. I would have happily flown over to see him if that was what he wanted.

Sadly, he didn't.

He told me it was for the best that we left it for a while to save either of us from getting hurt. I was in way too deep for that, but he somehow reasoned that we would be too far away and too long apart for us to try and stay together. I found myself numbly agreeing with him and tried to be as cheerful as I could about it. The last thing I wanted to do was to beg him not to end it and sound desperate. So that was that. I forced myself not to contact him that week, knowing that I was going to see him at Knebworth anyway.

The Saturday of the concert, my friend Paul, the owner of the nightclub Elysium, arranged for a car to take me and my friend Michelle to the gig. He was hosting the VIP tent backstage so was looking after all the celebrities. I arrived feeling happy and relaxed, but slightly nervous that I was going to see Max. It was a hot summer's day so I just had a metallic-silver string bikini top on, which made my boobs look great, but on the bottom I had my old faithful faded dungarees and trainers because it was going to be a long day and I knew it would get chilly later.

I saw Rob before I saw Max. He had just landed in his private helicopter and was being marched through to his dressing room. He said hello to me as he passed, and within five minutes Max was at my side.

'Rob told me you were here,' he smiled. 'He said you looked really fit.' My heart melted and I ached for him. He looked even more gorgeous than the last time I had seen him. He stayed beside me for ages before he had to go on stage, and he told me a few things to look out for that he was going to do especially for me during the gig. I was very friendly and held it together well, even though I was dying inside. All I wanted to do was beg him to reconsider splitting up.

Michelle knew I was hurting bad, and she was a star. She went round the backstage area chatting to everyone and making me join in. We had a very nice time and then suddenly we had to leave that area to go and watch the concert. It was amazing – the biggest outdoor event I had ever been to, and the atmosphere was electric. The first few tunes were great and Michelle and I were singing and dancing along to all the old Robbie classics. Then came the moment I had been dreading: a curtain came down to hide the band while Max played piano and Rob sang 'She's The One' and a couple of tunes from the *Swing When You're Winning* album. Rob always dedicated the set to his mum and Max's mum who, Rob said, was 'sadly in heaven'. A few weeks earlier, on one of the European gigs, Max had broken down on stage. He had phoned me straight after the gig in need of comfort and we had both got quite emotional. It might have been because it reminded me of the death of Kim, or Max's own pain about his mother, or the fact that I was devastated that we had split, or a combination of all three, but I started to cry. Michelle wrapped her arms around me – which made me worse. Suddenly I was sobbing – big, heavy sobs that hurt my chest. I can honestly say that I never want to feel pain like that again. Once I started, I couldn't stop. I cried for the rest of the concert and until about three o'clock in the morning. Every time I thought I couldn't have any more tears left, more tears came. I have never cried that much in my life.

After the concert there was a party in the Elysium tent and I spent the whole night curled up on a sofa over the back with my face buried in Michelle's lap, sobbing. It was a physical pain. I was hurting more than I had ever hurt in my life. People kept coming up to Michelle to ask if I was all right. 'She's fine,' she kept saying, 'just tired.' I didn't see Max after the concert, but I didn't want to. He had gone straight back to his hotel, and his brother had told me to come too, but I physically couldn't stop crying. At that moment I felt like I was going to die of a broken heart.

Max was the first man I had truly loved just for being him. All my other boyfriends had been a security blanket helping me to deal with the scars of my bullying or making me feel safe. Max I just loved for being Max.

CHAPTER THIRTEEN

A Bit on the D-Side

A week after Knebworth was the day of the premiere for *American Pie: The Wedding*. I had been filming all day for Television X – nothing seedy, just presenting it and recording links for shows. The red-carpet arrivals for the premiere were at half-past six, and I didn't finish filming until five. I had an hour and a half to get ready and pick up Fran – I had asked him to come with me as all my friends with normal jobs don't like staying out too late in the week and I knew this was going to be a late one. My make-up was already done from the filming, so all I had to do was choose an outfit and put it on, which I did at the studio. Claire, a really lovely girl from Television X, helped me choose what to wear. I had had some designers drop a few things off to me that morning and I settled on the tiniest black miniskirt, a black pinstripe shirt undone to show a good amount of cleavage and black stiletto boots. Not an amazing outfit, but it did the job.

Fran was ready to go, so he jumped in the car along with a three-person film crew from Sky who were making my documentary *Jodie Marsh Laid Bare* at the time. They had been with me all day at Television X and I got along really well with them. This was the first premiere I had taken them to, so they were quite excited to see the reaction as I stepped out of the car. There were another three people from Sky waiting for me by the red carpet so that they could have footage from both angles – in and out of the car. As we pulled up and one of the security men opened the door, the fans and paparazzi went nuts. It was such a buzz, but quite scary at the same time. I was really well known in England by this point, but I remember clearly that when I arrived there was a big group of Japanese girls at the front of the barriers. They were calling out to me and screaming hysterically that they loved me. I should have stopped to sign autographs, but it freaked me out because I had never thought people would get that excited over me. So, after posing for pictures, I headed straight for the door of the cinema. Once inside, Fran and I settled down to watch the film. They always have a warm-up guy come on before a film, someone funny to get the crowd going. That night it was Richard Blackwood. He picked on a few people in the audience and said how nice it was of them to come. Then he turned to me and simply said, 'And we have Jodie Marsh in the house, ladies and gents, and boy has she got great boobs!' Richard is now a friend of mine, so thanks for that, Blackwood – I'll get my own back one day!

After the film, which was hysterical, Fran and I got our driver to take us to the after-show party at Café de Paris. There we met up with Shane Lynch from Boyzone and all the members of D-Side (whom I'd never heard of). It was free drink, and we were definitely taking advantage of that. As with all these parties, however, it soon began to fizzle out and we decided it was time to go to another party at Wellington. At this point I had been making polite conversation with Shane and hadn't spoken to any of D-Side, but, when they clocked that we were leaving, Dane came quickly over to me and his first words were, 'You look like you need a cuddle.'

I thought I had been doing well at putting on a brave face, something I found myself doing a lot since Kim's death, but it felt like he had seen through it. Finally, I thought, a bloke who understands. That, combined with his thick Dublin accent – something I have never been able to resist – and the fact that I was pining for Max, made me invite him to Wellington; before I knew it we had left the party hand in hand and jumped into his car. I didn't actually get into his car on purpose, but he had exactly the same car as ours – a blacked-out Voyager which people in showbiz use all the time. Temporarily blinded by the paparazzi outside, I jumped into the first blacked-out Voyager I saw. Inside the car were the rest of D-Side who quickly began chanting, 'We love you, Jodie!' They were a great bunch of lads – very down to earth and lots of fun.

We arrived at Wellington to face yet more paparazzi and an angry-looking Fran – he had been left to get our car on his own. As we all walked down the stairs and into the club, who should be the first people we saw but a tanned and gorgeous-looking Max with his dad! My heart skipped a beat and I dropped Dane's hand like it was molten metal, but I managed to hold it all together and went straight over to say hello. His dad was lovelier than lovely to me. We had spoken on the phone loads of times by then, but we had never actually met until now. It made it even more difficult for me that his dad was so nice, I think, because it reminded me of how much I had lost. I had never really got on that well with any of my previous boyfriend's families, but Max's dad told me how beautiful I was and that he thought I was a really genuine and lovely girl. I responded by telling him that he should be very proud of his son as he was a diamond, and we hugged lots.

In the meantime, Fran must have told Max that I was there with Dane. He was obviously on the wind-up because he looked quite pleased with himself. Max confronted me straight away and wanted to know if I was seeing Dane. I told him the truth. 'No,' I said, 'I only met him tonight. But I can't put my life on hold for you, Max.' My chest tightened inside, and the hideous pain that I had been trying to block out came back, but I managed to make polite chat with Max and keep calm. I was determined never to let him know how much I had cried over him, or how much pain I felt. I thought somehow he might come back to me one day if I showed him how strong and together I was.

Dane was unwittingly making things very awkward for me. All I wanted to do was talk to Max and his dad. Dane kept coming over and offering me drinks or trying to hold my hand; I kept telling him to go away and give me five minutes. I think I told him that Max was an old friend of mine who had some problems so I needed some time alone with him. Dane never cottoned on and Max gradually got the hump and decided to leave. His dad didn't even want to leave, but Max told him it was time to go. As I watched him walk up the stairs, he turned to look at me one last time. I pretended not to see him as I pulled Dane towards me for a dance. All I wanted him to see was the fun-loving Jodie that I knew he loved. It was that or break down and cry.

Half an hour later, as Wellington was closing, we all left to go to Trap, where Fran now worked. By the time we had sunk a few more bottles of vodka there, I was pretty much nearing passing-out stage. I think I was trying to blot out the pain I was feeling. All I remember is Dane's manager telling me to go home and that Dane was going to come with me. An argument then ensued between him and Fran, who told him it wasn't wise for Dane to go home with me. The manager was arguing that, if we liked each other, there was nothing he could do to stop it and that it was none of Fran's business anyway. While all this was going on, I grabbed Dane and we left through the front door. I hailed the first black cab I saw and we were on our way to Essex. I couldn't be bothered with people arguing over me or telling me what to do; I had hit self-destruct mode and I wanted to do something bad to make me forget about Max.

In the taxi on the way home I drunkenly changed out of my premiere outfit into jeans and a T-shirt and laid my head on Dane's lap while he stroked my hair. Even though I knew I had no feelings for him whatsoever, it felt nice to have some male attention. I was desperately hoping that being with Dane would make me forget about Max. Back at my house, I managed to fix us a strong vodka and Red Bull each and we lay on the sofa with a Michael Jackson DVD playing. All I remember from then on are two things: Dane was really impressed with my plasma-screen television, and we had sex. I can't even remember how it started. I know I thought to myself that I didn't really want to have sex with him, but when he stroked my stomach and my porn-star tattoo (with which he was obsessed, having seen it in a lads' mag) it felt nice and – after getting a bit tingly down below – I thought, Why not? When I'm hurting I do stupid things to numb the pain. It didn't last very long, but I remember thinking, drunk as I was, that it wasn't a bad session, although it wasn't particularly good. We both fell asleep straight afterwards and woke up in the morning to a rough hangover and a beautiful day.

I'm not the sort of person to kick someone out first thing in the morning, so I asked Dane if he wanted to spend the day with me and maybe go into Brentwood to get some lunch. He accepted so we showered and I changed (he had nothing else with him) and I drove us into town. We went to my friend's pub because it has a lovely courtyard, and by this time my film crew were back with me. They wanted footage of me and Dane as they had interviewed him on the red carpet the night before and they were most amused that I had ended up pulling him. Dane was fine with that, and we larked about for the cameras. A little while after arriving, we spotted a paparazzi guy lurking in the car park behind the pub. He was kneeling down beside a car taking pictures of us with a super-long lens. I didn't really care by then – I had blatantly walked out of three clubs holding Dane's hand the previous night, so I knew the papers would already have something to say about that. A couple of hours later, Dane's tour manager arrived to pick him up as he was due to be in the studio. We swapped numbers and promised to see each other again soon.

I was right about the papers. The next day they were full of the fact that Dane and I were a couple. I also got a phone call from Max. He was preparing to leave for LA and joked that Dane looked like something from the movie *The Lord of the Rings*. He had obviously seen the papers, and I knew he was annoyed but was trying to make a joke of it. Again my heart ached, but I gave him the big-'un and told him I was a free agent now and could do what I liked and that, actually, Dane was a really nice guy. He was having none of it, but promised to call when he got to LA.

I saw Dane a few more times after that, once at the launch of the Sky channel TRL and once at the birthday party of my friend Linsey Dawn McKenzie. We turned up to both events holding hands and looking like a couple. The press loved it and all the papers and magazines ran pictures of us: model and pop star – a journalist's dream. Even if they weren't writing nice things about us, they were still writing about us. We snogged at both events, but we never slept together again as I always made sure I took friends along as well so that I didn't get left on my own with him. It's not that I didn't like him, but I wanted to forget about our first drunken night together. I thought that, if I acted like it had never happened, I could date him normally for a while. I felt awful for having slept with him so easily, and wanted to prove to him that I was actually a nice girl.

In the end, he blew it. It was the day of the Blue concert in Chelmsford, Essex. D-Side were supporting them and Dane had invited me along because it was so close to my house. My film crew were thrilled: by this time they had given me a 'Jodie Cam' – a camera of my own to film things when they weren't around. They were scared they were going to miss something! Since I had access all areas, they felt I should definitely take advantage of it and film as much as I could of the concert and what happens backstage. I took my friend Becky and between us we filmed some amazing stuff of the boys warming up on the side of the stage, as well as the whole performance from the press pit right at the front of the stage. Because we were in Essex as well, the fans were amazing and were screaming for me as much as for them. God, I love Essex!

When the concert was over, we had all planned to go

to Trap – obvious choice: free drink! Dane and I went in separate cars – we had gone to the concert separately, and in any case I wanted to go home and change out of my combats into something sexy. I met him at the club a few hours later wearing a ripped and bleached denim mini, denim boots and a white vest. He told me I looked great and we started drinking. After a few hours, I realised I hadn't seen him for a while. I was in the VIP section upstairs, and when I peered over the balcony I spotted Dane just in time to see him snogging another girl at the bar.

My heart sank. All right, Dane was never going be the next Max, but I had hopes for him being a potentially nice boyfriend. I swiftly left with Becky and she called all men cunts the whole way home in the car, which made me laugh. Even though it was hardly true love with Dane and we'd got off to a really bad start, I was thoroughly disappointed. I began to feel Becky was right and all men were arseholes. Dane called me the next day full of apologies, but, like Calum, he'd blown it. I had more pride than to take him back; I forgave him, though, and told him we would be friends. A few months later, I bumped into Bryan from Westlife who told me that Dane had a long-term (and obviously long-suffering) girlfriend back in Dublin. He said that, when the story had broken in the newspapers, Dane had told her that we had been forced to hold hands by his record company to gain publicity. I confronted Dane about this, and he admitted it was true. I was his bit on the side and he had completely used me for publicity. I lost the tiny bit of respect I had for him after that and to this day, although we still speak on the phone occasionally, things are quite strained between us. The rest of D-Side, on the other hand, are top boys and I often go out clubbing with Derek and Damian. Damien even came with my mum and dad to support me when I later appeared on the TV show *The Games* (more about that later). Thanks, boys. Love you lots!

CHAPTER FOURTEEN

The Biggest Mistake of my Life

The day after I split with Dane, Fran was on the phone in high spirits. He wanted me to come to Trap that night and I wasn't going to say no. Once there, he showered me with compliments and held my hand all night. I loved the attention. Deep down I think I knew that I was on the verge of cracking the high and mighty Mr Cosgrave. I was no longer just a Page 3 girl. Since the army belts, my profile had rocketed and I was making daily appearances in all the newspapers. Suddenly I was a credible girlfriend in his eyes.

Fran offered his bed again for the night. Once back at his, we lay in bed talking with the lights off. 'I suppose there's no point asking you for a shag,' I half joked. I'd made a couple of drunken attempts to get him into bed over the previous couple of months and I didn't expect this occasion to be any different.

To my surprise, he jumped up without any warning,

straddled me and pinned my arms to the bed. 'You want a shag?' he asked. 'I'll shag you all right.'

Suddenly, after all those months of desperately wanting this moment, I wasn't sure if I did any more. In my head I was screaming, No, I don't know! I'm not sure! I was only joking! It wasn't that I didn't want sex, but I wasn't sure if I wanted it like this. I always imagined our first time to be really special. We had grown so close, and I loved him like a brother. For all his faults, he had always looked after me, kept horrid men at bay, been there when I needed a good cry and generally stuck by me. I had known we would get together one day; I just wanted it to be right. But somehow I now found myself feebly murmuring, 'Yeah, I do.'

Fran was like a wild man. He kissed me all over before going down on me. He licked and nibbled me until I could take it no more, and found myself demanding that he shag me. He did so with brute force. It wasn't the best sex I had ever had, but it was rough (how I like it) and I felt satisfied that he had finally succumbed to me. We fell asleep in each other's arms.

The next morning, I woke up to his boner poking me in the back and I didn't waste any time in taking advantage. Afterwards, we lay chatting. He told me that there was no going back now. He told me that he wanted us to be a couple and that he had been in love with me for a long time. I found this revelation quite shocking. All along, I thought that I had been the only one with any feelings, but he insisted that seeing me with Dane had killed him. Hearing all this made me feel happy and secure. Fran might have messed me about, but I had always known I would get him in the end, and here he was, professing his undying love. I agreed that we should commit to one another. That day, as we wanted to be together away from the prying eyes of the press and everybody in London, we decided to go to Manchester. I had nothing with me except the clothes on my back, but I drove us there anyway. On the way, and on Fran's suggestion, I phoned and booked the penthouse suite at Manchester's best hotel. Once there, we realised that we had no clothes to go out in that night. I didn't even have a toothbrush or any make-up. We made a hurried trip to the city centre and blew £2,000 in an hour on all the things we needed to spruce ourselves up for a night out.

I had been to Manchester not so long ago doing a TV job for ITV, so knew all the best places to go out. Becky and I had spent an amazing night with Jonathan Wilkes, Richard Blackwood, Alex Sibley and Andrew Newton. We had hit all the clubs and danced for hours without being harassed by paparazzi. Even the local people had left us pretty much alone. I took Fran to the Sugar Lounge and the Living Room, and we ended the night in an exclusive little members' club I had found called the Circle. Once back at the hotel, we stayed up all night chatting and decided that we should tell everyone we were together and make it official. All in all, the weekend cost me over four grand (Fran didn't have any money on him) but I thought it was money well spent.

The press, as it happened, didn't clock for quite a while that we were together – we had been pictured out so many times together as mates that they didn't notice a difference. We told all our friends and family, though. Fran's mum was over the moon. I had met her a few months previously when his parents had come for a visit from Dublin. She had apparently told Fran then that he should be with me and that I was the 'nicest girl' she had met of his friends. She had also seen how good I was with Fran's little boy Josh, and loved it.

The first few months of being with Fran were good. We did all the usual things that couples do in the early stages of a relationship: we spent a lot of time going to restaurants and the cinema, and generally lived in each other's pockets. It wasn't long, though, before Fran was up to his old tricks. Just as was the case when we were mates, Fran managed to have some kind of hold over me by playing mind games. The first of these came when he confided in me one night that he had been out with Cat Deeley. He claimed that she had been in love with him but he had ended it because she became too clingy. He went on to tell me that he had also been out with Emma Bunton and that she too still had a thing for him. To say this now sounds mad, but it really bothered me at the time. It made me feel like I was lucky to have him and that I should be grateful he wanted me. I was determined not to lose him. He would often tell me during a night out that someone had come on to him or that another female celebrity fancied him. I remember him chatting to Lisa Scott-Lee one night in Ten Rooms and, when he had finished, he came back over to me and said, 'God, can that girl make it any more obvious how much she likes me?'

These little digs started to make me feel slightly insecure. He also made it very clear to me that he didn't like the skimpy outfits I wore. Often when I emerged from my dressing room in a daring number, he would laugh in my face and tell me I looked ridiculous. It was because of this that I started to cover up more, and within a few months I didn't go out unless I was wearing trousers or a suit. Partly I wanted to please him, but partly he had made me believe that I did look stupid.

Fran loved the limelight. Every time we stepped out in public together, he held my hand tightly so that he would be in all the pictures. Often he would do things like grab one of my boobs or my bum for the paparazzi, therefore guaranteeing that he would be in every shot that got used. On one occasion, on our way to a red-carpet event in Kings Cross, he sat in the back of the car and told me that he wasn't happy with the way I dealt with the paps. He said that he was fed up with the newspapers always using shots of me on my own and that he would have to teach me how to exit a car so that we only got pictured together. That night, he said, I was to get out from the same side as him and immediately hold his hand. I did as I was told and made sure they didn't get a shot of me on my own. I wasn't particularly bothered what pictures they took but I wanted to make him happy. After posing on the red carpet and entering the venue, I turned to Fran and asked, 'Was that OK?'

'No,' he replied, and went on to have a go at me for 'pulling sexy faces'. Apparently I still hadn't shown him enough attention in front of the press.

The premiere for *Scary Movie 3* was showing one night and I had been given tickets. I had been in bed all day with what I thought was the start of flu so didn't want to go, but Fran insisted – he said that he would use the tickets and go without me, which was enough to make me get out of bed. Much as I thought I loved him, I didn't trust him as far as I could throw him and certainly didn't feel comfortable with him being at celebrity events when there were apparently so many females who fancied him. As I put on a new white trouser suit, Fran asked if he should also wear a suit. I told him he should, and he appeared ten minutes later in the exact same suit which he had bought a week after me because he really liked my one. He had said at the time that we wouldn't wear them together, but he obviously had other plans. 'What are you doing?' I asked him.

'Well,' he said, 'we could be the new Posh and Becks if we go like this.'

I was too ill to argue. I didn't want to go to the premiere anyway, and I didn't care what I was wearing, let alone what he wore. We turned up to the film looking ridiculous. We looked more like Bill and Ben than Posh and Becks. Still, Fran was over the moon that we made all the magazines the following week and, if he was happy, I was happy.

Fran liked to belittle me. He mainly did it in front of people, and one occasion he not only upset me and made me feel stupid, but he also seriously pissed off my good friend Linsey Dawn McKenzie. Fran and I had his son Josh for the day and we were looking after him at my house. Linsey was over for a visit and we had spent the day chilling out in front of the TV and going through some of my photo albums, laughing at all the snaps of our mad nights out. Linsey pointed out that, between us, we had a lot of celebrity mates – my albums were full of famous faces and we agreed that it would be lovely to look back on them in years to come. That got me thinking: Josh was only a toddler and here he was, sat on the sofa with Jodie Marsh and Linsey Dawn, two of Britain's most well-known glamour models. 'Think how many men would love to be in his position,' I said.

I turned to Fran and said that he should start making a scrapbook for Josh for when he was older. I explained that, by the time he was sixteen, he would probably enjoy looking at pictures of himself with the likes of me and Linsey. 'Are you completely fucking mad?' Fran replied. 'Why on earth would I want pictures of my son with two birds who get their tits out when his mother is from Atomic Kitten?'

Shocked and hurt, I tried to reason that I was sure any teenage boy would like mementos like that. It was something Fran could give him, father to son when he was old enough to appreciate it. Linsey jumped in to defend me, saying that she thought it was a fabulous idea and that Josh would love it. 'You're mad,' Fran repeated. 'You're hardly famous. Josh is surrounded by real celebrities every day of his life.'

Now that he had deeply offended both of us and made us feel completely stupid, Linsey and I exchanged incredulous glances and didn't speak to him again for the rest of the afternoon. I apologised profusely to Linsey the next day on the phone and she demanded to know what I was doing with him. She told me she had never met anybody so arrogant and rude in her whole life and that I could do a hundred times better. Agreeing with her, I wondered what made me stay, but confessed that I didn't have the strength to leave him.

Fran's club Trap was being refurbished so it wasn't open to the public. Because of this, he didn't have any money. It meant I paid for everything. Crazy as it sounds now, I didn't think he was using me, I just saw it as a normal part of a relationship. I thought that you were meant to support each other through hard times, and support him I did. After we split, I added up how much I must have spent on him. It came to over £60,000. At the time I didn't think anything of it. If he wanted clothes, we would go to Selfridges or Harrods. We would split up to trawl the men's and women's sections and meet back up at the end so I could pay the bill. His bill would always be in the region of £700 and I would pay it without hesitation. Looking back now, it angers me that I spent that sort of money on him and it frustrates me that I didn't see how much he was using me. Somehow he had this hold over me that I couldn't shake off. Even when Trap reopened, Fran still never seemed to have any money. He was always asking to 'borrow' money from me – which was hardly borrowing, as I knew I would never see a penny of it again – and I paid for everything we needed to live on. I paid for his food, his toiletries and even his taxis. He had moved in with me in Brentwood soon after we got together, and was getting the train up to London each night to work as he didn't drive. As I dropped him at the station every night, he would ask, 'I couldn't have twenty quid for the train, could I, babe?' I always gave it without question. I justified it by telling myself that he would do the same for me if things were the other way round. As always, I looked to my parents to show me what the perfect relationship should be like: I knew that either one would give their last penny if it meant the other being happy.

At Christmas, Fran made it very clear that he wanted a watch – not just any watch, a Breitling diamond-encrusted one costing £8,000. I shuddered at the thought of how expensive that was and, for the first time in our relationship, questioned whether he was worth spending that much money on. In the end I felt like I didn't have much choice. Fran was all about show. Unless he looked the right way or had the right things he wasn't happy, and his idea of expressing affection was to shower somebody with gifts or give them the most expensive thing he could find or afford. He never understood that the little things count more or that, as the old saying goes, the best things in life are free. He thought that love meant splashing out for that person at any cost, and he made this very clear to me in the lead-up to Christmas.

I agonised for ages over what to get him. It strikes me

now that I must have known how wrong our relationship was not to automatically want to buy him the watch. If I had truly loved him, the money wouldn't even have come into it. That clearly wasn't the case. Deciding against the eight-grand watch, I went on a number of shopping trips and bought him all of his favourite things: a couple of new pairs of Timberlands, three new pairs of jeans, about twelve T-shirts, six woolly hats, two beautiful silver rings, a stack of DVDs, a £1,000 leather jacket from his favourite designer – oh, and I bought a whole home gym for him which my dad spent hours setting up. I thought that would be enough but, as I sat down to wrap all the smaller presents on the morning of Christmas Eve, I realised that in Fran's eyes it probably wouldn't be sufficient. He had gone on about the watch so much and stopped to stare at it so many times in the last few weeks that I suddenly felt guilty that I hadn't bought it for him. He had made it clear that he thought diamonds were the ultimate gift for a loved one, and had hinted so many times that he would love me forever if I bought him something like that. Insanely, by lunchtime on Christmas Eve I had rung every jeweller in both the Lakeside and Bluewater shopping centres to see if anybody had the exact watch in stock. Most of them didn't keep such expensive items, but I got lucky with the last shop I called. They had one in and said they would hold it for me.

I left my house at midday with my brother and didn't get home until eight o'clock that night. With the mad last-minute Christmas rush, it took us eight hours to get to Bluewater and back. I made my brother promise not to tell my mum and dad how much I had spent on the watch, as I knew they would be horrified (they didn't like Fran that much in any case). When we finally got home, I wrapped it up and put it under our tree, feeling sick. Suffice to say, Christmas was a good day. Fran opened his presents with half-hearted thanks, saving the watch until last, when I finally got a proper reaction to a gift. Even though I could have kicked myself for spending that much on him, it was the only present I knew he actually appreciated.

Once Trap had reopened, Fran and his business partner sat me down one night 'for a chat'. Fran told me that they had discussed different ways to get press for the new club and they had come to a decision. I wasn't allowed to be photographed anywhere except at Trap. Fran reasoned that the papers were still printing pictures of me constantly and I was obviously still in demand. If I was only photographed there, they would have to print that I was at Trap and the club would receive some free publicity. I was not particularly happy that my boyfriend had slapped a ban on my going to other clubs, but I agreed that I would do it for him anyway. Being the mug I was, I still wanted to please him.

His plan worked and soon Trap was all over the papers. I invited other celebrity mates there and they got pictured coming out too. Trap was suddenly the place to go. A few months later, however, Fran and his partner sat me down for another 'chat'. This time they said they didn't want me to be pictured outside Trap any more. There had been a huge piece on me in *New* magazine that week. Their comment had been 'Somehow Jodie managed to evade the fashion police.' Fran and his partner had decided that I didn't have the right image for the club and was bringing it down and making it look cheap. In what had been the biggest insult and blow in my relationship with Fran so far, I swallowed my pride and told him lovingly that I would sneak in and out of the back door from now on.

New Year's Eve was just around the corner and we, or should I say Fran, had decided that we were going to spend it at Trap. Even though the club ran itself and he really didn't have to be there, he made a big deal of 'needing' to be there. I had only spent one New Year's Eve away from my parents, and I wanted to continue the tradition. Fran and I argued about it for a month until the day came and, as Fran wouldn't budge, it was go or be without him. I went and had quite possibly the worst night of my life. The last time I had seen Kim alive was the night before New Year's Eve the previous year, so it was a very fragile and emotional time for me; Fran, on the other hand, spent the whole night getting drunk with his business partner and left me sitting on a sofa alone in the VIP room. None of my mates would come as they all had family things to go to or had stayed with my brother in Brentwood, not wanting to pay hundreds of pounds for a taxi home from London on the most expensive night of the year. Since the day Trap had reopened, Fran had not let me venture outside of the VIP room alone. He didn't like it when people recognised me or asked for autographs, and he definitely didn't like men approaching me, even if they were harmless fans. He had once thrown two guys out for telling me I was fit, and he told a guy who was obviously a big fan wanting an autograph to 'piss off'. We had had countless rows over it, as I had always made a huge effort to accommodate fans or people wanting autographs. I thought of them as an essential part of my work – after all, they were the ones who bought magazines with me on the front. Fran didn't see it like that. He hated me getting any attention whatsoever and therefore banned me from moving off the sofa at 'our' table other than to go to the toilet.

As midnight came and went, I began to feel more and

more emotional. I missed Kim, I missed my other friends, I missed my brother and I missed my mum and dad. Eventually, I couldn't hold the tears any longer and they flowed freely. Luckily no one was really around to see them and I sobbed and held my knees as I buried my head in them and rocked on the sofa. It was all too much. The biggest night of the year came and went with me sitting alone on a sofa in a dingy club. My boyfriend was nowhere to be seen and I ached to be with the people that cared about me. Silently I made a vow to myself that I would never again be away from the people who mattered on a special night like this.

When Fran finally surfaced from the main club, he was steaming drunk and didn't seem to be too bothered that I was crying. 'Why did you come if you knew you'd get upset?' he shouted at me. I couldn't believe what I was hearing! 'Why don't I call a cab for you?' he asked.

'No,' I stammered, 'I don't want to spend the next two hours in a car alone.' He tried to persuade me to leave but all I wanted was for him to comfort me or sit with me. Unsympathetic, he told me that he had to show his face in the club. I wasn't going anywhere looking like I did, so he left me alone again for another hour and a half. The next time he came back I was huddled in a corner. My eyes were red and puffy from crying so much and he still had no sympathy. All he kept saying was that I should have stayed with my brother. I knew that now, but it was a bit late to do anything about it. By the time we left the club, we weren't even speaking. I hadn't even had a drink and he was paralytic. We got into bed at half-past seven the following morning and, to add insult to injury, Fran admitted that he hadn't really needed to be at the club after all. I hated him with a passion.

Once we were living together, and Fran had decided I was the love of his life, he started to become more and more jealous and paranoid. Not only did he not like me having fans, he didn't even like men looking at me, and he certainly couldn't cope with my ex-boyfriends. Early in our relationship he brought up the subject of Kian. It was during a clearout of my flat when we were looking at old magazines and he found an article about my relationship with him. He sat and read it. I told him not to as I knew it would give him the hump, but he wouldn't listen and threw the magazine to one side when he finished. He wouldn't speak to me for an hour after he had read it and, when he finally did, it was to ask, 'So, how exactly did you fucking feel about Kian?'

Not wanting an argument, I said simply, 'It was just a bit of fun, Fran.' And that's all it was.

'Really?' he replied. 'I thought you fucking liked me at the time. What about our kiss at the house? Man, I still can't get over the fact that you went with him!'

I was shocked. 'If I remember rightly, babe, you were the one that told me to go back to his that night. I wanted to be with you more than anything. I had laid myself practically on a plate for you and, when you still didn't want it and told me you couldn't be seen with a Page 3 girl, you encouraged me to go back to Kian's.' I was so furious that he even had the cheek to question my motives.

I tried to end the conversation there so as not to get involved in another huge bust-up, but he wouldn't have it. He carried on questioning me. Did I love him? Did I fancy him? Was the sex good? Did I ever think about him now? I answered all these questions with a resounding 'No!' in all honesty – well, the sex had been OK, but I wasn't going to admit that to an already incensed Fran. He refused to drop the conversation until I lost it with him and shouted that it was his fault that I went with Kian in the first place.

'I was testing you!' he screamed back. If I said yes, I was a slut who didn't deserve his romance; if I said no, Fran said that he would have wanted to be with me. I couldn't believe that, after all this time, Fran was trying to pin that on me. He could have had me any time he wanted me back then. Why did he need to wait for a big star to fall for me and for me to knock him back before he wanted to be with me? The truth was that Fran always thought he could do better than me, and, when nothing better came along and suddenly a major celebrity wanted to be with me, it had pissed him off. Even so, he still managed to make me feel bad that I hadn't passed his 'test of love', which shows how manipulative he could be. I spent the afternoon trying to convince him that I loved him with all my heart.

Considering Fran had been Westlife's minder for a short while and still claimed to be good friends with them, he didn't have a lot of good to say about Kian. After the row was over, he spent a good half-hour slagging him off to me: 'Of course, he couldn't fucking sing anyway! The rest of the band would cover him on stage. He was always out of tune. I'd stand in the wings with the sound guys wincing every time he opened his mouth. Even the rest of the band are embarrassed by his singing. On the records, his voice is always re-mastered!' Not particularly interested, I didn't bother giving a reply, but Fran continued to slate him. 'He's an arrogant little prick as well. No one likes him. He used to slag you off when he was seeing you. He told the whole tour bus that you licked his bumhole. It makes me feel fucking sick!'

Outraged by his comments, I bit my tongue and fumed silently. I knew that Kian had bragged to the other boys in the band and to his minder Paul that I had been dirty in bed. Paul had told me on a drunken night out that Kian didn't stop talking about me. It didn't bother me that much. I tell the girls everything about a guy's performance, so I saw it as quite normal. Fran had to turn it all around though and try and make me feel cheap. He had a way of doing that like nobody else.

Around November time, Fran and I had a huge bust-up over something trivial, as usual. He decided that he didn't want to come home, so he slept at the club for a few days. After three days, I called him to say it was silly that we weren't speaking, and he broke down in tears. I asked him why he was crying but he wouldn't say. 'We've been friends all this time,' I told him. 'It's ridiculous to end like this.' I wanted at least to be friends with him, and even in the three days I had missed his company.

After a long conversation, and more tears from him, he finally admitted that things had gone too far to be friends. When I asked why, he said he couldn't tell me. I pushed him for an answer but he still wouldn't say. After another hour of heated conversation –by which point I was furious – he blurted out that he had slept with someone else. In the three days we had been apart, he had shagged another girl! I was hysterical. I had started the conversation wanting to patch things up, but ended it a crying wreck and unable to believe I had meant so little to him.

He begged my forgiveness, and in my hurt and confusion it was all I could do to accept his apologies and tell him we could start again. He still wanted to be with me, but didn't see how we would ever get through it. I didn't have a clue either, but I was willing to try. The pain I had felt all those years ago with Dave Milner came flooding back, only now I wanted to deal with it differently: the first time around I had lost the guy; this time I wanted to fight for him.

One day, when my mate Alex was over and we were reading magazines, Fran got the raging hump. A magazine had run a picture of the two of us with the usual caption: 'Jodie Marsh out on the town with boyfriend Fran Cosgrave.' Fran threw the magazine on the floor in disgust and practically spat in anger. 'Why do the bastards always do it?' he shouted in a huff.

'Do what, Fran?' I asked.

'Put your name before mine, as if you're the celeb and I'm not. Why can't they just say "celebrity couple"? It really fucking winds me up!'

Alex's face was an absolute picture. She turned away so as not to catch my eye and make me laugh. The next day she called me and asked, 'Who does he think he is?' Fran often kicked up a fuss about me being famous (or rather, in his eyes, not being famous). He hated the fact that I had worked my way up from being nobody to being one of the most photographed people in the country. After his comments to me before we got together that I was just a Page 3 girl and that he was embarrassed to be seen with someone so low down the celebrity ladder after going out with a high-profile star like Natasha, I felt a burning desire to prove to him and to others that I was capable of more.

It was not long into our relationship that I became concerned that Fran was an alcoholic. Until we really started living in each other's pockets I hadn't paid too much attention to his drinking habits, but one night it dawned on me that he had just drunk two whole bottles of Jack Daniel's to himself, plus a load of bubblegum cocktails and a few glasses of champagne. I had also become accustomed to his long stints in the toilet during the day. For a month or so he had passed it off as 'having a bug', but I began to suspect his diarrhoea was down to the ridiculous amounts of alcohol he consumed. When he started to vomit at the end of each night, I became quite worried. I asked him if he thought he drank too much and he denied it, but the truth was that Fran drank more than anybody I have ever known.

Night after night, at closing time, we would be sitting in the club with the lights off and the cleaners sweeping the floor, and Fran would pour himself another triple JD and Coke in a pint glass. I would always say, 'Do you really need that last one, Fran?' and he would tell me to get off his case: he had had a hard night working and needed it to relax. Actually, all he ever did was sit and get drunk in the VIP room – the bloke didn't know the meaning of hard work! Even on a Sunday, which was his day off, he would get drunk at the dinner table. His drinking worried me and, to be quite frank, it annoyed me too. How were we supposed to have a normal relationship when he was pissed all the time? His back and neck were covered in big hard lumps. They weren't squeezable and didn't ever seem to go away. I assumed they were something to do with the alcohol.

Another side-effect of the alcohol was the fact the Fran could no longer get a hard-on. I later found out that he had been taking Viagra since the day I met him. For ages it hadn't bothered me as I hadn't given it enough thought but, as each alcohol-fuelled day wore on and the sex never differed, it began to grate on my nerves. It felt OK, as all sex does when you get down to it, but, as with all blokes on Viagra, he just banged away at me without emotion as he tried to pleasure himself. Each time we made love, I began to feel cheap and dirty – there's nothing nice about being shagged by a drunken, sweaty bloke on Viagra. Sometimes I would have to stop him, as he would make me sore from the harsh, continuous grinding. He always took ages to come and would often get annoyed if he couldn't, blaming it on me. He would scream and shout insults at me, and stomp into the living room to watch TV, leaving me in tears in bed. I knew it wasn't my fault. I had never had any complaints in bed before – in fact, quite a few of my lovers still rated me as the best they had had – but somehow he always managed to make me feel terrible about it, and belittled me over and over again.

Added to all of this was the fact that Fran had the grossest foreskin I have ever seen. It was so horrid that I felt physically sick when I gave him a blow job and I had to stop doing it as I gagged every time. He used to sit on the sofa playing with his knob – like all blokes do – but he did it in a really weird way. I don't think he even realised he did it, but it made me feel ill. He got the raging hump with me over the lack of blow jobs, and it caused yet more rows. I told him that I had never liked doing it to anyone. Well, what was I supposed to do? Tell him the truth that his foreskin made me want to puke? I don't think it would have gone down too well…

You may be wondering after hearing all this what the hell was I doing with him. Bloody hell – now I've written it all down, I'm thinking that too. Well, he did have some good traits. On Valentine's Day, for example, he told me to be dressed and ready at eight o'clock. On the dot of eight, a car pulled up at my house with 50 red roses in the back – it was one of the rare times that Fran had money – and a giant teddy bear. The driver took me to the Oxo Tower, where Fran was waiting to greet me and we had dinner overlooking the Thames. Two weeks before Christmas and my birthday, he asked me to go to Liverpool with him to look at a club he was thinking of getting involved with. When we got there, he told me he had to go and meet the club manager at her house. He asked me to go in with him, and when I entered the woman's living room I saw the most beautiful vision in the whole world: four tiny, fat bulldog puppies with lumps of wrinkly skin and squashed faces. 'Happy birthday and Christmas, babe,' he said. 'Pick one.' I burst into tears and fell to the floor to let them crawl all over me. I chose the most handsome one, a shy little boy, and called him Paddy. Fran knew that I had always wanted a bulldog, but, having six dogs already that my parents looked after while I was away, I didn't think it fair to get another. Bulldogs were also really hard to come by, hence the journey all the way to Liverpool. At £2,000, I have no idea how Fran afforded him, but I wasn't going to start asking questions. With my bundle of joy wrapped up in my arms, I left Liverpool a richer person. Paddy was like a new Pixie, and he never left my side.

Fran also shared my love of films. I have about 800 DVDs and watch at least four a week. I would sit up late at night and watch films, and Fran, being a night owl too, would join me on the sofa and massage my feet or hands while we watched one together. We both also loved clubbing and music, and it was nice to be with someone I had so much in common with.

When he wasn't drunk or showing off, Fran was a genuinely nice bloke. He did try to make me happy and we spent lots of cuddly moments on the sofa at home talking about our hopes and dreams and generally being loved up. But that's all I've got to say about his nice side. Back to reality...

Fran loved being with celebrities, but he rarely made time

for 'normal' people – unless he could get something out of somebody, he saw them as useless hangers-on or, in his words, 'fans'. I realise now of course that the irony is that he was the biggest hanger-on I have ever met. I never seemed to be able to get it through his thick skull that my friends were real friends and they were what mattered. He only liked my celebrity friends. Unbelievably, it took him eight months of seeing my mate Lauren before he actually remembered her name.

For this reason, Fran hadn't won over many of my friends. In fact, they despised him and didn't hold back from telling me so. They thought he was rude, selfish and just using me for my fame and money. My brother hated him on sight, so much so that they nearly had a fight the night they met, and my parents weren't keen on him either. You would have thought I'd have listened to everyone around me, but still I defended him and hung on in there. God only knows what was wrong with me. Could I blame Kim's death? I was still grieving after all. Could I blame my bullies from school? I still had major insecurities underneath the surface. Could I blame the fact that I was heartbroken by Max? Not a day went by when I didn't think of him. Or was it just the classic case of wanting to tame a bastard? To this day I don't know. Maybe it was all those things; maybe it was also partly that I'm a mug, a sucker for hanging on in there when the going gets tough; maybe I felt the need to make Fran fall for me hook, line and sinker. I didn't just want him to be mine as a boyfriend; I wanted him to love me like he had never loved before. On the one hand I hated him and couldn't live with him; on the other I needed his appreciation and respect and couldn't live without him.

He drained me financially and mentally. I was

desperately unhappy but I didn't know what to do. He had destroyed my confidence and I was a wreck of a girl who couldn't walk into a pub on her own. I needed him, I thought. He was sought after by the likes of Cat Deeley, Emma Bunton, and Lisa Scott-Lee (or so he told me). I should feel grateful he wants to be with me, shouldn't I? I questioned myself over and over again. Should I stay with this sweaty, alcoholic, soul-destroying man, or should I muster the strength to leave? Fran quite neatly took that decision away from me.

During an argument in the car on the way home from Trap, Fran started slagging off my friends yet again. 'They're all hangers-on,' he said. 'They only like you because you're famous.'

'They were my friends long before I was famous,' I defended them, 'and I love each and every one of them.'

'They're slags and bitches,' he shouted at me. 'They don't care about you.'

I lost it with him. 'How dare you?' I screamed. 'Who the fuck do you think you are? My friends mean more to me than anything. They have stuck by me through thick and thin!'

Suddenly he cut my rant short. 'If they're so fucking great,' he yelled back in my face, 'how come I've shagged one of them?'

Silence.

'You've what?' I quivered.

'I've shagged one!' he screamed at me again. Not quite believing my ears, and not sure if I even wanted to know who, I stared at him open-mouthed until he quietly said, 'Jess.'

I didn't speak another word to him the rest of the way home. My brother was in the car as he had been out with us that night. He hadn't said a word during our row but, when we arrived back at the house, he turned to Fran. 'Best you don't stay here tonight, mate,' he told him. With that, Fran got back in the car and ordered the driver to take him back to Trap. 'Are you OK?' Jordan asked.

Surprisingly I was. I couldn't even cry. It was like months of torture and pain were over. I couldn't give him another chance, and I didn't even want to. I went to sleep a little bit dazed and woke up the next day feeling like somebody had switched a light on in my head. Not even a tiny bit sad, I thought that I would at least have to find out from Jess if it was true. I waited until she texted me, which I knew she would. The text said: 'HI BABE, WONDERING IF U AND FRAN R ABOUT 2NITE. FANCY DOING SUMTHIN?'

'WHY'S THAT BABE?' I replied 'SO YOU CAN FUCK FRAN AGAIN?' No point beating around the bush, I thought.

She texted back: 'I DON'T KNOW WOT UR TALKING ABOUT.'

'FRAN HAS TOLD ME EVERY SORDID DETAIL SO NO POINT LYING.' He hadn't, but I have always been good at calling people's bluff.

'WHAT'S DONE IS DONE,' she replied. 'IT'S IN THE PAST, WHY DON'T YOU FORGET ABOUT IT?'

This was all I needed. Jess had been one of my closest friends for nine years. I had practically taken her in as a sister when she had no one else to turn to during hard times. My parents had treated her like a daughter and we had all gone out of our way for her. I sent a simple text telling her to stay away from me and that I never wanted to speak to her again. I think I added a 'slut' on the end for good measure before calling Becky. 'I need some help, babe…'

Later that night, Becky and Alex were round mine wearing rubber gloves and helping me put all Fran's things into dustbin bags. I wanted every trace of him gone from my house. We actually had quite a laugh as we stuffed his mildewed clothes, still damp from sweat, into the bin liners. Everything had to go, and it took us four hours. Fourteen bin bags later, having piled them up outside on my driveway, there was just one last thing to do: the photo of me and Jess that I had had blown up was in a frame on top of my TV, and it needed to be got rid of. To make clear to Fran the reason we were splitting, I placed it neatly on the very top of the pile of bags. Just to embarrass him further, we laid a load of his white boxers we had found stuffed in a carrier bag out on the floor next to the pile. They had huge brown poo stripes down them, and we arranged them with the skid marks showing so that he would know we had seen them. We also found about 50 tablets of Viagra, still in packets. We kept those and dished them out to our other mates.

Something we also found that we thought was hilarious, if slightly weird, was a pink corduroy skirt of Natasha's. Considering he had called her a 'psycho-bitch from hell' the whole time I had been with him, I didn't really understand why he had kept an item of her clothing. It was folded neatly inside a shoebox containing some hideously cheesy modelling photos that Fran had made a mate take of himself. I found the whole skirt-keeping thing a little scary. We joked that perhaps he wore it when no one was around, and laughed at the thought of him parading round in the pink mini. Still, it seemed very stalker-like and totally went against everything he had said about Natasha. If you hated someone that much, surely you don't keep such mementos of them? The whole time I had been with Fran, he had slated Natasha to me, telling me he only stayed civil to her for the sake of Josh. When they had split, the papers had said that Natasha had dumped him, but he told me in confidence that he had actually dumped her. He said that he had ended it after a holiday where she had beaten him over the head with a lamp. He said that she was paranoid, controlling and violent. I don't even know Natasha, but I would put money on it that Fran treated her the same way he did me. It was him that was controlling. If he did half the stuff to her that he did to me then I feel for her, I really do. The truth is that she probably got to the end of her tether with his constant lies and power trips, and kicked him out, as the papers had said all along.

I don't think a man could have felt any lower than Fran did when he arrived to collect his things. I stood and smirked as he loaded the bags into the waiting car. He hissed in disgust at the picture of me and Jess, and squirmed with utter mortification at the skid-marked pants, which he now knew had been seen not only by me, but also by Becky and Alex. Becky thought that we should have kept them and put them on eBay for everyone to see – I loved the idea but didn't think I could honestly be that cruel. His humiliation on my driveway was compensation enough.

I thought back to a time halfway through my relationship with Fran, when Max had returned to the country having finished working in LA. He called me for a chat and confessed that he had really missed me. I told him I had missed him too. 'Can we meet up?' he asked.

'Yes,' I told him, 'of course.' We arranged a time and place. My heart still jumped every time he phoned, and I was desperate to see him. Breaking the news to him that I was with Fran had been horrific. He had called me for a chat a few weeks after going to LA. It was six in the morning and I had just got into my car outside Trap to go home after a night's clubbing. Fran was beside me in the passenger seat. We had been 'official' for a week and as Max launched into 'Baby, I've missed you…' I had to cut him short and tell him the news.

I heard the tone of his voice change as I said, 'I've got something to tell you. I'm not single any more.' The last time I had spoken to him, I had just split with Dane, and he was glad of it. He had made no bones at how annoyed he was with my new partner. I'd laughed it off, telling him that we weren't serious and that Dane was a passing fancy. Fran, however, was a different kettle of fish, and Max knew it. Max had known I'd been close to Fran as Fran had often called me up first thing in the morning while I was lying in bed with Max. He'd never mentioned this before but told me now he had always thought Fran had a thing for me and that he knew it was only a matter of time before we got together. He sounded really down and my heart ached – I knew I had just ruined for good the possibility of Max and I ever making a go of it again.

This time when he called me, however, he sounded more upbeat. We hadn't spoken since that hideous conversation in my car, but I was delighted to hear from him. I assumed he had decided that it was better to be friends than nothing at all, and I couldn't wait to see him. The conversation then turned. 'I can't wait to see that beautiful little arse, babe,' he said.

'Max,' I laughed, 'be a good boy, you know I'm taken now.'

'I can't, babe. I've missed you and I need to see you.' He then recalled some of the amazing sessions we had had and told me that we had some unfinished business. 'You know we're going to be together again one day, babe,' he said.

I found myself agreeing to a secret liaison with him. If I

was honest with myself, Fran didn't even compare to how I felt about Max. Max still was the love of my life and every inch of my body wanted to be with him. We decided that Fran didn't need to know and the day was set. I called an urgent meeting with the girls. Once Becky and Michelle were at mine, I confessed that Max wanted to see me and that I was going to go. They were happy for me. They had picked up the pieces of my shattered heart after I had split with him, so they knew how much he meant to me. Plus, they didn't like Fran.

A day before I was due to see Max, however, something began to niggle at me. I had always thought it wrong to cheat on a partner, having had it done to me in the past. I had also always firmly believed that what goes around comes around, so I started to worry about the karma of me cheating on Fran. I called Max in a state of panic. 'I'm so sorry, babe,' I told him. 'I can't do it.' It wasn't that I didn't want to – more than anything I wanted Max to hold me in his arms and never let me go. It wasn't even that I cared enough about Fran, if the truth be known. I'd have shit in his face and dumped him on the spot if I thought Max would have me back. It was purely about having morals. I explained to him that it wasn't right and that I couldn't bring myself to cheat on somebody. He grudgingly accepted it. I wasn't going to admit to Max that I would dump Fran for him, but at the same time I wasn't going to cheat. If Max wanted me back, I reasoned to myself that he would have said so. Instead, he wanted a sordid affair. It was obviously about the sex for him and, while I would have gone running if I were single, I wasn't, so I didn't.

Instead, Max turned up unexpectedly at Trap that night. He knew I would be there and didn't have a lot else to do so thought he would come and see me anyway. He called me from outside the club and asked me to get a doorman to let him in, which I did. Fran was ever the gentleman to his face and we spent the night sitting together at a table in the VIP. Each time Fran went to the toilet, Max placed a hand on my thigh and looked suggestively at me. He told me I looked amazing and kept leaning his face in to mine so that we were almost close enough to kiss. I think he was trying to see how far he could push it. I didn't tell him to stop – I couldn't! Every bone in my body loved him inside and out. The only time I pushed him away was when I saw Fran heading back from the toilet. The night ended with Max cuddling me for slightly longer and a little bit tighter than he should have done, and Fran and I rowed the whole way home. He was complaining that he'd had to entertain an ex of mine. I don't really know why I'm telling you all of this now, other than to say that, after Fran ended up shagging Jess, I suppose I wish that I had gone through with the dirty deed of seeing Max behind his back. By the time of the split with Fran, Max had a new girlfriend. By being with Fran – the serial cheater – and by being unable to cheat myself, I had missed out on an opportunity to be with the one I really wanted. I really could kick myself now. But with Fran and Jess gone from my life, I decided it was time to concentrate on getting my career back on track. *The Games* was going well and I had lots more lined up for the future. I found myself happy to be free from the clutches of Fran – until, that is, a bombshell hit a week later.

CHAPTER FIFTEEN
The Decision

A week after I split with Fran, Becky and Lauren (that's the school teacher, not the stripper) came over to mine to have a girly night in. I happened to mention to them that my boobs were really heavy and that my period was late. I laughed that I had better not be pregnant, but I never really thought that I might be – I just presumed that the stress from the break-up was having an effect on my body. They exchanged glances. 'Actually, babe,' Becky said, 'I thought earlier on in the week that your boobs looked really big. Do you think you should do a test to be on the safe side?'

The hairs on the back of my neck stood up as I realised she was serious. 'I can't be. I'm on the pill, I'm sure I'll come on soon.' But I didn't convince myself, let alone her, as I realised that actually it did seem feasible. For a few weeks I had been struggling with the gymnastics in *The Games*. Every time I did a forward roll, I felt sick and dizzy which was something I had never had a problem with before. Unusually for me, I had become quite tearful and couldn't understand why. If I was pregnant, it would all make perfect sense. I had a test in my bathroom cupboard, and the girls insisted I go and do it. I told them I wasn't ready – if it was positive, it didn't bear thinking about, but I promised I would do it at some point later that night.

A few hours went by and I thought of nothing else but my heavy boobs and sickness. Although I tried to be jovial and join in with the conversation, the realisation that I might be pregnant had set in so I knew that I would have to take the test. I slipped off to the toilet, pretending I needed a wee, and did the test alone. As I stood waiting for the result, I felt nothing. My fingers trembled as I held the stick. Please, God, I thought. Don't let me be pregnant.

As the little line appeared in the window of the stick, I froze.

I waited a full ten minutes in case it changed, but it didn't. Still numb, and unable to string a proper sentence together, I unlocked the bathroom door and walked slowly upstairs still holding the test. When I reached the top of the stairs, my face must have said it all. I crumpled as they rushed to cuddle me. 'I'm pregnant,' I sobbed.

They walked me back to the sofa and sat me down. 'We're going to deal with this, babe,' Becky told me.

'You're not going to go through this alone,' added Lauren.

Becky decided that she would take the following day off work to be with me. It was a Sunday night and I had training for *The Games* in the morning. Not wanting to tell anybody that I was pregnant, and not knowing what on earth I was going to do, I didn't want to be left alone. Unable to discuss my options that night, I just sat and cried. Immediately I felt different. I *felt* pregnant, and had an instinctive urge to protect my stomach. As I sat and gently cradled my belly on the sofa, I knew that I was going to want to keep my baby.

It took me another two days to tell the people that mattered. My parents had to know, as did my agent, Jeff. As I told them, they each offered their undying love and support and told me that, whatever I decided, they would stick by me. I didn't want the press to find out, but I knew that I couldn't carry on with my training for *The Games*. Jeff took on the responsibility of telling the head of Endemol the news. He granted me as much time off as I needed, but obviously didn't want to me pull out of the show. He understood what a horrible situation I was in, and sympathised, which eased the pressure on me to perform. I took a few days out to consider my options.

I had enough money to raise a child alone, I had the support of my friends and family and, most importantly, my maternal instincts had kicked in and I wanted to have the baby, for whom I already felt a huge love. On the down side, I hated Fran with a passion and hadn't spoken to him since the day he picked his stuff up from mine. Fran also already had a son. I couldn't help but compare it to the way I had been brought up. My parents were still married after 32 years and my brother and I had been raised lovingly by both Mum and Dad. I had never agreed with abortion but, faced with this huge decision, I suddenly understood why women had them. I wanted the baby, but I didn't want to be tied to Fran forever. Moreover, I had never envisioned having a child out of wedlock.

I decided to hold off making any kind of decision for a while, and booked a scan with a private clinic. Linsey Dawn drove me there on the day and came in with me for support. Neither of us wore make-up, and we wore baseball caps and the dodgiest-looking tracksuits we could find so that we stood less chance of being recognised. It was after they had given me my scan picture and told me that I was eight weeks and five days gone that I broke down to Linsey and said that I thought that Fran should know. She agreed, and said that I should wait until we were back at hers and then call him. But I couldn't wait. Much as I despised him for all he had put me through, he had also asked me on numerous occasions when we were together if I would have a baby with him. It was time to tell him that I was carrying his child and I didn't want to leave it a second longer. Outside the clinic, Linsey and I sat on a bench and I nervously called Fran's number. 'What?' he said abruptly when he answered. I knew it wasn't going to be an easy conversation.

'Don't talk to me like that, please, Fran,' I said. 'You were the one who cheated, remember? Just be nice and listen for a minute. I've got something to tell you.' He shut up and let me continue. By now I was in tears and was struggling to get the words out. 'I'm pregnant. I'm sitting outside the clinic looking at the scan picture.' I knew that I wanted to keep the baby but also knew that it would mean patching things up with Fran.

The reaction he gave was not the one I was looking for. 'You fucking lying cunt!' he screamed down the phone. 'Fuck off and leave me alone. You're not fucking pregnant, you're an attention-seeking little bitch!'

Gulping back the sobs, I tried desperately to reason with him and convince him that I wasn't lying. Linsey was furious and tried to get me to hang up on him. Fran heard her in the background, called her a 'lying slag' as well and then hung up.

I have never spoken to him since.

A week passed as I wallowed in my pain. I have absolutely no idea how, but that week the newspapers found out that I was pregnant. A journalist friend told me that I had been spotted by a member of the public outside the clinic in North London. For a week, the papers ran stories about it. Fran had been asked to comment and all he would say was 'I don't give a fuck if she's pregnant.' Reading this hurt even more. I felt like someone had ripped my insides out.

Trying to be logical, I wondered how I was supposed to bring a baby into this world with a father like Fran. What would I do when the child was eight or nine and started asking where his daddy was? I didn't think I would be able to live with that much hatred inside me, and I certainly didn't want to inflict that on a child. I would have been a bitter old hag of a mother who had nothing but nasty things to say about the father, and I couldn't go through with it. I take off my hat to single mums and I would definitely not rule out being one. I think I'd do a great job, with or without a bloke, in bringing up a child, but Fran was a different story. It sickened me to the pit of my stomach when I thought of him and in the end, feeling such venom, it didn't seem fair to bear a child. It gradually began to dawn on me that the one thing I always thought I had been dead against was actually starting to look like an option. How much I loathed Fran had played too big a part in deciding what to do. I honestly didn't feel like he had left me with any choice.

I booked the termination for a week later. It was the most awful decision I have ever had to make and it still haunts me today. I know that, when the time comes when I *am* ready to have children, it will hurt even more viciously. Every day I have to live with myself that I killed a baby in my own stomach.

Back on the road to recovery, I had a public appearance booked in Belfast. I asked school teacher Lauren to come with me and we hopped on the plane with my minder. Once there, we found we had been booked separate hotel rooms, and they were huge. I had a suite and it was beautiful. I was in need of a little pick-me-up after the horrific mess that was Fran, so as we got ready that night we were feeling really naughty. In all the time I've been famous, I have never acted like a celebrity. I'm the least diva-ish person you could meet. My make-up artist Sadie makes more demands than I do (but always blames it on me, saying, 'Jodie wants a Twirl!' when she fancies chocolate or 'Jodie wants chips' when we have food). I'm never stroppy unless someone upsets me first, I have never thrown my weight around and I have never wanted special treatment. For the first time since I'd become well known, however, Lauren and I decided that we would both act like stars.

After I finished my PA at the club, we sat in a roped-off area of the VIP room and proceeded to get very drunk. Belfast appeared to be full of fit young men, so we took advantage of it and decided that my minder should go and tell the ones that we hand picked that they were invited back to my hotel for a drink. Without hesitation he approached six blokes we had chosen, none of whom knew each other. 'Jodie Marsh would like the pleasure of your company back at her hotel tonight for late drinks,' he told each of them in turn. They all agreed immediately, which I found amazing and hilarious.

My minder drove Lauren and me back to the hotel – it was only two minutes away – while the boys were told to walk and meet us in the bar. All six of them turned up. I couldn't believe that they were willing to come along. They didn't even know each other, but they were all prepared to have a go at pulling one or both of us. We sat up drinking with them for another three hours and had a scream, but when the time came that we wanted to go to bed, and having realised we didn't actually fancy any of them, we just upped and ran, leaving my minder to deal with it. 'I'm afraid Miss Marsh is tired now, so it's time to call it a night, lads,' he told them. I felt a bit bad for stringing them along, but when I was hit with the drinks bill the next morning the guilt soon faded. It certainly perked me up though: for the first time since splitting from Fran, I was beginning to realise what effect I could have on other men.

One of these men who fell for my charms was Major James Hewitt. We had filmed a show together called *Celebrity Penthouse* where we had been locked in a house for 24 hours. I was with Fran at the time and had been on my best behaviour. The only thing I did that was slightly outrageous was to give James a pair of my knickers and a poster from *Ice* magazine of me wearing them. Needless to say, he got a little hot under the collar. James and I had got on really well and, as soon as he read in the papers that I had split with Fran, he called to ask me out. I was very busy so couldn't give him a day, but I did have a spare ticket to a premiere. It turned out that James was already going, so we arranged to meet there and I took my brother.

The film was good. Jordan loved James and, after five minutes of conversation, turned to me and said, 'You should marry this one, Jodie.' He had hated every single one of my boyfriends, so this was a first. Nothing had even happened between James and me, but Jordan wanted it to. James is a real charmer: when you meet him, you can't fail to like him, regardless of whether you're male or female. He had my brother in fits of laughter from our very first conversation, and I knew it was going to be a good night. Whenever my brother was out of earshot, though, James didn't hesitate to come on a bit more strongly. He told me how wonderful I looked, before saying in his thick, Sloaney accent, 'You're making me feel very naughty!'

I wasn't looking for a relationship by any means, but James was lots of fun and knew how to make a girl feel special. He might be worth a snog, I thought. James had told me that he was mine for the night: I could do with him what I wished. On that note, I told him that, after the premiere, I'd like to go to Funky Buddha. James hadn't been to a nightclub in years and wasn't used to partying all night – his idea of a good time was going to a swanky restaurant or the theatre. Nevertheless, we jumped in a car after the film and rocked up at the club where a crowd of paparazzi were waiting. It was a Tuesday night and Funky was the best place to go, so they always waited outside. Once settled at a table, we ordered a couple of bottles of vodka and mixers and set about getting drunk. By the end of the night, James was twirling me round the dance floor like something from *Saturday Night Fever*. After a good hour's dancing, he pulled me in towards him and tilted my chin up towards his. As he covered my lips with his, awful as it sounds, all I could think was, Princess Diana has kissed these lips! We snogged openly for a good half an hour. I knew I should have been more discreet, but was too drunk to care by that stage. I could feel that James was, shall we say, quite turned on. Oh, all right, he had a rock-hard boner and it was digging into my stomach – he's a lot taller than me! His fingers did a little wandering. I had a really short skirt on and, as I joked that he was making me wet and had better stop, he wasted no time in having a little feel. I let him touch me for a split second, then pushed him off, suddenly embarrassed. For some reason the fact that he was a lot older, combined with the fact that he was ultra posh, made me feel a bit like a silly little girl and I came over quite shy. We made our way back to our table where my brother was in full pulling mode and was chatting up a couple of pretty girls with James's best mate. We sat holding hands for the rest of the night and carried on kissing. Occasionally James would try to put his hand between my legs and I would push it away, saying, 'Not in front of my brother, James!' The night soon came to an end and we said that we would speak soon.

The following day, James texted me to say that he had really enjoyed himself and that we would have to do it again soon. Somehow our text conversation turned sexual and, within five minutes, we were furiously exchanging filth. He told me what he wanted to do to me (I couldn't even repeat it!) and I told him he was going to get it when I saw him. Our texts became very graphic and I even sent him some dirty pictures of myself – much to his delight. He phoned me half an hour later to say that I was 'a very naughty girl'. We arranged another date and he told me that this time the night was going to be arranged by him. He had loved Funky Buddha but now wanted to show me what *he* did for enjoyment. All he told me was that we were going to a fancy dinner first, so I rushed out to buy a posh dress, as I knew I couldn't wear one of my usual fun outfits.

On the day, I asked James to meet me at the hairdresser's where I was getting my hair done for the night. I was excited to see his reaction when he saw what I was going to be wearing. When he arrived, I was still in the chair in my tracksuit. When I was done, I went out to the back of the shop to change and had three hairdressers helping to do up the straps at the back of my dress. As I made my entrance back into the shop, James said aloud, 'Wow!' He had started drinking wine with the receptionist and seemed to be quite tipsy but I was glad he approved and we made our way into the waiting car.

The 'dinner' that James had asked me to go to actually turned out to be a jewellery showcase, and as soon as I walked through the door, £150,000 worth of diamonds were placed around my neck to wear for the night. I actually felt like a princess. Even though the diamonds were great, however, the event wasn't that happening and I made it clear to James that I thought we should go somewhere else. He agreed and said that he wanted to take me to one of his favourite places in London. Back at the car, he ordered the driver to take us to the Lancaster Gate Hotel. The porter opened the car door for us and we were greeted like royalty. James was clearly a regular: the staff loved him and it showed. We were taken through to the restaurant, where we sat at the bar and ordered drinks. We both felt a little peckish and ordered some food. James had some fancy French dish and I had a bowl of chips – you can take the girl out of Essex and all that…

After we had eaten, James wanted to sit and 'lounge' with a cigar and some red wine. All I could think about was the party I was missing at Wellington. Even though I had vodka lemonade in front of me, it wasn't quite the same. James must have known something was up and asked if there was anywhere else I wanted to go or anything I wanted to do. I didn't want to rubbish his choice of events or places, but it just wasn't me. I felt uncomfortable in my dress and couldn't help but notice the stares of the posh women surrounding me. 'Do you mind if we go somewhere a little more lively?' I asked him.

'Of course not,' he replied.

We left the hotel to find about twenty paps waiting for us. Someone had tipped them off that we were there. James shielded me as we waded through the scrum and climbed into the car, and we shouted at the driver to go to Wellington. What followed was quite possibly the scariest thing I have ever experienced. The paps were obviously desperate to get a picture of the two of us, and I can only think that, because I was wearing a posh dress for the first time ever, it made them even more eager. They jumped into their cars and on to their motorbikes and chased us from the hotel all the way to Wellington. Now, I have had my fair share of paparazzi attention – they have followed my every move on nights out since the days of the army belts – but this was totally different. They surrounded us as we drove through the streets of London. Motorbikes rode dangerously close to the side of the car and the guys even pointed their cameras at the car window while they were moving. Our driver was stressed and trying to act like a bit of a hero: he drove faster, which in turn made the paps drive faster. We drove for a full ten minutes in this scary, high-speed convoy, followed by at least four or five cars. A few cars had burned us up at the lights – they had obviously guessed where we were going, and they wanted to get there first.

Once we got to Wellington, the paps fell over themselves to get a picture. James and I exited the car as elegantly as we could and fought our way through the mass of photographers. Once inside the door, I escorted James downstairs and we spent the next hour being bombarded by people who wanted to meet him. Wellington was a regular haunt of mine and I knew practically everyone in there, but James had never been before. After his performance on the first series of *The Games*, it seemed he had quite a lot of fans. Jake the owner gave us free drinks and looked after us. After an hour or so, James went off to the toilet. A load of my friends had turned up, including Calum, and I had been preoccupied with them for a while. James hadn't been left on his own however – he had been chatting up a woman who had approached him. When he hadn't returned from the toilet half an hour later, I checked my phone and there was a text from him: 'I'M REALLY SORRY DARLING BUT I FELT TIRED AND HAD TO GO. I'VE HAD A WONDERFUL NIGHT, I'LL CALL YOU TOMORROW.' It was something of a relief to me, as all night I had felt that I was acting like something I wasn't. Now I could let my hair down. I went on to get pissed and snog Calum, but left alone after a good night's partying.

I genuinely liked James, and still do, but after that night I realised that he wasn't for me and that I didn't want anything further to happen between us. He is such a lovely guy and I don't have a bad word to say about him. The only thing that made me realise he wasn't right for me was noticing how different we really are. He loves good food and posh restaurants; I'm happy in Pizza Express. He loves a cigar and a log fire; I prefer dancing on a table in a club. He can talk for hours about a good red wine; I drink only milk, water and vodka (although not together!). He lives in Chelsea; I'm from Essex. It said it all – he wanted to drink brandy in a hotel lounge when all I wanted to do was swing from the chandelier in Wellington. There were too many conflicts of interest and, aside from that, I had not long been single. I couldn't even begin to think about starting a new relationship and, even if I did, he was too much of a ladies' man for my liking. James had flirted with and charmed every female he met that night. It didn't bother me in the slightest, but I knew that in the long run, if I was going to be with a bloke seriously again, he would have to love me and me alone.

CHAPTER SIXTEEN

Playing Games

A month or so later, *The Games* started on television. Ten of us had to go into a house in Sheffield where we would have no contact with the outside world for a week, and each day we had to compete in a different sporting event. I stayed up the night before, having my hair done – we didn't start till midnight, so with all the fag breaks it was six o'clock before we were finished – and my car picked me up at seven, so I was shattered as I set off for the show.

I had become very close to Lady Isabella Hervey during the four months of filming, and I was looking forward to spending the week with her and her dog Cleo, who she was taking into the house. I was also excited to be meeting the boys, as we had been kept apart until now: I immediately bonded with Pat Sharp and Jarrod, winner of the Mr Gay UK title; I already knew Shane Lynch from the party scene in London so we got on well; the 'Millionaire Major', Charles Ingram, was completely mad but loveable; and

Romeo was the shy heartthrob. The first day was really good. I won the first event on the rowing machine, which felt amazing as my parents had come to support me and were sitting in the audience. My mum cried when I won, and I was ecstatic that I had done her proud.

By day two it had started to become difficult. Isabella and I didn't get on with TV presenter Katy Hill at all. I had known Katy since I was five years old – she was big sister to Naomi, the girl who got off with my boyfriend Dave in my house. So although Katy had been like a sister to me when we were children – I had practically lived at her house and she had even worked for my parents as a waitress at one of their parties – I hadn't seen her since I was fourteen years old and had that big falling out with Naomi. On the first day of filming the training in January, I had walked in all smiles and rushed to hug Katy. She stuck her hand out and said with a smile 'Nice to meet you.' I stepped back, shocked and said, 'Pardon?' Again, she said, 'Nice to meet you, I'm Katy.' I thought she was joking. Surely she knew who I was? I had been best friends with her sister for nine years and, although I hadn't seen her since, she must have known I was the same Jodie Marsh from Brentwood. Incredulously, I asked if she was serious that she didn't know who I was. She replied, 'Sorry, I don't read tabloids.' I said that I was, in fact, the same Jodie Marsh who used to come to her house every night after school. It suddenly dawned on her and she said she was pleased to see me. I let it go, not wanting to cause tension on the very first day of filming.

By the time we were in the house together, things reached boiling point, as Katy had been calling Isabella 'Victoria' (her sister's name); Isabella, being the youngest and least known, was feeling positively put upon. Having become such firm friends, I vowed to her that I wouldn't let Isabella be upset.

It all came to a head one day out in the stadium. Each day we had to go and rehearse that night's event off camera so that we all knew what we were doing for the live show. As we sat on the grass, Katy made a bitchy remark to Isabella and Isabella bit on it. She shouted at Katy to leave her alone, and asked why they couldn't just get along for the sake of living together for the rest of the week. Katy went into one, saying that Isabella had a complex and that she shouldn't be so paranoid. I took over the argument and told Katy that actually I thought Isabella was right.

When she asked what I meant, I told her about what I felt when she didn't remember me and said that, after working with Isabella five days a week for four months, she might have got her name right. Isabella had been in tears before about Katy calling her Victoria; Katy had said to camera that she hadn't meant to do it, but she still found it amusing. She again said she didn't know who I was and that she didn't read tabloids.

'No, but I bet you read *OK!* Magazine, don't you?' I replied. She answered that she did and I said, 'Well, I've been in that every week for a year!' She had no reply. Not wanting to have too much of a go at her as I knew I was winning the argument and she was lost for words, I finished off with 'Look, it doesn't matter anyway, Katy. The point is we've got to live together for the rest of the week. I don't want to argue on camera as we'll all look silly, but I want everyone to get along. Can we all agree to put our differences aside and be nice to each other for the sake of getting through this programme? I don't know about you but I'm here to make money for my charity, and that's all I care about. Now please, can we all shake hands and make up?'

I thought I was being very diplomatic about it all. There was no need for a screaming match. If we acted like adults, we could see this through and do what we came to do. Katy agreed and we all had a bit of a hug. Linda Lusardi, who had been nice to me while I was going through the horrendous pregnancy situation (even phoning me up outside of *The Games* to offer advice and sympathy) had become Katy's friend since we had entered the house, but she too agreed that we should all try to get along. Hugging done, we carried on with rehearsals and were back in the house an hour or so later.

But we just weren't going to get along. As soon as we were back in the house, and back on camera, Katy went into the bedroom and broke down in tears, with Linda comforting her. Isabella and I asked what was wrong and Linda told us that we had really upset Katy earlier. She said that Katy felt victimised and that we were both being horrible. I'd had enough! I felt like screaming. I reasoned with her again that she had been wrong to call Isabella 'Victoria' all the time. I didn't want to bring up my issues with her as they hadn't been documented on TV. I stood my ground and defended her until there was nothing left to say. Poor Isabella became a hate target for the fans at the stadium each night. We entered the pitch each night to the sound of 9,000 people booing Isabella. She was 21 years old, was the youngest of the group, had never been on TV before, hadn't done *anything* wrong and was getting booed. I was looking like a bitch on camera and was furious. The crowd had taken a massive liking to me so each night I put my arms round Isabella and waved for the crowd to cheer for her. It worked a little bit, but not as well as I would have hoped.

After all this, and still not anywhere near recovered

mentally from the hell of the termination, I became more and more fed up inside the house. I was the only vegetarian and, by the look of it, the only person who had lived on junk food all their life. My meals each day consisted of dry brown rice and a few vegetables. Every day I asked if I could possibly have a jacket potato or some chips, but never had any joy. Apparently the food had been carefully planned out to give us energy. In fact, it was doing the opposite for me: having lived on pizzas, chips, bread and pasta for the last 25 years, I couldn't cope with the emptiness in my stomach – the dry brown rice was tasteless and didn't fill me up. By day three I was lying on the sofa, unable to move and in desperate need of a chip buttie. When the fitness trainer came in, I moaned to him that I needed proper food. He said he would see what he could do, but nothing changed.

That night in the stadium, my mum sneaked in a bag of chips and threw them to me from the stands. She had bought them just outside the stadium and put them in a special bag that had kept them hot. Every night directly after the live show, a couple of people had always been ordered to go straight back to the house because the live viewing continued on E4. I managed to get out of it each time, preferring to stay in the stadium to sign autographs and meet the fans. That night, however, I was forced to go straight back to the house. Lauren, Becky, Michelle and all my other friends who had been watching the show religiously had looked forward to the night that I was one of the first to come back. They told me afterwards it had been the most disappointing TV they'd ever watched – apparently it took me half an hour to eat the chips and I groaned orgasmically all the way through. They had stayed up every night for that!

Later that night, after coming last yet again in my event, I sat and chatted to Isabella in the garden. I said that I felt like I was letting the fans down. Each night there were thousands of people there to see us. Many of them cheered for me religiously and I kept coming last. During the early stages of training I had suffered a groin strain which hadn't healed and made it difficult for me to run. The doctor had wanted me to pull out of the events that involved sprinting, but that would have meant no money for my charity so I wouldn't do that. Added to that was the month I had taken off from training while I was pregnant, and now I was feeling weak from hunger and desperate to talk to my mum. I contemplated how shit I was and how I hoped the fans weren't too disappointed. I couldn't believe how nice they were and how much they rooted for me. Isabella told me not to worry, and said that it was great I was even there. She gave me lots of cuddles and said that Cleo could sleep on my bed for comfort. I waited for everyone to go off to sleep and sat in the garden with a cigarette to wallow in my sadness. A lone tear rolled down my cheek.

Jamie Theakston later told me that he and the crew had watched that from the live cameras and it had brought tears to their eyes. The following day I was still feeling terrible, and a comment from Shane made me cry so much that I demanded a phone call to my mum otherwise I was walking off the show. We had been talking about ex-boyfriends, and all Shane had said was that Fran seemed like a nice guy. After all the months of hurt and pain and feeling like I had been left with no choice but to abort my own child, his comment seared through me like a knife. I went to pieces. The producers, frightened that I really was going to walk off, let me call my mum. She cried down the phone with me and begged me to be strong. She told me that she loved me and that lots of people were rooting for me. I was only allowed five minutes with her, but it made me feel a hundred times better. I dried my eyes, apologised to Shane for my outburst and carried on with the day.

That night a girl called Vicki brought a banner she had made for me to the stadium and gave it to Charlie Dimmock to give to me. It cheered me up even more. It was covered with pictures of me she had cut out from magazines and had the words 'Jordan who? Jodie is No 1' written on it. It came with a note saying that I wasn't letting anybody down and that they all thought I was great. As I sat in the garden with Isabella, marvelling over the banner, she gave me a good talking-to. She reminded me that I was there to make money for my charity; not only that, I was doing it for Kim – my chosen charity was Refuge, which fights domestic violence against women. I had chosen it because of Kim, and knew by now that two women a week were killed by a partner or ex-partner in England and Wales. Isabella told me that she loved me and that I had been her rock throughout the show – if I walked, she would too.

Thanks to my mum, the banner from Vicki and Isabella's friendship, I decided to stay; not only that, I decided I was going to enjoy it. At the time I had felt like I should have pulled out of the programme as soon as I found out I was pregnant. I needed to be with my family. I wasn't OK mentally and it showed. In retrospect, I'm so happy that I saw it through as I ended up raising a lot of money for Refuge, so my thanks are due to Vicki Duffy, Isabella and my mum.

CHAPTER SEVENTEEN

Great Scott

When I finished *The Games* (having come last – hooray!), I took a much-needed week off and lay on the sofa at home doing nothing. After a while, though, I started to get bored so I hit the London party scene again. After clubbing it like mad for a few weeks with the likes of Ricardo, Calum, Dave Courtney and D-Side, I was beginning to feel normal again. It was on one such night out that I bumped into Scott Sullivan, Jordan's ex. I had met Scott before at a lap-dancing club where I briefly worked after Strings, and Jordan had asked me to dance for him, which I did. I hadn't seen him since Jordan had dumped him publicly on *I'm A Celebrity Get Me Out of Here!* a few months previously, and he was enjoying a boozy night out with his mates. I nodded a hello to him and carried on partying in a corner of the Embassy Club with Ricardo.

Later on that night, one of his mates approached me and asked if I would talk to Scott. He said that Scott was too shy to ask me himself. 'I'm happy to talk to him,' I said, 'but I'm not moving. He'll have to come to me.'

Five minutes later Scott was at my side. I patted for him to sit down. We giggled as we caught up on what we had been up to since the last time we had seen each other. One of Scott's mates joined us and, not realising that Ricardo was a man (he was in full drag), had been persuaded by us to lick Ricardo's toes – a great comedy moment, although the pleasure for me came in *telling* him that Ricardo was a man. Scott and I exchanged numbers at the end of the night and said that we would stay in touch.

He texted me the next day to say that he had enjoyed my company, and asked when we were going out again. Thinking he was a lovely guy, and quite fanciable, I texted him back that I had four tickets to a premiere the following week and asked if he wanted to bring a friend and join me and a girlfriend. He said he would love to, and we carried on texting each other in quite a flirty fashion right up until the night of the premiere. I didn't want to like him – but I couldn't help myself. He was a gentleman and funny with it. He was only 21, but I've always been a sucker for the young ones. Scott had said he would meet us in London and I arranged for my driver, Vince, to pick me up at home and take me to meet Scott at the Ritz Hotel, where he and his mate would jump into our car and we would then go to the film.

Waiting at the Ritz, I became quite nervous. I hadn't felt excited about a bloke for what seemed like forever, but now I definitely had butterflies in my tummy. When he walked in he looked gorgeous. He was wearing ripped, faded jeans and a simple white shirt. He jumped into the car and we took off. The press went nuts on the red carpet – they loved the fact that I was with Jordan's ex. If I'm honest, I knew that they would, but didn't particularly care. I genuinely liked Scott by now – what girl wouldn't fancy him? He was extremely handsome. After posing for all the pictures and doing the usual interviews, we made our way into the cinema but, standing in the foyer, we decided that actually the film didn't really interest us that much and we weren't that bothered about watching it. Unable to walk back outside to the throngs of waiting press, I called Vince and told him to drive to the back door of the cinema. Laughing hysterically like naughty schoolchildren, we ran down a fire exit and sneaked out the back door. Vince had the car doors open waiting for us, and he drove away quickly before we were spotted.

We were all hungry so we asked Vince if he knew of any good places to eat. He drove us to a Turkish restaurant he knew of that he thought we would like, and waited outside as we ate a huge meal of kebabs (and chips for me). After we had eaten, Vince drove us back for the after-show party – we were bang on time! That party wasn't much better, though, so we decided to move on to the best place to be on a Monday night: Ten Rooms. Pat Sharp happened to be in there with his beautiful wife Monica, so we spent the night getting drunk at a table with them. Scott and I were getting on like a house on fire, and by the end of the night I was sitting on his lap with his arms around my waist. He and his mate ended up staying at my house – we just didn't want the night to end – and Scott and I cuddled each other to sleep. For the first time since Max, I felt all warm inside.

Scott and I spent a lot of time together over the next two weeks. He stayed at my house a few times, and I drove to Brighton and stayed at his. Scott rode motorbikes as a hobby and we spent hours in the fields at his house on bikes. He wouldn't let me ride a proper one (even though I had a bike as a kid), so I was subjected to riding the quad. It was great fun, though. I soon realised I had met someone with all the same interests as me, someone who knew how to have fun, someone who was spontaneous and someone who, for the first time in my life, came from the same background I did. Scott's parents were very well off, but they had earned every penny of it. They had built up businesses and now lived in a huge mansion in the countryside near Brighton. By an amazing coincidence, Scott's parents had also built him a house on their land, next door to theirs. I had never met anyone who lived the same way as me. It seemed like a match made in heaven. Scott's parents had brought him up to have the same manners and respect that I did. He was the perfect gentleman – but dangerous on a bike, lots of fun, knew how to give good cuddles *and* he was good in bed. I couldn't have asked for more. The press had a field day and slated us for pairing up, stating that it was all for publicity, but I can assure you that Scott and I were as real as my tits.

A few weeks into our relationship it was Scott's birthday, so I went to Brighton to celebrate with him and his friends. We all got very drunk and ordered taxis to take us home. As soon as Scott and I got in our cab, I started to feel a bit fruity. We hadn't been alone all night, so now I felt like taking full advantage of him. We started with – how can I put this? – a little oral pleasure, and Scott sank back into the seat to enjoy it. It was dark, so I didn't think the driver would notice. One thing led to another and before we knew it we were having sex – me sitting on top of him, knickers to one side and my miniskirt hitched up. Too desperate to wait until we got home and being the thrill-seekers that we both were, the sex got more and more noisy. After a minute or two of my bouncing getting harder and his moans getting louder, the car suddenly screeched to a halt. The driver didn't even turn round to look at us. 'Either stop what you're doing,' he shouted, 'or get out!' He refused to drive an inch further with us shagging in the back. I had shagged in taxis before and, perhaps surprisingly, never had a driver complain. In fact, when they let me carry on, pretending to be oblivious, I always tipped them by a large amount.

Feeling once more like a couple of naughty schoolchildren, we gingerly parted and adjusted our clothes. I got a nervous giggling fit the rest of the way home – and needless to say the taxi driver didn't get his tip. I was mortified to think that he might go to the papers, and could just see the headline: JODIE THROWN OUT OF TAXI FOR SHAGGING!

What I loved most about Scott was that he was spontaneous and fun. One morning, after staying at his and waking up to go and feed the ducks on his pond, he drove me into Brighton town. He parked the car, walked me down to where the trampolines were lined up along the sea front, paid the guy for two and we spent an hour bouncing in the morning sun. It was exhilarating and mad. He made me feel like a teenager with a crush again – we even went for a milkshake afterwards. My favourite game had always been run-outs (a more difficult version of hide-and-seek) and I remembered years before, when I was with Garry, he called my friends and I childish because we wanted to play it one summer's evening. Scott, however, wouldn't have batted an eyelid if I had said, 'Let's play run-outs.' In fact, he'd have rounded up all his mates and run off into the nearest forest. I could be as childish and stupid as I wanted with him. It wasn't because he was immature; it was because, like me, he didn't want to grow up.

Just after his birthday, I moaned to Scott that I hadn't had a holiday in three years. He said, without hesitation, 'Where do you want to go, babe? I'm up for a holiday.' That very day we booked to go to Paphos in Cyprus. We each paid for a friend to come with us, feeling that it was too soon to go alone, and set off the following day for a week in the sun.

Cyprus was lovely, although when we arrived at the hotel we found three paparazzi waiting for us – God only knows how they found out, as we hadn't told anyone we were going. They had checked into our hotel and then spent the week snapping us from their balconies. Scott and I discovered during that holiday that we had even more in common – neither of us wanted to spend the whole holiday on a sunlounger, so we did every fun thing we could: we hired out speedboats and jet skis, we went paragliding, wakeboarding and go-karting. We had a blast. The hotel was one of the best in Cyprus and we lapped up the luxury. When we couldn't be bothered to do anything, we floated round the swimming pool on a huge double lilo we had bought.

The sex was amazing, too. One evening at around six o'clock when all the sunbathers had gone in for the day, Scott and I were still lying on loungers by the pool. Realising we were alone, I started to play with him and put my hand up his trunks. Within five minutes we had made each other come. The sun was beginning to set and I'm sure a man from one of the balconies overlooking the pool got a great view of the whole performance. It was exhilarating to do it so openly and out in the fresh air, and the excitement of possibly being caught added to the thrill. Scott and I then went on a mission to find a new buzz sexually. We both got off on being dangerous, and loved the adrenaline buzz. Our best shag in Cyprus was when we hired a jet ski for about the fourth time that week with the sole intention of shagging on it. We rode it out towards a shipwreck and, a mile out from the beach, switched the engine off. Scott turned round so that his back was against the handlebars, and I straddled him. It was exciting and passionate. The sea salt covered our tanned bodies and the fact that we were once again having sex in broad daylight thrilled us both. We rode back to the shore grinning like idiots.

Once the holiday came to an end, we arrived home happy but feeling like it hadn't been enough. The following day, sitting in a pub, I said to Scott that I really wanted to go back to Barbados. I hadn't been there since the time with Garry, and he had ruined my perfect vision of the place. I had been scared to go there ever since. I thought that being back there would only mean bad memories and that it would bring back the terrible time I'd spent with Garry there, which I'd tried to forget. Scott, on the other hand, made me feel safe and happy. He persuaded me that it was time to face my demons and revisit the place I had loved all my life. He had never been there, so was very up for going. We went to a travel agent's, booked the soonest date we could get and boarded the plane a week later, just the two of us.

I am so glad that I conquered my fear of going back to Barbados. Scott managed to make me forget all about Garry, and we had a wonderful time. Even though we stayed at the same hotel as I had before, I got a thrill out of showing Scott round the island. We hired out a Mini Moke which we toured round in and put to very good use sexually – many a warm night was spent shagging over the bonnet down a dark lane. We got ever more outrageous in terms of where we had sex, even going so far as doing it on the back seat of the open-top Moke in broad daylight at the side of a field.

After everything I had gone through in the last year, Scott was exactly what I needed to perk me up. He made me feel young and happy and full of life. He reignited my passion for dangerous sex – and being 21 he had a constant boner. Joy.

On about our fourth night in Barbados, however, we had a huge row. One of Scott's mates was also in Barbados by coincidence and we had arranged to go out for dinner with him and his girlfriend. I felt ill with a stomach cramp and was lying on the bed. I fell asleep for a little while but told Scott beforehand that, if I felt better when I woke up, I would get ready and we would go. If not, he was going to go without me. When I woke up, however, Scott was dressed and ready and about to walk out the door. It resulted in a huge row. I now felt OK to go but didn't have enough time to get ready. Scott wasn't prepared to wait for me and walked out, leaving me sitting in the hotel room on my own. I wasn't upset, more furious that he could do that to me. He knew how difficult it was for me to see Barbados as a nice place since Garry. I sat stewing in the room for ages until Scott texted me and asked me to join them. They had finished the meal and were going to a nightclub. Not in the mood to go out now, but not wanting to sit alone any longer, I asked him to come and pick me up. The night turned out OK: we spent it in an exclusive members' club on the west coast, got drunk and danced all night.

The rest of the holiday went without a hitch, but something had changed after the night we had the row. I felt differently towards Scott, as I had seen a side of him I didn't like and I think it made him realise that he wasn't actually ready for another full-on relationship. We cuddled each other the whole way home on the plane and slept in each other's arms. When we got to Heathrow, my brother picked me up and Scott's mate came for him. We kissed passionately on the tarmac outside the exit, but I knew our relationship was over.

An hour later I was sitting in my bedroom, going through all the unopened mail and faxes I had been sent about work. I came across an invitation for that very night from *FHM*. It was their 100 Sexiest Women party, and as I was one of them they wanted me to go. I called a mate and asked if she was up for partying. She was at mine within an hour. I didn't have anything to wear as I had been in holiday mode and had forgotten all about the party, so I sat on the floor of my dressing room rooting through my clothes. I wanted to show off my tan and I wanted to stand out – I didn't want to go to the 100 Sexiest Women party and be a wallflower! My eyes scanned the room for something to wear and rested on my collection of belts hanging over a rail. I wish I had something as good as the army belts to wear, I thought. Then suddenly I saw them – my two diamond belts. One I had bought for myself, another had been a Christmas present. I normally wore them with jeans but now I saw them in a different light. Suddenly they looked like an outfit!

As I pulled them off the rail and tried them on, I knew I had to do it. The army belts had been good, but these were better. They were the new, updated, expensive version! I hurriedly flicked through my skirt collection and decided that none of them were good enough. If I was going to do it, I had to do it properly. I darted round the room in excitement, looking for something to wear on the bottom, and my eyes were again drawn to my belts. Suddenly I saw the perfect thing. It was a thick, black, studded belt. I had bought it in Brighton with Scott with the intention of wearing it as a skirt one day. It was only an inch shorter than the length of some of my skirts anyway. I tried the whole outfit on and giggled. It was completely outrageous, but looked good. I tottered over to my mum's house, wanting to get another opinion. I was slightly scared of my mum's reaction as I thought she might say it was too much (or rather too little), but she loved it. In fact, she squealed with delight. She said, although I was outrageous, she thought I looked beautiful and said that if she looked like me she'd wear it!

That sorted, I did my hair and make-up and the car picked me up an hour later. When I arrived at the party, the press went nuts. They couldn't believe that I had worn such a daring outfit and, more to the point, couldn't understand how I was managing to keep it on. The belt 'skirt' was held together by a single stud. The party was great. A selection of the world's sexiest women were there, and we drank pink champagne, ate strawberries and danced on the mirrored dance floor, which I absolutely loved!

After a while we felt it was time to move on and called our driver to take us to another club. At the second venue of the night, the belt on the bottom, which I had bragged wouldn't come off, suddenly burst open and fell to the floor. I was left standing in my diamond belts and a black thong. Embarrassing is not even the word! My mates fell about laughing as I bent down to retrieve the belt from the dance floor – all I can say is it's a bloody good job clubs don't allow photographers in! We partied at another four clubs that night and were so drunk by the time we got in the car that we made Vince take us through the 'drive-thru' McDonalds while we sat on the bonnet of the car and tried to order through a poster (thinking that it was the speaker box).

I made all the papers the next day, and the *Sun* really went for it. I decided that I didn't need a man. For once I was going to concentrate on my career: it was obvious I was still in demand, and I thought I had better make the most of it.

CHAPTER EIGHTEEN

Feeling Blue

A few weeks later, Becky and I were in Great Yarmouth for T4's Pop Beach party. As soon as we arrived, we joined up with Joe Swash and Ray Panthaki from EastEnders, and I spoke to lots of famous faces I hadn't seen in a while – Lemar, Big Brovaz, Emma Bunton and Girls Aloud to name a few. We were sitting on a bouncy castle, and after an hour or so Blue came up to say hello. Antony sat down with us. I had met him a few times out clubbing, but had always thought he was rather rude – a bit full of himself and arrogant. The last time I had seen him was at the FHM party. He had been lurking around; as I emerged to face him, I said, 'Hello, Blue boy, where's the rest of your fit band?' He stammered a reply and I joked that I would be up for an orgy with the four of them.

As he joined us now, he admitted that I had terrified him that night. I hadn't been serious (oh, OK, maybe a tiny bit), but he had thought I was a maneater. That combined with what I was wearing had left him lost for words. Today, however, was different. I was in simple pink combats and a pink vest. There wasn't anything remotely scary about me and, for the first time, Antony and I struck up a normal conversation. He ended up spending the day with us and paid me lots of attention.

I had always thought Antony was the best looking in Blue. All of them are lovely, but Duncan is a bit too clean-cut for me, Simon is too serious and Lee I had known since he was young as he had gone to stage school with my brother. I have always liked a man to look like a man – wonky nose or a hairy chest and pot belly don't bother me in the slightest, as I find these traits masculine. Give me a real man over a plastic-looking Peter Andre any day! All in all, therefore, I was quite flattered with the attention I was getting from Ant.

The next day he called me and asked if I wanted to go to Toast in Hampstead. It was a bar I regularly went to on a Monday night and he was going with his sister and a group of mates. I invited Becky, Michelle and a few others and we joined Ant at a table near the back. Ant was a complete gent and paid the entire bill at the end of the night. The following day he was on the phone again, wanting me to meet him at a bar in Loughton. I was doing a photo shoot but said that I would join him when I finished. We met up and got quite drunk; I decided I should eat something, so he walked me to the Chinese over the road and paid for my food. As we sat waiting for it to arrive, he leaned over and kissed me. It was a beautiful, if somewhat drunken, moment – he was a *very* good kisser. I had fancied him on sight and, having spent a few days with him, also realised that he was actually a really nice bloke.

What followed was the most intense whirlwind

relationship I have ever had. I practically moved into his house and we spent *every* day together for the next two months. We cuddled on the sofa, we watched films, we went shopping, we ate in restaurants and went drinking together. Ant was very loving and always needed reassurance and attention. He didn't like to be on his own so would need to see me as soon as he was back from a job. I was busy too, but we spent every spare minute together.

Ant was very willing to please, so much so that my friends nicknamed him Eager Beaver (EB for short). One night, after telling him that I loved him in a suit, I got dropped at his house after a PA in a nightclub. He had just done a gig with Blue and, when I walked into the darkened lounge, I was greeted by the sight of hundreds of candles, romantic music playing on the stereo and Ant wearing a black suit. He knew how much he turned me on in his suit and I just jumped on him. We slow danced round his lounge for a while before ripping each other's clothes off and making love on the sofa. His house was beautiful: it was done out almost identically to mine, which I liked, all in cream, with big leather sofas and stone floors. He had a huge TV like mine and we slobbed out as much as we could in front of it. I loved his efforts (although the candles and suit were slightly lost on me due to my drunkenness after the PA), and appreciated the lengths he had gone to.

On another occasion, I was performing 'Do You Think I'm Sexy' with the *FHM* girls on stage at G.A.Y. Antony was doing a concert with Blue the same night, and he apologised profusely that he wouldn't make it back in time to see my performance. He even went to the length of getting one of his backing dancers to call me to tell me that Ant was sorry he couldn't be there. Ten minutes before I went on stage, however, I was nervously practising the dance routine with Myleene Klass when the dressing-room door flew open and in walked Ant. He had made his driver go like the clappers and had planned to surprise me all along. I nearly cried with happiness. No bloke had ever gone to such lengths for me before – it was like the fairy-tale romance I had always hoped for. Nothing was too much trouble for Ant. He came to visit my grandmother in hospital with me, and even took me to a wildlife park, where he was terrified of all the animals. He knew that I was a big animal lover and organised it with the manager of Paradise Wildlife Park in Hertfordshire that we received VIP treatment all day. I was allowed to go into all the cages with the animals, and even hand-fed the lions! I was in my element. He knew how much it meant to me and he loved the fact that he had made me so happy. He wouldn't come in to any of the cages, though, and was particularly terrified of the birds of prey. I did manage to get him to hold one, and I still laugh when I look at the pictures. Ant is leaning as far away as he can from the bird on his arm, with a look of fear in his eyes. Bless him. I have always been the sort of idiot that will try to pet any animal, no matter how big or dangerous, but Ant wasn't having any of it. He didn't try to hide how scared he was and hopped about all day in a panic. I laughed all day and buzzed from the experience of getting to touch, hold and feed all the animals. Ant was the perfect boyfriend in that respect.

The only down side to having Ant as a boyfriend was that he was very insecure. For the duration of our relationship, he must have asked me *every* day what I saw in him. 'I've always fancied you,' I would repeatedly tell him. 'I think you're beautiful.'

'But you could have anyone you want,' he would reply.

I couldn't tell him enough that I didn't want anyone else,

and he never believed me when I told him how sexy he was. He kept saying that he had always been known as the fat ugly one in the band, and I told him continuously that he shouldn't listen to the nasty people who wrote such things. 'I get called names too,' I said, 'but that hasn't bothered you, has it? You made your own mind up, you didn't judge me by what someone who has never met me has said.' Still, I couldn't persuade him that I honestly did fancy him loads. I loved his round belly and flat nose – they were a part of him and I've never wanted a perfectly formed guy who pumps iron and eats healthily. So, Ant, if you're reading this, once and for all the world to see – you are gorgeous. You always will be. You have the looks and charisma of a young Al Pacino and in my eyes you are still one of the most fanciable men in Britain! Doesn't mean I like you though.

Although I knew it wasn't true love I was feeling for Ant, I thought that we definitely had something special. A week into our fast-paced relationship, Ant wanted 'The Chat' about the press. For the first week, we hadn't been anywhere that paparazzi tend to frequent, and the press knew nothing of us, but we knew that we wouldn't be able to keep it a secret forever. Ant said that perhaps we should just be honest and that he didn't mind if we were seen together. Something in my head told me that it was too soon to make it public and, while I didn't want a repeat of the sneaking-around-with-Max situation, I thought we should wait a little while. I had grown to realise that, in the world of showbiz, secret was better as then you didn't have to justify yourself to the world when a relationship didn't work out. Ant was very offended that I felt this way. He took it to mean that I was embarrassed to be seen with him and I spent a day trying to make him understand that I adored him but that I didn't want our relationship to be about getting press. I wanted it to be real, which to me meant doing things that normal couples do, not turning up to red-carpet events holding hands for the nation's press to gossip about. Also, I wanted to prove to Ant that I wasn't with him because he was in Blue.

The press often wrote nasty things about me that made me sound like a desperado who would do anything for fame. That isn't true. Just for the record, I don't go to two-thirds of the things I'm invited to. I only go out if I fancy it and the drink is free – why not? Yes, I enjoy being famous and all the perks that come with it but, in my own time, when I'm not working, my idea of a perfect day is to be curled up on the sofa with my dogs and a good film. I don't do the set-up pictures that 95 per cent of celebs do. (Yes, shock, horror, nearly all of those pics you see of celebs kissing in parks or out shopping aren't real! They're set up to look like they were papped and the celeb takes a cut of the money when they're sold.)

So now you know that, when I am papped, they really have hidden in bushes or followed me for the day against my consent or without my knowledge. I love being known and I wouldn't change it for the world but I firmly believe in keeping it real. My life hasn't changed in the slightest since I've been known. My friends are still the same friends I had from Brentwood and I've always been a die-hard clubber. Anyway, after a year and a half of having very well-documented relationships, I wanted one that was private and mine to enjoy for a while without having to answer questions on what my partner was like. I think Ant eventually understood where I was coming from, but he made it clear he wasn't happy about it. I began to feel dread: it reminded me of Dane from D-Side who got publicity for himself out of it. Still, I pushed those feelings to one side and carried on enjoying the attention.

While we were dating, Ant and I were invited separately to Jennifer Ellison's birthday party. We fancied a night out, so we decided to go. I wanted to wear something a bit special, but didn't have any new outfits that hadn't already been seen. I decided to make something, and took the scissors to a pair of designer jeans. Within five minutes I had cut the bum and crotch out and turned them into a pair of chaps. While I was doing this, Lauren popped over to pick up a signed picture to auction for charity. I pointed at the bum of the jeans lying on the floor. 'How about that instead?' I asked her. She loved the idea, so I signed them and told her to buy a paper the next day which, if I was photographed, would contain the picture showing where the cut-out bum had come from. She went away very happy.

At the party, I spent all night by Antony's side. Nobody knew we were together – we must have just looked like good mates. Bizarrely, Antony's ex-girlfriend was there, and halfway through the night she was in a row with him. I sat very uncomfortably as she screeched at him, wanting to know when he was going to buy her a house. She dragged me into the argument. 'What would you do, Jodie Marsh? I know who you are! What would you do in this situation?'

I tried to be diplomatic. 'As long as the father of my child saw the child regularly, then I would be happy and would go to any lengths to make sure that things were smoothed over enough for the child to have a good relationship with its father. But I don't think that a celebrity party is the time or the place to be having such a public argument – I've already spotted a journalist lurking close by trying to hear what we're talking about.'

'Oh, what would you fucking know?' she screamed back at me. 'You're just a dumb blonde who gets her tits out.'

Charming! Antony stuck up for me and told her to leave me out of it. Luckily Ray Panthaki was there too and he calmly tried to smooth the situation. She ended up turning on him, so Antony and I made a swift exit to our waiting car. We sped off to Elysium to chill out and, once there, Antony collapsed in my lap. He was so fed up with all the rows and couldn't believe that she had caused one in public. I cuddled him for an hour on the sofa and we left sleepily.

A few weeks later, it was Ant's birthday. He arranged a party for friends and family in a local bar and we got all dressed up for it. We still hadn't gone public about our relationship, but we still spent the night in close proximity to each other. All of his family knew, and aunts and uncles that I hadn't yet met were coming over to say with a wink, 'Hello, I believe you are Antony's special friend!' Ant proceeded to get completely drunk, and we moved on to a club when the bar closed. We had only been there for half an hour when Ant fell over in a drunken stupor and passed out on the floor. His friends decided it was time for him to go home and it was left to me to drive him. As I was in my two-seater TT, I couldn't take anyone else. It took two men to get him into the car and, once we were back at his, I realised I was going to have difficulty getting him out. I tried for ten minutes to wake him up, but to no avail. I realised I would have to carry him somehow, or drag him. It was that or leave him in the car all night. He was so out of it that I was worried about him. I kept having visions of him choking on his own vomit so I knew that I would have to get him out. Antony was like a dead body. I lifted each leg out one by one and turned his body to face me, and he immediately started to fall forwards. I crouched down underneath him to try to prop him back up, but it was no good – he was a dead weight and too heavy for my small frame. He carried on falling and I stayed underneath to cushion the fall on to his gravel driveway. We were then both lying on his gravel driveway. I tried to lift him but after five minutes realised that I wouldn't be able to.

I left him lying on the drive while I went to open his front door. Back at his limp body, I hooked my arms under his from behind and dragged him with every inch of strength my body could muster. Once inside, instead of just putting him on a sofa, I stupidly tried to get him upstairs into bed. I dragged him all the way up the stairs. To this day, I don't know where I got the strength from. People say that, in times of crisis, it's amazing what the human body can achieve and I've heard of people finding superhuman strength to lift cars off trapped children. All I can assume is that I found my inner power for that one night. Once in the bedroom I realised there was no way I was going to get him on a bed; instead, I stripped him off on the floor and laid a pillow under his head. I took the duvet off the bed and placed it over him. Then I sat down to catch my breath.

I spent the night on the floor with him. I slept with my head on his chest thinking that if he choked in the night, I would wake up. In the morning, he was feeling rough but laughed the whole thing off. I had taken pictures of him slumped on the floor to embarrass him, which he proudly showed to his mates later on. He thanked me for looking after him but found the whole story hilarious as I relayed to him how I had dragged him from the car. His mates all told him he had found a diamond and said that they would love a girl who would do that for them. He gave me lots of cuddles that day, and I saw the funny side too.

I wouldn't say that Antony had a drinking problem. It was more that, when he did drink, he just didn't know when to stop. If I started to feel tipsy or sick I would stop drinking immediately, but he never did. One time, we had been out to a club. When we got home and got into bed, we had a session and Ant immediately rushed to the toilet straight afterwards. I think all the bouncing had affected him and, as I lay waiting for him to return, I suddenly heard a loud retching noise and I lay there wondering what to do. We hadn't been together that long and I thought he might be too embarrassed to have me watch him being sick so I pretended I couldn't hear. After a few more minutes, a feeble 'Babe' came from the toilet and I jumped up to see to him. He was hugging the toilet and looked up at me with his puppy-dog eyes. It was all I could do not to laugh as I stood and rubbed his back.

He carried on being as loving as ever. He even arranged tickets for my mum and me to see a Barry Manilow concert that had sold out after an hour – sad, I know, but hey, you can't help what you like and I have been going to see Barry Manilow with my mum since I was five years old. My mum was so happy she cried and hugged him in thanks. It was quite funny because, for the first time since I'd had famous boyfriends, my mum actually knew who this one was. She doesn't watch any TV really and didn't have a clue who Kian or Max or Dane were. Calum she knew because she'd fancied his dad when she was young and thought he was gorgeous, but she had actually been a big fan of Blue. She knew more Blue songs than I did – and went a bit giggly the first time he came round. I found it amusing and cute.

Two months into our relationship, it was his sister Natalie's birthday. I had arranged a guest list and a VIP table for her and her friends at Funky Buddha, and we all set off in the car that night to cause carnage. It meant the press were going to get shots of us together, but by then we had palmed everybody off by saying that we were just good friends and that Antony was working on some songs with my brother – which he was. I got ready that night at Antony's and chose a cute see-through dress. I had his hairdresser put all my hair up for me, as Antony liked it that way. Once inside the club, we ordered lots of vodka and sat down to get drunk.

Lots of Nat's friends had turned up, and they included a load of pretty girls. I thought nothing of them until I noticed that Ant seemed to be enjoying the female attention a little too much. One person he flirted shamelessly with was Brooke Kinsella who used to play Kelly in *EastEnders*. None of the guests except Ant's family knew that we were a couple, so I couldn't do anything but stand and watch. There had been rumours in the press for a while about something having happened between Antony and Brooke, but he had assured me that they were all lies. Ant didn't even seem to notice as I sat with his dad and fumed as his flirting became more and more obvious. It was like he had forgotten I even existed and spent most of the night with Brooke. I knew I wasn't being paranoid, and I have never been a particularly jealous person, but a woman gets a sixth sense for things like that and I knew there was more to it than just a bit of banter. I really got the impression that Ant fancied her like mad. I didn't think it was her fault – after all, she didn't even know we were a couple – but I was so angry at Ant. Still, I couldn't say anything and I wasn't going to embarrass myself by causing a scene.

In the car on the way home, a very drunk Antony told me he loved me. I was in a mood about how the night had panned out, but he was too drunk to notice. He sent me about five texts (his dad was in the car) saying that he couldn't wait to make love when we got home; but once we were back at his house, he promptly passed out, leaving me to sit and watch television. In the morning, Ant was oblivious to the fact that I was annoyed. I didn't want an argument, so I didn't mention his obvious thing for Brooke. The seeds had been sown, however, and it played on my mind for the next few days.

Later that week, I was having a well-earned rest at home with the girls when Ant's best friend Tony called me in a state of panic. They had gone to a bar in Islington and Ant had got drunk to the point that he was now unconscious and lying on the pavement outside the bar. Tony wanted me to come and pick him up and take him home as he had work in the morning and couldn't afford a cab. It was midnight, I was in my pyjamas, Bec and Lauren were over and I really didn't want to do the 60-mile round trip to get him and take him home. After his birthday, I didn't think I would physically be able to lift him again, and I didn't want a repeat of him lying in the driveway. I mulled it over with the girls, who agreed that I shouldn't go; but in the end I felt guilty, got dressed and left.

When I arrived in Islington an hour later, Ant was being propped up against a wall by two men who managed to get him into the car and put a seat belt round him. His head hung down on to his chest and he didn't wake up. Having left the house in such a rush, I realised on arriving at the bar that my phone battery was dead, so Tony handed me Ant's phone. I drove back to Ant's in silence. I was still slightly hurt and confused by his behaviour the other night and I was starting to get fed up of Ant being drunk. By the time we reached his, I realised that, yet again, I was going to have to drag him out of the car. He wasn't waking up for love or money. I repeated the whole sorry performance of his birthday and spent half an hour dragging him to the door of his house. Luckily, once inside, he came to a little bit and managed to crawl up the stairs with me behind him holding his bum so that he didn't fall. Once on the bed, he passed out again and I struggled to undress him as he was lying face down. I managed to get some of his clothes off and turned him on to his side.

I went downstairs to get myself a glass of water when his phone rang. It was Tony. 'How is he, babe?' he asked.

'Fine,' I said. 'He's asleep.'

'Will you spend the night with him?'

'Of course,' I told him, and hung up.

As I sat in his lounge, it hit me that things weren't right between us. He spent most nights drunk; he had flirted outrageously with Brooke in front of me and, for the first time since we had been together, ignored me all night – it was blatantly obvious he fancied her; he was no longer capable of having night-time sex as he always passed out when he got home. And something else struck me as strange: that week he was going to Egypt for a few days to do a concert with Blue. He was due home on the Saturday. Normally when we spent any time apart, he would arrange with me well in advance that we would hook up the minute he got back. This time, though, he hadn't even mentioned seeing me when he got back.

With all these thoughts swirling in my head, trying to make sense of it all, I did the unthinkable.

As I picked up his phone, I knew I shouldn't be doing it. I felt sick at myself, and totally ashamed that I had resorted to this. I had had ups and downs in life, but I never thought I was neurotic enough to go through somebody's phone. I knew I was behaving ridiculously, but justified it to myself by saying that he would never have to know and that I had some kind of right – after all, it seemed pretty obvious to me that he had feelings for Brooke, and he wasn't bothered about seeing me when he got back from Egypt. I reasoned that I needed to know if I was wasting my time. As I went into his text message outbox, the first one I saw was one to 'Lucy Jo' – Lucy Jo Hudson from *Coronation Street* with whom he had been linked in the past: 'PLEASE STAY AT MINE SAT NITE BABE? I'LL B BACK FROM EGYPT IN THE AFTERNOON THEN WE'LL AVE A MAD ONE X X X.'

It was all I needed to see. Feeling sick with anger and disgusted at myself for going through his phone, I lit a cigarette and took a minute to decide what to do. I definitely wasn't going to stay there. He wasn't even aware of the fact that I had brought him home, and I thought it better if he woke to an empty house. Besides, in my eyes our relationship was over. I went to his kitchen, found a pen and paper then set about writing him a letter telling him it was over. The only problem was, I realised I would have to admit going through his phone if I was to give a reason. I thought about lying. I had a friend in *Corrie* so thought that I could say he had spilled the beans. In the end, my stupid old morals took over again and I thought it best to be honest. I wrote him a note that said I was truly sorry, thoroughly disgusted at myself and that I hoped he could forgive me, but I had gone through his phone. I then went on to say that I had seen enough to know that it was over. I apologised again, and finished by saying I hoped he would still want to be my friend. I went upstairs, placed it on his bathroom sink so I knew he would see it straight away, and went home.

I was woken at seven o'clock the next morning by my

phone ringing. It was Ant. He had seen the letter and wanted to explain that he and Lucy were just mates. I wasn't convinced. He spent a good half an hour trying to make me believe him, and seemed to have totally forgiven me for reading his text. Result! I thought. I had imagined that it was going to be me that had some serious apologising to do, but no: he was ashamed that yet again I had come to his rescue when he was drunk, and he still seemed to want to be with me. He reasoned that I had boy mates who stayed at my house, which was true, and that I had never so much as kissed them – also true. I began to come around. We finished the call saying that we were both going back to bed for a while and that we would speak later.

When he called again that afternoon, his tone had changed. He no longer felt so comfortable with the fact that I had looked at his phone, and wanted a row about it. I couldn't be bothered to argue, said sorry again and hung up. It's over, I thought. We obviously weren't going to resolve this easily and, on top of all of that, I knew what I had seen in Funky Buddha. My eyes hadn't deceived me as I watched him drool over Brooke and hang on her every word. I switched my phone off and spent the day in bed.

A week after splitting with Ant, his dad Mike called me and asked if I would come to the house. He wanted to put a business proposition to me and said that we both stood to make a lot of money. Knowing that Ant was away, I went. Once there he asked me what had happened with Ant, and I told him the full story from beginning to end. Red-faced, I admitted looking at his text message and said that it was over between us. What happened next shocked me beyond belief. Mike *begged* me not to give up on

Antony. He told me that the whole family had fallen for me and thought that I was the nicest and most intelligent girl Ant had ever gone out with. I shook my head. 'It's too late,' I told him.

'Please, Jodie,' he implored, 'please give him one more chance, please don't give up on him.' And he broke down in tears, which set me off.

As we sat and cried together in his lounge, I tried to explain that it wasn't about giving him a second chance. *He* had decided at the last minute that he couldn't cope with me looking at his text, and *he* wanted to end it. Mike wouldn't have it, and I ended up staying at the house for a painful three hours. I loved Ant's family as they were so similar to mine – tight-knit and supportive of each other – and they always made me feel very welcome. They had accepted me straight away as his girlfriend, and I felt honoured that Mike was going to so much trouble to sort the pair of us out. In my heart, though, I knew it was over, and there wasn't a lot I could really say to make it better. I explained to him that all my life I had fought for men. I had been cheated on, bullied and each time I had been the strength that had kept the relationship together. I didn't want to fight any longer; I wanted somebody to fight for me. I told him how sorry I was and that I would always be there for Ant if he needed me. I left in a blur of tears and confusion.

Another one had bitten the dust. I didn't have the energy or the willpower to fight for him. He had worn me out with his constant need for reassurance, and I was bored of picking him up off the floor drunk. I was sad that it had ended; but another part of me was fed up to the back teeth with men. Although I should have been off men by now, after Garry and Fran and some of the shits in between, I wasn't. I still craved sex and affection and love. Subconsciously, I made the decision that I was going to stay single until 'the one' came along. I didn't believe myself that I would – I had jumped from relationship to relationship over the years, scared of being alone. My biggest weaknesses in life were chocolate, fags and men. I didn't think I'd ever get by without them. Back to being single, I carried on working hard and hoping that round every corner I would find Mr Right.

CHAPTER NINETEEN
Charity Works

Back in the days of Click, I met Dane Bowers. I was so drunk that I considered snogging him – until, that is, my mates slapped me round the face and dragged me away by the hair. I bumped into him again at an Eminem concert. I had been completely mobbed by the fans outside and escorted backstage by the police. They were worried for my safety as the crowds were quite lairy and all wanted to touch me or get a picture. It only took one person to recognise me before about 50 were on top of me. My friends had freaked out and the police were alerted.

Once backstage, Dane and I had a nice chat. I was seeing Max at the time so wasn't interested in Dane romantically, but he seemed friendly enough. We then continued to bump into each other regularly and became friends. He would often be DJing at clubs I went to, so we would party together. We became so close that we would stay at each other's house and go to restaurants together. Even though

Dane never became my boyfriend, he certainly acted like it. From the moment we became friends, he would tell me that he didn't like what I wore. I used to tell him to shut up as it was none of his business and wondered why the hell he cared. Dane was always very opinionated and never held back from speaking his mind. He told me repeatedly that I looked better without any make-up and that he thought my outfits looked cheap.

My friendship with Dane was a funny one. We shared a love of nightclubs and PlayStation, but we didn't have much else in common. At times we got on really well; other times we were at each other's throat. He wound me up talking to me like he was a boyfriend, when in fact he was just a mate and I didn't think he warranted any say in what I wore or did. Still, many a night was spent together at his or my house, playing PlayStation and having deep discussions – or rows. Our arguments weren't proper arguments, more a clash of egos trying to outdo each other and gain the upper hand. They were always in jest and we grew to enjoy trying to aggravate each other. On the one hand I found Dane quite sweet and enjoyed his company, on the other I found him a stroppy little boy who had a lot of growing up to do. One day I texted him, but he didn't reply straight away. Wanting an answer, I sent another text an hour later and, knowing that it would wind him up, I added, 'PRICK' at the end of the text. It wasn't meant nastily, we often called each other names and I laughed as I wrote it. A minute later, my phone beeped and it was a reply from him. It simply said, 'I'M WITH MY SON, YOU ARSEHOLE.' I hit the floor laughing. For a girl to be called an arsehole was more insulting than anything – it was worse than being called a cunt! I mean, there are a lot of stronger words you could use but 'arsehole' in the context he'd sent it seemed so harsh. He sent the text with such venom and anger that I knew that I was supposed to be offended, but I found it so hysterically funny that my cheeks hurt laughing. That was Dane all over. He was moody, childish, quick to bite and a treat to wind up. I showed all my mates the text, who also thought it without a doubt the funniest text they'd ever seen. We spent the next few months saying 'You arsehole!' to one another. I'd like to extend my thanks to Dane for providing me with endless laughter over that.

One night at his house, we had a huge row. We had been playing on his PlayStation and chatting and, as usual, things had got heated. Dane went off on one of his normal rants about my image and told me that he didn't think anybody respected me. I begged to differ and explained that my outfits served a purpose. They had got me where I was today and made me a lot of money. Dane wouldn't have it and asked me if I would consider covering up more. I told him that I would, but not just yet. I enjoyed myself, I liked the way I looked and I didn't feel the need to change that. Dane then spent half an hour trying to convince me to cover up in public, and even told me that it would help my career and get me more work. I argued that my skimpy outfits were partly to do with how well I'd done and that I didn't think I'd get more work by covering up. The *Sun* and other papers loved my flesh-baring outfits. He wouldn't listen to a word I had to say, and was so confident in his opinion that he offered to manage me. If I let him tell me what to wear and how to act for one month, he would change the public's perception of me. 'Don't be so ridiculous,' I told him. 'Wearing proper clothes might make a few more women like me, but it's not going to do wonders for my career.' I was famous for things like the belts and quite happy with how my career had soared.

Two days later was the *DodgeBall* premiere. Knowing that Dane was going, and wanting to prove a point, I decided to go in the skimpiest outfit I could possibly find. I wanted to make a real entrance and I wanted to piss him off in the process. Getting ready on the night, I chose just a bra and knickers. It was the most daring and ridiculous outfit I had ever worn, but I jazzed it up with accessories to make it look special. When I arrived, the paparazzi went ballistic. Every time I tried to leave the red carpet, they screamed at me to stay. On walking into the bar, I waited smugly to see Dane's reaction. His face, when he finally walked in, was a picture. His jaw hit the floor and he turned away in disbelief. He didn't speak to me until the after-show party. For added fun, the organisers had arranged for all the celebrities to change into trainers and play matches of dodgeball. On my first match, I was lined up to play against the boy-band team, which Dane happened to be in. As we stood head to head before the game, Dane simply said, 'I hate to admit it, but you look fucking fit.' Sweet. He hated me dressing skimpily, we had argued for hours two nights before about it, yet still he was forced to admit that I looked good. I loved it.

Much later that night, the party-animal celebrities – myself, Calum, Ricardo and Dane – headed off to Wellington and then Chinawhite. Dane made a beeline for me. He started off being quite nice, but the conversation quickly turned to my outfit. He said that, although I looked good and carried it off, he still thought I looked cheap and that people didn't respect me. 'Outfits like that make you look like a slut,' he told me. 'I know you're not, but other people don't.' He insulted me over and over again, making supposedly valid points for which I had an answer every time. He wouldn't let me get a word in edgeways and, too tired to argue any more, I resigned myself to hearing him out. After an hour's heated conversation, I called him a prick and went home. I would have the last laugh, I told myself, when the pictures hit the papers.

I didn't just have the last laugh – I had a full-on comedy show! The *Sun* called the next day and said they wanted to do a photo shoot with a difference. They wanted to dress me up in the frumpiest clothes they could find and photograph me in very little make-up. I agreed as I was up for a laugh, and the following day on the front page they printed a huge picture of me in the bra and knickers (£17 for the set from Topshop) at the *DodgeBall* premiere with the headline: MORE SHOCKING JODIE PICTURES INSIDE! Sure enough, inside they ran a full-page picture of me looking like a geeky 40-year-old, surrounded by little pictures of more of my famous outfits, including the belts. The geek picture was shocking all right: I was dressed head to toe in tweed with thick cream tights and brown flat shoes. On the day of the photo shoot, I got a friend to take a picture of me on my camera phone. I sent it to Dane with the words, 'I'VE TAKEN YOUR ADVICE AND DECIDED TO COVER UP. I THINK I LOOK REALLY GOOD AND EVERYONE ELSE AGREES. IT'S DEFINITELY GOING TO TURN MY WHOLE CAREER AROUND. I'VE BEEN TOLD I MIGHT EVEN MAKE IT AS A PROPER MODEL NOW! THANK YOU AGAIN DARLING.' I made the front page of the *Sun* because of my nutty dress sense, something which I told Dane was a large part of being Jodie Marsh. Not only that but I had done it wearing a bra that cost £12 and a pair of knickers that cost a fiver. Unlucky, the celebs that paid thousands for their designer dresses that night!

I've never heard from him since!

Needless to say, I'm not ready to hang up the belts just yet. In fact, I probably won't be ready to do that for a long time.

Every night I go out is like going to a fancy-dress party for me. I don't take myself that seriously, and I don't think I look particularly amazing, I just enjoy playing at dressing up. My outfits aren't always worn to please myself – sometimes I do it to piss people off! I enjoy being the centre of attention and I'm very much in touch with my sexual side. I suppose a lot of it stems from the bullying. Often I feel more confident in a silly outfit as it's down to me that people look – they're not looking at me dressed normally and laughing. That would hurt beyond belief. If I make people look at me then I can handle their remarks. The bottom line is that the way I dress is a part of me. It's fun. Nobody can say I'm not creative, and I like to look different. It might not do me any favours when it comes to finding a nice boyfriend or making people respect me but, at the end of the day, the people that matter know who I really am.

Dane could go to hell for all I cared. He wasn't my boyfriend, he had no control over me and I wanted an easy life. I wasn't too sad at the loss of his friendship – I had enough friends who *didn't* give me grief – and I was still hoping to find Mr Right. Boyfriends had come and gone, but I hadn't given up hope that I would meet someone again soon.

I was single for months after I split with Ant. It wasn't that I didn't want a guy, I just didn't find anyone that met my standards. It seemed that people only wanted me for a shag or as a trophy girlfriend because I'm famous. So, instead of jumping into a relationship with the first half-decent bloke who came along, I kept all men at arm's length and only made friends with them. Something that the God-fearing Shane Lynch said to me during *The Games* has stuck with me, and it became more meaningful after I split with Ant:

sometimes people enter our lives and we are too quick to place them in the wrong category. In other words, we might meet a bloke who we fancy, and jump straight into bed with them, when really they weren't placed in our lives to become a lover, they were placed in front of us to guide or help us or just to become a friend.

Although I was desperate for a shag (the rampant rabbit is totally worn out), I was very laid back when it comes to men. I didn't even go on a date in months. I realised that only I can make myself happy, and I don't need a bloke for anything in my life. I make my own money and I have the best friends and family a girl could wish for. I would rather have my dog Paddy by my side than another fame-seeking wannabe or sponging, drug-taking cheat. I spent months doing things that make myself and other people happy, not running around after a man.

A few months back, Linsey Dawn invited me to a charity do thrown by Linda Robson, the star of *Birds of a Feather*, in aid of Fight for Life. Once there, I got chatting to Linda and told her that I would do anything I could do to help the charity. Linda was really sweet and told me that she would be in touch. A little while later, I happened to bump into Yvonne, one of the women who runs Fight for Life. She had heard that I was willing to help and asked me if I was serious. I told her I was and, three days later, I was on my way with my brother to a hospital in London. Linda, Yvonne, another lady called Nikki, my brother and myself were going to spend the day giving out toys to terminally ill children.

I knew it was going to be difficult, but nothing prepared me for the sight that greeted me as I walked into the first ward. A tiny little boy, who could have been no more than eight, stood smiling at us. He was attached to a drip and had no hair. He was frail and gaunt. His skin was so thin it looked transparent, and his eyes were sunken and yellow. My brother turned away in tears and had to leave the ward to compose himself. I wanted to be strong and do what I went there to do. I knew that, if I went anywhere near my brother crying, it would trigger my own tears, which were welling up behind my eyelids, so I stayed away. The girls from Fight for Life had told me before we went in that we couldn't get emotional – the kids didn't need to see us upset. When my brother broke down, I had to turn away, fight back my own tears and carry on into the ward. Someone else went to see to Jordan while Linda and I got on with giving out the presents.

I can put my hand on my heart and say that it was the hardest day of my life. I have never felt so humbled and emotional. The children were adorable – so happy and playful. Everything I had ever done in my life suddenly seemed so insignificant. Things I had previously seen as a problem now seemed pathetic. Most of the little children, although delighted with the toys, didn't know who Linda or I were. I felt that we were doing a great thing but I really wanted to do more. 'Are there teenagers here?' I asked. I was told there were, so I asked if I could see them. Although we didn't have any toys left (not that they would have wanted them), I thought that, if they recognised me, it might cheer them up. Walking into the teenage boys' ward was the best part of the day for me. I was right in thinking that it would cheer them up. Boys who were weak and depressed sat upright in their beds and even stood up to have their pictures taken with me. They all grinned from ear to ear as I signed photographs for them. I chatted to them individually, spending five or ten minutes with each one. My heart felt like it was going to burst with the sadness of their suffering and not knowing how long they had left to live, but also with happiness that I had made their day. Now, I'm not telling you all this for you to think, What a lovely girl Jodie is, far from it. It was the hardest and most life-changing of days. It made me think that no matter what goes wrong, there are always people going through worse and, no matter how many nasty people in this world, there are always people like Nikki and Yvonne who work tirelessly to bring happiness to others. To bring a sparkle into somebody's life or to grant somebody their last dying wish is something I think only a very few special people can do. Most of us run through life at a fast pace, worrying about our jobs and trivial things like whether we should eat that last biscuit. I felt like I had been in the presence of real-life angels that day, and I promised to do as much as I could to help in the future. One of the nurses, who worked directly with Fight for Life by telling them what they needed to raise money for, took us on a tour of the hospital. She showed us all the equipment bought with the money the charity had raised, including a sensory room, and my eyes were opened to something new. My priorities would be different from now on.

I'm not going to give up doing what I do – I need to stay in the public eye to be able to continue to help on a larger scale – but what I witnessed that day somehow made all the times the papers and magazines had called me a slag seem all right. As Mae West once said, I don't care what they call me, as long as they call me. From now on, they can call me a slag all day long if it means staying famous enough to make a difference.

I took my motorbike test in the summer, after getting the buzz of riding bikes again from Scott and bought myself a powerful Yamaha R6. Its top speed is 180mph and it does 0–60 in three seconds. I get more of a buzz from riding that than from anything else I've ever done (with the exception of a bungee jump). Surprising what a throbbing piece of equipment between the legs can do to a girl!

The guy that took me through my lessons and tests, Paul, became a very close friend. Throughout the weeks of lessons, I told Paul my life story. Talking to him was like therapy and helped me with psyching myself up to writing this book. We had bundles of laughs as I dropped his bike (the one I learned on) twenty times a day. I'm only five foot two and had difficult holding it up at traffic lights. The bike became known as Jodie's bike and every day I broke a brake or clutch lever off as it smashed to the floor. Everyone around me, with the exception of Paul, my dad and Jordan, didn't want me to ride a bike. They thought it was too dangerous and that I would end up killing myself. I wouldn't listen and, even after crashing and rolling down the road on my first day of lessons, I didn't give up. I wanted to do it for myself. I'd always been an adrenaline junkie and this seemed like the ultimate buzz.

One thing is for sure – I'm never taking another exam for the rest of my life. Put me on live TV or naked in front of a room full of people and I'll be fine but, at 25 years old, sitting the theory test and then doing the practical was so stressful. I was a bundle of nerves and anyone that thinks doing a U-turn on a 500cc Suzuki with nearly bald tyres is easy can piss off.

The funniest moment came for me one day when I was following Paul to Lakeside. We hit a huge roundabout and Paul got through, but I got caught at it in the traffic. Coming to a stop, I didn't put my foot down quick enough and the bike fell on top of me. After freeing my leg from underneath and standing up, I looked ahead for Paul. No sign. By now, cars had come to a stop all around me and blokes had jumped out to see if I was all right. Two men had picked the broken bike up and one guy asked if I was alone. I told him I wasn't, but still there was no sign of Paul.

Amused, I stood for five minutes with the men, not wanting to take my helmet off for fear of them recognising me. Eventually Paul headed back to the roundabout. He had gone on ahead to the car park, feeling confident enough that I would follow without a problem. I swear the guys must have been thinking I was that girl off the Zovirax advert, that underneath I was some hideous-looking beast. When I finally lifted my visor to thank them, I was on the back of Paul's bike and driving off in the direction of B&Q to buy a new brake lever. We rode off to screams of 'It's Jodie Marsh!' I cringed in embarrassment but gave them a cheeky grin and they saluted me.

Passing my test was a day of joy for me. Afterwards, a load of us went to the pub and got pissed and I ended up in a club, still in my motorbike leathers. I now own a set of pink leathers and a pink helmet. It had to be done. I'm also the only female road-tester for *Motorcycle News* and Ducatti have given me a free bike.

Another thing that came out of learning to ride happened on the night after one of my long chats with Paul, when Lauren and I sat down to write a list of all the people we'd slept with. We came up with a formula for how to achieve the perfect match in a man based on previous lovers. We're going to write a book on it one day and help women everywhere. It's going to be called *The School Teacher and the Sexpert*. More than ever, since discovering this formula, I haven't wanted a relationship, let alone a one-night stand, unless it's with the one I'm going to marry. I feel good about that fact. I'm in control and calling the shots in my life.

A few months ago, I was approached by the charity Beat Bullying. They wanted me to attend the launch of their website to get them some publicity. I said I would be honoured, but I knew that the papers wouldn't be interested in a picture of me or any other celebrity turning up to a bullying event. I had jumped off a 1,000-foot aerial slide a few months before for the Royal National Institute for the Blind, and they hadn't even printed a sniff of it. Knowing that they are only ever interested in scandal and never in the good work I do, I dressed up in an army camouflage bikini and smeared army cam cream over my body. They still weren't interested and, although I raised a good deal of money on the day, the charity could have done with the exposure. I wasn't prepared to let that happen for Beat Bullying. I had always wanted to be famous for two main reasons – so that I could show my bullies from school that I was worth something and so that I could help other children and teenagers who were victims of bullying. I have read so many stories in the newspapers about children who had killed themselves because of bullying. It broke my heart, but I knew I stood more of a chance than others of making a difference. I knew what these people were feeling – I had been there myself.

A while back I had given a load of interviews about my own bullying ordeal to various different magazines. ChildLine got in touch, Esther Rantzen herself called a meeting with me and I was delighted by the fact that I was finally going to be able to help. I sat and explained everything I had been through, and told the panel of directors, including Esther, that I really wanted to get involved. I said that it was all well and good celebrities turning up to events in aid of charities and being photographed, but that I *really* wanted to make a difference. I said that my dream would be to do a tour of schools and actually go in and talk to the kids. I thought that the kids would sit up and take notice if I went in – I know that, if a celebrity had walked in to my school years ago, I would have paid attention. Esther loved it. She told me she was overwhelmed by my compassion and thought I would be a perfect ambassador for ChildLine. She gave me a tour of the offices and showed me the call centre where they took calls from bullied children. Esther liked all my ideas and couldn't believe how much I was willing to do. I went home the happiest I had ever been. Finally, I was going to be doing something worthwhile.

A few days later, however, ChildLine called. They were very sorry, but they didn't think I had the right image for the charity. Around that time, the papers and magazines had been exceptionally nasty, labelling me a slag and calling me cheap. Not a day went by when someone didn't call me trashy or a slapper – and all just because I wore skimpy outfits. Well, sorry, all you evil, bitter journalists out there that have caned me without even knowing me, but the last time I checked, wearing skimpy outfits doesn't make you a slag. Anyway, as a result, ChildLine weren't able to let me become an ambassador and they didn't want to organise the tour of schools. I felt like someone had ripped my heart out and smashed it in two. I had worked so hard for all those years trying to get somewhere. I wasn't a bad person. I wasn't nasty to anyone. I just wanted to put my fame to good use – which is more than I can say about a lot of celebrities I meet – and here it was being thrown back in my face. I hope you're proud of yourselves, I thought about all those pitiful critics who had nothing better to do with their lives than be nasty about me for no reason.

It took me a long while to get over the rejection from ChildLine. I didn't think it was Esther – she had adored me – I think it was one of the stuffy old women on the board. She obviously thought that as a 60-year-old she would have more influence on the kids. Even so, I was gutted and felt like I'd been kicked in the stomach.

Beat Bullying, however, didn't have the same attitude. Once I explained that I wanted to do as much as I could, they scheduled a meeting. I went to meet the girls who ran the charity and repeated everything I had told Esther. They sat and listened for half an hour and, when I had finished and amid tears from all of us, they jumped up and hugged me. They said that they would be extremely proud to have me on board and I told them my idea of how we were going to get press. Instead of me turning up to the event in normal clothes, I thought we needed to do something big. I hit on the idea (and I told them not to put me in a straitjacket before I shared it) of me being made up to look like I had been beaten up. No make-up, just cuts and bruises on my face. I had never been seen without make-up before, let alone looking like I had been beaten. The girls loved it. They said it would be powerful, hard-hitting and surely couldn't fail to make people stand up and take notice.

We booked a top film special-effects guy for a week later, and I went to the offices of Frank PR who were donating their services to the campaign. The make-up was amazing: by the time I was done, nobody could look at me – I actually looked like a victim of a serious beating. We went outside to do the pictures, which we did through the Press Association. It meant that nobody would have to pay for them and that they would give them away for free. Hopefully, it would make people want them even more. Everyone wants something for nothing, right? The pictures were released the next day, when the website launched and it fucking worked! It was huge. Most papers, including the *Sun*, the *Star* and even *The Times* ran the pictures. The press went nuts on the day and film crews turned up to capture it all. We made *London Tonight* that evening, and *GMTV* wanted me on the following morning. I can't tell you how happy we all were. Our efforts had paid off and, as a team, we had succeeded in getting coverage on not one, but two primetime slots on ITV. Beat Bullying were elated and I was on cloud nine. We cried tears of happiness after the press conference and celebrated with tea and biscuits. Funny, only three magazines out of about fifteen printed the beaten pictures the following week, even though they didn't have to pay for them. Just shows you what a caring bunch the people are that run these things. You try and do some good and nobody wants to know! Forget the kids that have killed themselves, print another set-up picture of celebs; after all, I'm sure they need the money more than the kids need help! Forgive me for sounding bitter but, really, we wonder why there's so much violence and destruction in the world today.

The outcome was that we organised a tour of schools and I am officially an ambassador for Beat Bullying. The website – www.bbclic.com – is the best website I've ever seen. It's like a computer game and you have to pick a character to be when you log on. Try it – you can be me if you like!

I then went into hospital having somehow caught chickenpox (at 25 I was laid up in bed looking like a two-year-old with camomile lotion on all the spots), which lasted for three weeks, before it turned into shingles in my ear. I was rushed to hospital and put on a drip (which, having a needle phobia, didn't go down too well) and morphine. The infection made my inner ear swell, which in turn, pressed on the nerve that controls the facial muscles. For a scary week, the whole of the right-hand side of my face was paralysed! I can honestly say that it would have hurt less if they'd just cut my ear off. Before I fully recovered the doctor let me out, as I needed to finish my book.

I have to say a big thanks to my mum, dad and brother and all my friends for bringing me chocolates and flowers and films to watch while I was housebound. I know you were all scared of catching it too, so massive thanks for caring enough to risk it. The doctors and nurses at Harold Wood hospital were amazing too and put me in a private room with a sign above the door saying Sarah. They refused to admit to anybody that I was there, so that the press wouldn't turn up and even told my dad that 'Jodie Marsh' wasn't at the hospital one day when he called to find out if I was OK. Gems!

Linsey Dawn became pregnant by her lovely boyfriend, the footballer Mark Williams, and they asked me to be godmother to their child. I accepted straight away and told them it was a huge honour.

I was on *Frank Skinner* and *Ready Steady Cook!*. *RSC* arranged for Antony to come on with me. A few weeks before I went into hospital, however, I bumped into Antony in a club near me. He ignored me all night and I thought, Charming, until, after the drink had got the better of him, he approached me for a row. I had been ill and so had not turned up to a charity event his dad had organised the previous week and he laid into me for not showing up. Initially, I was going to help with the event but pulled out when Antony and I split, not feeling too comfortable about working with his dad. Anyway, he started saying horrible things and I argued back that he was the horrid one. After everything I had done for him, he wanted a row because I had been too ill to go out for a piss-up. Things got heated and ended in the doormen having to pull us apart. His mates were rowing with my mates; it was like a scene from a Western film.

After things had calmed down, his lot continued to shout 'Slag' at me from across the club. That is, until Lauren marched over, slammed her hands down on the table, looked straight at the instigator and said, 'Look me in the eye and tell me you really believe she's a slag!' He couldn't. He hung his head in shame and left the club two minutes later.

That done, I decided that I really couldn't go on *Ready Steady Cook* with Antony and pretend everything was OK. I phoned up to pull out and they told me that they would pull Ant instead of me. I asked Isabella to do it with me and she said yes. (I had tried to stay friends with Ant but the boy with the smallest knob I'd ever seen made it impossible… Oops, did I just say that?)

I did a lot of soul-searching last summer with school-teacher Lauren and Paul the motorbike instructor and I have realised that men are not an essential part to me being happy. If I can go months without sex then I think I'm doing all right. I signed a contract with *Zoo* magazine to continue to be their 'sexpert' for another six months. Oh, by the way, I did actually write the column myself and boy was it frustrating! Plus I have to be the only sexpert in the world who isn't actually having sex.

The charity work is fulfilling me more than anything I've ever done. I haven't given up hope that one day I will meet the man of my dreams. My list of requirements is getting longer though, so I might be waiting a long time. He's got to be fit and strong, able to shag at least three times a day, be a vegetarian, love animals, ride a motorbike, have his own dreams and ambitions, make his own money, think that Paul Weller is a music legend, get on with my family, make time for my friends, know what it's like to lose a best friend, want to come and visit terminally ill children with me, let me dress how I want to dress, understand my job, defend me to anyone that slags me off, put up with my forty-a-day habit, want four children, love clubbing but not drink every night of the week, want to live in the countryside, share the bed with five dogs if need be, not be jealous or patronising or try to control me, not take drugs, not be fame-seeking or pretentious, want to come to my brother's gigs with me, love watching DVDs, be prepared to watch *Dirty Dancing* at least once a year, enjoy going to concerts, cuddle me when I'm down and kiss me when I cry, make me laugh, be proud of me, understand that a foot massage is an important part of a relationship and love me more than he's ever loved anyone before in his life. Just in case you were wondering! Failing all that, I might just turn lesbo. As long as she doesn't have a big hairy bush, I think I might just cope.

I have had huge highs in my life so far and massive lows. I have overcome intensely cruel bullying, I have got a man off drugs and made him turn back to them. I have worked my arse off to get where I am now and I have lost a best friend to murder. I don't look perfect and I haven't had any surgery, in secret or otherwise, other than to correct my broken nose. I'm a good, honest, decent person. I could have been a lawyer but I chose to do something else. Something that, although there are times I wonder if I made the right choice, I get a great buzz from doing, make great money from, get to meet amazing people and am in a position to help others not so fortunate. I don't want praise or sympathy for the bad things I have been through. I just want to be able to continue in an amazing job (perhaps with a little less criticism, thank you, Carole Malone, 3am, Garry Bushell and the rest of you, you know who you are) so that I may continue to help others and live a nice life.

I have been sad and happy, I have felt true love and immense pain. I am not the person I have been portrayed to be for the last two years and soon I'll do something to shock the lot of you. I'll prove that I do have talent and something to offer. I have played dumb for the entire duration of my career and let the insults go over my head (most of the time). I always keep it real and I don't bullshit. On top of everything, I'm still here and I'm still going strong. And I'm proud of that.

It was midnight on a cold November Wednesday night; the house was quiet apart from my tapping on the computer. I was drained emotionally from having written this whole book myself, alone, from start to finish. I have cried writing it, stressed myself out in thinking it isn't good enough and laughed until my cheeks hurt. I have done my best and I hope it's good enough. I hope that I'm an inspiration to somebody somewhere that's either been bullied or is being bullied or that's gone through the pain of a death.

I hope you enjoy my tale as much as I enjoy living it. I realise how lucky I am to have such an amazing group of friends who have stuck by me and been there throughout the years and a family that leave me lost for words with the support and love they have shown. Paddy is still the absolute light and soul of my life and, as I sat there with him by my side snoring gently, I had a feeling that life, no matter what it throws at me, was going to be just great.

It takes no talent, no brains and no character to criticise. Only God can create a flower but any foolish child can pull it to pieces. When people are hostile or rude, when they say cruel or unkind things, it is invariably a reflection of their own troubled spirit rather than a reflection of you.

CHAPTER TWENTY

Kenzie, My Little Chimp

There I was, happily single. I hadn't had a bloke in ages and wanted it to stay that way. I had decided to wait until I found 'Mr Right'. Then I happened to turn on the TV while a cheeky little chap called Kenzie was in the middle of a laughing fit on Celebrity Big Brother. I don't usually watch those kinds of shows, but from the minute I saw Kenzie's face I was hooked.

I was filming a TV show of my own at the time, *Jodie Marsh Live and Turned On*, for Television X. I was on the road with a film crew and my make-up artist Sadie. We travelled the country looking for the weirdest of the weird. People with fetishes, swingers, foot slaves, vampires, grown men who pretend to be schoolgirls and a group into Pony Play, where they dress up as and act like horses, even living in stables full of hay.

We had a great time, even if we were slightly freaked out more than once. In between filming, I would watch *Celebrity Big Brother* whenever I could. The more I watched the more I realised that I was falling for Kenzie.

His happy and innocent nature captured my heart. I loved how much he laughed and how unaffected he was. I know it sounds stupid, but I felt like I already knew him – loved him, even. I knew that if we ever met we'd hit it off big time.

I remember sitting in my parents' living room one night watching the show. I told my dad that I fancied Kenzie and that I was 'going to be with him' very soon. He laughed and pointed out that I didn't even know Kenzie, and that it was just a TV show. I wouldn't listen. 'Mark my words – I *will* be with him!' I said. All my friends knew I had a big crush on him, too. Most of them fancied Jeremy Edwards, but not me. Kenzie was the man for me. I knew that if I met him he would be my next serious love.

As luck would have it, I found out that the guy who books my nightclub PAs was also Kenzie's manager. Touch! I called him and told him clearly that I fancied Kenzie and that I wanted to ask him on a date as soon as he came out of the house. Ridiculous as it sounds, I had fallen for Kenzie, hook, line and sinker. He was the burst of energy and fun I needed in my life and I wasn't going to rest until I met him. His manager wasn't sure if I was being serious, but I convinced him that I was.

After Kenzie came out of the *Big Brother* house, I called his tour manager a few times, hassling him to give me an answer on the offer of a date. He kept telling me Kenzie was busy. I felt that I was being fobbed off and tried to think of ways to meet him or get a message to him. I didn't need to worry for long. Exactly one week after Kenzie came out, I was sitting at my usual table in a nightclub in Essex when a young boy that I recognised from Kenzie's band, Blazin' Squad, walked up to me with a smirk on his face and said, 'Kenzie's over there!'

'Well, what are you doing standing here then?' I said. 'Go and get him!'

As Kenzie made his way over, I had just enough time to excitedly fill in my mates on what was happening. Kenzie smiled confidently and asked what I wanted to drink. He sat down, and within minutes he had his arm around me and we were grinning at each other like idiots. My friends were great, hanging back and giving us some space; his friends, on the other hand, got a bit excited and kept coming over. Kenzie was embarrassed by their antics and kept apologising. They weren't doing anything wrong; they were just drunk and excited that Kenzie was being chatted up by Jodie Marsh, I suppose. As we talked, I found out that earlier in the night I had walked straight past Kenzie in the club and not even turned around when he called my name. I hadn't seen him. It also turned out that Kenzie's tour manager had put my offer of a date to him in such a way that it hadn't sounded serious. His mates had spent the week winding him up about it, digging out lads mag pictures of me to show him. Once we'd cleared this up, Kenzie and I got to chatting, getting to know each other and having a little cuddle.

One of his friends got into a fight at the end of the night. It got a bit messy and the police were called. Kenzie wanted to see what was happening, but I stopped him. I explained that some photographer would snap him and he'd end up all over the papers for being involved in a nightclub brawl. Kenzie agreed and I sorted it out with the club manager – a friend of mine – that we could stay behind until it was all over. When the coast was clear, a group of us went outside. My friend Lauren was driving that night, and Kenzie, being a gentleman, walked me to her car. When we got there, his mates asked me what I was doing for the rest of the night.

'Taking Kenzie home with me,' I replied and guided him into the back seat.

'I'm being kidnapped,' he joked, as Lauren drove off, leaving his mates open-mouthed on the street.

Back at mine, Kenzie and I stayed up all night chatting. We had a little kiss, but nothing more. I knew I had been right about my feelings for him, but I didn't want us to jump straight into bed. I wanted him to get to know me properly.

I was filming the next morning, in the Isle of Dogs, and Kenzie decided to come with me. When I turned up for work with him in tow, the girls in the studio giggled and winked at me. Kenz and I stayed in my dressing room for a couple of hours, until his tour manager came to pick him up. He left, telling me that he would call soon. An hour later, he did. He asked if he could come back for the afternoon and I happily said yes. He lay on the sofa in my dressing room and I spent all my rehearsal breaks with him. He did have to go eventually, as he was working that evening, but we arranged to get together the following night in the club where we'd met. With that, we had another cheeky kiss and we left each other, grinning from ear to ear.

The next day, we texted each other back and forth a few times and the plan for the evening was still to go clubbing. I was working on the new Johnny Vegas show that day and wouldn't be finished until nine o'clock. I had arranged to meet everybody at my house at about ten o'clock and we were going to go straight to the club from there.

The Johnny Vegas show was good fun. Huey from Fun Lovin' Criminals was also a guest on the show. I had met him with his girlfriend in a club years ago, not that he remembered me. He asked to be introduced and I gave him a cheeky smile, saying, 'We've met before,' while shaking his hand, then I turned to walk away, leaving him to think about it. The whole way through the show, all I could think about was Kenzie. I was so happy and couldn't stop smiling.

When the show finished, I got changed in about 30 seconds and literally ran to my car. I checked my phone and saw I had a text from the manager of the club we had planned to go to. It said that I couldn't bring Kenzie to the club: it was over-21s that night and Kenzie was only 19. I immediately called him and begged him to let Kenz come with me, but he wouldn't budge. I had to come up with some silly excuse to give to Kenzie and thought that I'd be able to persuade him to come over to my place instead. We were planning to meet there anyway and a night in with a group of my friends would be just as much fun.

Just as I was about to call Kenzie, I got a text from him. It simply said, 'I ain't coming out now.' It was really blunt: no kisses, no 'hi babe'. Nothing. My first thought was that he'd heard about the club and had the hump. I called him to see if he was OK and he was really off with me. He sounded totally different: grumpy and distant.

I kept asking him what was wrong and eventually he blurted out, 'Well, people have told me not to trust you and that you're just using me for publicity.'

To say I was horrified doesn't even come close to how I felt. My heart sank and tears welled up in my eyes. I felt sick and wanted to hang up. If it had been any other bloke, I would have. It was different with Kenzie. In the one night and one day I'd spent with him, and in all the time I'd been addicted to watching him, I'd fallen for him. My head was screaming at me to hang up and never again talk to this guy who was acting like a judgemental, no-brained twat, but my heart was telling me to talk to him, to explain that he had it wrong and to make him understand the hate that's out there, not just for me but for everyone in the public eye.

After all, Kenzie was only 19 and had only just become famous. He probably had managers and advisers around him, telling him what to do. I'd been a household name for a lot longer – and no one tells me what to do. I certainly wasn't about to let someone change the lovely, sweet Kenzie into just another stuck-up arsehole of a celebrity. I knew the words coming out of his mouth weren't his and I knew that he didn't mean them. Over the next 45 emotional minutes, I managed to reason with Kenzie that whoever had put these evil thoughts into his head was totally wrong.

If there was anyone who didn't need publicity, it was me! I go to maybe one out of every 20 things I'm invited to. I don't do set-up pictures and I don't have a publicist making up stories about me and feeding them to the press. I'd even said to Kenzie the previous day that we should keep our relationship secret for a while, to get some quality time together before it became a media frenzy – as it eventually would, no doubt. By the end of the conversation, Kenzie felt really bad. He couldn't believe that he had listened to other people and not waited to make up his own mind. He apologised over and over again and I told him not to worry. I was still shocked and hurt but, above all, I knew I didn't want to lose him.

I told Kenzie the truth about the club and he agreed to come over to mine. My friends Jonny, Emma and Lauren were there. Kenzie didn't really speak for the whole evening and I didn't try to make conversation with him, either. My eyes were sore from crying and I was trying to pretend to my mates that everything was OK. It wasn't an easy night for Kenzie. He felt bad about having made me cry, and about being so stupid as to let others sway his opinion. But at least he got to come over and see me relaxing and having fun with some of my best mates. It was just a normal evening at home: we watched some music DVDs, had a little sing and dance, got into some deep chats and made each other laugh. With every burst of laughter and every meaningful conversation, I could see Kenzie sinking lower into the sofa. I could see that he knew how wrong he'd been to believe the lies he'd been told and that he felt like an arsehole for upsetting me the way he did.

Eventually, everyone left at around four o'clock in the morning and I was left alone with Kenzie. After I'd seen the last of my mates to the door, I came back into the living room and Kenzie was standing up and waiting for me. He grabbed me, pulled me in tight for a cuddle and told me that he would never judge anyone again. He apologised for about the thirtieth time and begged me to forgive him and forget that it had ever happened. I smiled gently and told him that I would. I was still smarting a bit, but I knew that I would get over it. After all, I've had much worse in life!

Kenzie stayed that night, but we did nothing but kiss. From then on, we spent every single day together – but I made him wait until Valentine's Day to have his wicked way with me. And, when we did do the deed, it was great. Kenz had been in Blazin' Squad since he was 15, so he had always had his fair share of female attention. He certainly knew what he was doing and wasn't scared to show it. We were quite adventurous together.

One time, I was driving him home after a long weekend at mine. We knew we weren't going to see each other for a while, so, on the way, we found a remote spot behind some garages on an estate and pulled over to have sex. We were in my TT, which is quite small. I straddled him and rode him until he came. It was broad daylight so we hurriedly pulled our clothes back on afterwards and I dropped him back to his parents' house. I left him with a big smile on his face.

Kenz and I were extremely happy together. We laughed all the time and my friends said they had never seen me so smiley! We shared the same sense of humour and positive outlook on life. Even when things were bad, we found a way to laugh about it. The only problem was other people warning him off me – some of whom had never even met me! Then, we had a bigger issue: Kenzie's mum. From the minute I met her, I got the feeling she didn't really like me. Then again, if I'd have been Kenzie's mum, I probably wouldn't have liked me either! I was seven years older than him; I was famous for getting my kit off and for being a sex columnist; I'd had loads of boyfriends and I'm clever. Kenzie's mum still saw him as her angelic little boy who couldn't put a foot wrong. She probably thought that he shouldn't even have had a serious girlfriend, let alone one who was a glamour model that famously scored her ex-boyfriends out of ten on a T-shirt!

Kenzie's mum was never rude to me; she was just off. She was quite cold towards me and used to get annoyed with Kenzie when she felt he was spending too much time with me. She even used to send him texts with messages like: 'When am I going to see you?' or 'Can you come home now please?' I fully understood that she missed him, but I couldn't help it that Kenz and I wanted to spend all our free time together. We were both busy with work and did everything we could to be together in between. Kenz knew his own mind, anyway, and could have gone home whenever he wanted. The truth was that we felt lost without each other. Kenzie's dad was always lovely to me and I liked him instantly; it was just a shame about his mum. Despite everything – or maybe because of it – I desperately wanted her to like me.

I remember once taking Kenzie to a hospital with one of my charities, Fight For Life, where I was visiting the kids to bring them presents and cheer them up. The night before we went, we took a trip to the local Tesco, where I spent £500 on toys to give out the next day. As expected, the kids were delighted to meet Kenzie and loved having their pictures taken with both of us. Kenzie had never done any charity work or seen anything like it. It made him realise that you could do good things with your fame. The following night, we went to see his mum and told her all about it. She didn't seem impressed. From then on, I knew I was going to have a big struggle on my hands.

Kenz and I continued to be blissfully happy. We had the odd moment – who doesn't? – but on the whole things were great. He was always there for me when I needed him. One day, we were getting ready to go for lunch when I got a phone call from a close friend of mine. She told me the devastating news that her mum had just died. I immediately burst into tears and Kenz heard me and rushed in from the bathroom. He jumped on to the bed and put his arms around me. I spent two hours on the phone to her, sobbing and talking, and the whole time Kenzie sat with his arms around me. He didn't ask what was going on, he didn't move. He just sat and listened to me cry with my friend for two whole hours with his arms around me. He proved to me that day how much he cared.

One weekend, Kenzie had a PA in a nightclub quite far away. I went with him and we stopped at a service station on the way back to get some food. While we were waiting in the busy Burger King for our food, a voice that seemed to come from behind the counter shouted, 'Blazin' Squad are shit.' The whole restaurant heard.

Kenzie bristled, but I told him to ignore it. I'm used to the hatred and jealousy, and I know it's not worth retaliating. All these losers want is a reaction and if you bite you only give them what they want. A few minutes later, the voice from the back came louder again: 'Blazin' Squad are shit!'

I could tell that Kenzie wanted to have it out with the guy, but, again, I calmed him down. By now, everyone in the queue was looking at us and whispering. It was quite embarrassing but I thought our food would be ready soon and we could leave quietly without a fuss. Not so. A few seconds later, it came again: 'Blazin' Squad are shit and you're a wanker.'

Kenzie had had enough. He asked the guy serving us to find out who was shouting the abuse. The voice seemed to come from behind the counter but we couldn't see who it was. The guy serving us seemed not to know what Kenz was talking about, so Kenz very calmly said, 'If you don't go and get him, I'll come round there and get him myself.'

At this, our guy and all the guys in the kitchen started ranting back and forth at each other.

In the meantime, I whispered in Kenzie's ear, 'Babe, you had a Number One hit record at 15 years old and this guy is a loser. Let's just get our food and go. Don't let him wind you up, he's just jealous.' I was just trying to make him see sense and calm him down.

'You're right,' Kenzie said and shouted back at the guy not to worry about the idiot at the back and to just give us our food. He gave it to us and we left.

When we got back in the car and told Kenzie's tour

manager what had happened, he was furious. He said that if he'd been there he would have given the guy a smack.

We didn't think any more about it after that – until we got a call the next morning from a friend who told us, 'Have a look at the *Sun* newspaper.'

The headline read LOWER THAN POND LIFE and the story said it was me and Kenzie who were lower than pond life and that we had gone into Burger King and started a fight! It said that we thought we were something special and had been throwing our weight around. There was something about us kicking off when they got our food order wrong, and that we shouted at the serving staff that we were 'famous' and that they were 'nothing'. It was quite possibly the worst press I had ever seen about myself or anybody else. It made us both look like nasty, horrible twats who went around starting fights and thinking we were better than everybody else. All we had done was stop at a restaurant to get food during a six-hour drive, where my boyfriend, who had been abused repeatedly, asked to see the guy who was causing all the trouble. We left calmly and civilly, without an argument, and were dignified and adult about the whole thing. But not according to the *Sun* – none of whose journalists had actually been there.

The editor of the *Sun* and its showbiz writer appear to have a problem with me anyway, for no reason, but it was still a surprise. I texted the paper's showbiz writer, Victoria Newton, giving her a full picture of what had happened and asking her what she would have done in the same situation. She never had the balls to reply. Boy, did I take great delight when the shameful story broke about the *Sun*'s editor Rebekah Wade apparently whacking her husband, *EastEnders* star Ross Kemp, in a domestic.

Two days after the Burger King bust-up, Kenzie was

booked to appear on the TV show *Ministry of Mayhem*. We made plans to stay in a hotel near the TV studios the night before, and we made our way over to Kenzie's house from where we were going to be picked up. As we arrived at Kenzie's, I saw that his tour manager was standing in the street outside his house. He didn't look happy. He quietly asked to have a word with Kenzie on his own. I stayed in the car. Five minutes later, Kenzie was back in the car with me, his eyes red from crying. He had been told that his manager had stipulated that I was not allowed to accompany Kenzie on any more jobs, and that I definitely wasn't welcome at the hotel that night. They told Kenzie that the bad press in the paper that day was entirely my fault and that I was dragging him down to a disgraceful level.

Within minutes, I was in tears as well and Kenzie was threatening to pull out of his TV appearance if I couldn't go with him. I didn't want him to pull out, but I also thought that no one had the right to tell him who he could have as a girlfriend or whether he could take them on jobs with him or not. What difference did it make if I went to the hotel? But Kenzie's tour manager wouldn't let me come with them; it was more than his job was worth, he said.

Kenzie just kept crying to me, 'Why can't people leave us alone?' and 'It's my fucking life!'

While this was happening, Kenzie's mum came out to see what was going on. She saw both of us in tears and asked to speak to Kenzie alone. He followed her back inside the house, while I stood and chatted to Kenzie's tour manager. I argued that it wasn't fair for people to tell Kenz what to do. 'He's an adult,' I told him. 'It's nobody's business but mine and his.' His tour manager agreed and told me he felt sorry for us. The most outrageous part of the whole thing was that neither of us had done anything wrong. If anything, I had calmed the situation.

A few minutes later, Kenzie and his mum emerged. Kenzie went to speak to his tour manager and I was left alone with his mum. She asked me why I was crying. Finally, I thought, she's going to be a friend to me and understand. How wrong I was! When I told her how upset Kenzie and I were at people interfering in our relationship, she told me what she thought: I was a bad influence on Kenzie, she said, and all the negative press he had received lately was entirely due to him being with me. Shocked, I tried to explain that I had been the one trying to calm Kenzie down in the restaurant, but she wasn't having any of it. She looked at me with disgust in her eyes and I desperately tried to stop the tears from flowing as I attempted to make her see sense. It was no use. When she said to me that Kenzie wasn't interested in the press, that he was an 'artist' with a 'talent', that he only wanted to make good music and wasn't in it for the money, I had to laugh. 'No,' I said, 'he's the same as the rest of us – he's trying to make a good living, doing something he enjoys.'

She hit back: 'No, he's nothing like you – he's got talent and he's got a career. He doesn't do anything for money; he does it because he loves what he does and you are getting in the way of that.'

I was surprised. How little you know your own son, I thought. It was easier for her to see me as the source of all evil, rather than admit to herself that her son could ever do any wrong.

She wasn't prepared to listen to anything I had to say. She merely used the opportunity to tell me all the things she had probably wanted to say from day one: that I was a bad influence, that because of me Kenzie was getting bad press, that I was too old for him and that I was standing in the way of his career as an artist. She finished by asking me to stop making a scene on her street, as people were starting to look out of their windows and that she had to live here, unlike me. It was all bullshit. No one was looking out of their windows and I was hardly causing a scene. Yes, I was upset and I was crying, but through it all I hadn't shouted or even raised my voice.

How could I not be emotional? Kenz and I were head-over-heels in love by then and we hated being apart. As for the bad press – we hadn't done anything illegal, and there is a saying that all publicity is good publicity, no matter how bad it initially looks. Ultimately, there were no real grounds for Kenzie's mum and manager trying to split us up.

After our chat – or, should I say, controlled argument – Kenzie's mum stormed off, leaving me in floods of tears. Kenzie came back out and told me that he and his tour manager had come up with a plan: if I drove myself to the hotel and kept a low profile, no one would get in trouble. We set off in a convoy a few minutes later, with Kenzie in my car.

When we got to the hotel and checked in, Kenzie and I wanted to go straight to bed. We were both still upset and had the puffiest red eyes ever from so much crying. But Kenzie's tour manager insisted that we get something to eat and drink. He could see that we needed to calm down. He was a lovely guy and was totally on our side. He'd spent quite a lot of time with us and told us both that he could see how much in love we were. He said that he would do anything he could from now on to make sure that Kenz and I could be together – even if it meant sneaking us around in secret, God love him.

Earlier that day, when I packed my overnight bag, I had slipped in my Polaroid camera as a treat for Kenz. I thought we could take a load of dirty pictures in our hotel room as something a little different and naughty. With all the trauma that we'd just been through, I thought a little dirty-picture-taking now seemed an even better idea – a great end to a terrible day! Once we got to our room, I put on some of the sexy underwear I had brought with me and handed the camera to Kenz. He snapped away, getting more and more turned on as I posed for him on the bed. Then I changed into a black PVC bondage outfit that Kenz had bought for me. He told me that he had been embarrassed going into the sex shop, but had loved all the stuff in there. He was very excited at the prospect of seeing me in the outfit.

It was very naughty; held together by metal links, it was crotchless and had holes for your nipples to poke through. I loved it. It looked amazing, so Kenz took loads of snaps of me writhing around on the bed in it. Eventually, he couldn't contain himself any more and jumped on me. Before I let him go for it, though, I pushed him off and made him pose on the bed for me. I wanted some pictures of him for myself, so I took a load of him stark naked, holding his hard piece and looking sexily into the camera. When I finished, I let him take me from behind – and took some more pictures while we were at it. I've still got all the snaps. You don't think I would be silly enough to let a bloke hang on to those, do you? No, I have them for safe-keeping and I can't force myself to throw them out!!!

Let's just say, we had an amazing night of naughty and emotional sex. It had been a long day and we fell asleep in each other's arms.

As I said, Kenz and I had decided to keep our relationship

under wraps for as long as possible. I knew from past experience that the longer you remain away from public scrutiny, the easier and nicer it is. But this was all ruined for us one night by someone I thought I could trust. A friend of mine ran a nightclub that I used to go to a lot. It was a place where I was looked after and given special treatment. I took Kenzie there for a night out and we had a whale of a time. My mate Terry from the band E17 was with us and we danced for hours in the VIP room. Kenz loved it.

The next morning, I had to do a shop opening in Essex so I left Kenz in bed and promised to be home soon.

A queue of people had already formed at the shop and the lady at the front came rushing up to me and said, 'Congratulations on going out with Kenzie!' I asked her what she meant, pretending not to know what she was talking about. 'You're in the *Sun* today,' she replied.

A friend who was with me rushed out to buy a paper – which showed a load of pictures of Kenzie and me snogging in the VIP room. I was totally shocked. As soon as the shop opening was over, I called my mate at the club to find out what had happened. He told me that someone had taken the photos when he wasn't looking and had sold them to the *Sun*. My mate was as angry as I was and promised to make it up to me. I went home and got back in bed with Kenzie, showing him the paper as I slipped in beside him. It wasn't the end of the world, but we knew we'd now be in the firing line for other people's bitterness and jealousy.

Kenz and I had such an amazing time together. A few weeks into our relationship, I had all my teeth filed away to little stumps and veneers put on them, Hollywood-style. The TV show *Cosmetic Surgery Live* offered to pay for the work as long as I let them film it. I agreed without hesitation: it cost 20 grand and I wanted it done anyway. Poor Kenz had to spend the next six weeks lying awake at night with me beside him, screaming in pain! He was great, though, and looked after me the whole time. I had been told it wouldn't hurt but I was in agony. I'm not sure if I was just a big wimp but, either way, it was Kenzie who spent half the night feeding me painkillers and cuddling me better.

A few months into our relationship, I was refusing to go to his parents' house following the argument with his mum. This meant that Kenzie was now spending most of his time with me, but was also going home on his own every so often to see his mum. Around this time, Kenz and I decided to go on holiday together. When his manager got wind of this, he was on the phone and emailing us straight away with loads of offers from magazines to pay for our trip if we would let them have exclusive pictures of us. Neither Kenz nor I wanted to do this. We just wanted a normal holiday away together, like normal people. The last thing we wanted to do was go on holiday and work. Believe it or not, we actually wanted to book and pay for our own holiday!

As soon as Kenzie's manager found out, he hit the roof and got straight on the phone to Kenzie's mum. It seemed to me that they had teamed up against me and were doing everything they could to split us up. Kenzie's mum called him and asked him what he thought he was doing 'ripping his manager off like that'. Unbelievable. One minute, they were criticising me for using Kenzie to get publicity and money, and now I was being told off for deliberately turning it down! It was just another in the long line of problems that kept cropping up between me and Kenzie's mum and manager.

Just before we went away together, I asked Kenzie to sort

out a meeting between me and his manager. I wanted to get to the bottom of why – according to his rules – I wasn't allowed anywhere near Kenzie, yet at the same time his management team was still trying to make money out of our relationship. I thought it was time to clear the air. Something else was bothering me, too, and I wanted to talk to him about it. Basically, I had been set up on a hidden-camera TV show, a kind of British version of *Punk'd*. Two guys playing undercover policemen arrested me, saying that my car had been used in an armed robbery. The prank was very funny and I kicked off at them. It turned out my brother was behind it all.

When they came to make a second series, they told me I could set someone up to get my own back. Kenzie was the obvious choice, but out of respect I called his manager to give him the low-down. He hated the idea and told me that under no circumstances must I go ahead with it. He said that it wouldn't be a good thing for Kenzie to do and that he would only end up looking silly. I was gutted. I knew the producers weren't out to make anyone look silly and that it was just a bit of fun. I tried to talk him around, but he was having none of it. I called the producer back and told him that I wouldn't be able to do it. To make matters worse, Kenzie's manager then told Kenzie I was planning to set him up and he was gutted. Kenzie said he would have loved it (as I knew he would).

As if that wasn't bad enough, a few weeks later I was in London on a job, and Kenzie's driver, who was meant to pick me up, didn't show. I was left standing on the street for an hour. Kenz wasn't answering his phone and I didn't have a clue what was going on. Eventually, after an hour-and-a-half, Kenz called me laughing and said that he had just been set up on a TV show. His manager had arranged it behind my back with the producers. He obviously had a change of heart about the prank and had realised it wouldn't be such a bad thing to do.

With this and everything else, matters had reached boiling point and I was ready to explode. I really wanted to meet with Kenzie's manager to sort things out, and I went to his office to see what we could do. I was open and honest from the moment we got there. I asked Kenzie's manager what his problem was with me and what difference it made if Kenzie took me to the occasional job so that we could spend time together. I also asked what right he thought he had in telling Kenzie who he could and couldn't take to work with him.

As he answered, he couldn't look me in the eye at times. I felt he knew I was right in everything I was saying and in the end we agreed to stay out of each other's way – not that I had ever been in his way, but agreeing to it at least got him off Kenzie's back. We'd effectively called a truce. Not that I had any sort of vendetta, but I didn't like the man and probably never will. I'd done nothing wrong, but played along at the make-up game and things got a little better after that for both of us.

Finally, our holiday came along and we were in Barbados before we knew it. The first two days of the holiday were spent proofreading my autobiography. It was couriered to my hotel the morning of the first day and I had to check it thoroughly to make sure it was exactly as I had written it. I was worried mistakes might have been made in the typesetting, so I read it through twice and spent ages on the phone giving picture captions to the publishers. After the book was finally put to bed, we got on with enjoying our holiday. We had an amazing time! Although I was badly sunburned from the two days I'd spent reading the book outside with no sun cream on, we made the most of every single day. We went swimming with turtles, went on a party boat and got very drunk, and then went jet-skiing. I also taught Kenz to drive in the Mini Moke we had hired. Within a couple of days, Kenz was driving us around the whole island.

Once home, we both carried on working hard. I had my book tour looming and Kenz was busy in the studio. He was getting really excited at the thought of a new single coming out and would often talk to me about it. Because of my history with his mum and manager, I just couldn't get excited for him. I felt awful and didn't want to be negative but I couldn't help it. When he was jumping around all over the place about his new song, I would just do a fake smile and turn away. I desperately wanted to be happy for him but I just couldn't. By then, I'd really been through the mill with his mum, bandmates and his manager. Kenzie was finding it tough, too. He was dividing his time between me and his mum and also finding it increasingly hard to cope with everyone being nasty about me. I knew it wouldn't be long before I would have to make a decision one way or the other.

Even so, Kenzie joined me at the start of my book tour and we had a real laugh. He would come to signings with me and try to blag free books from the shops (which he often got). We had a blast and did photo shoots and TV shows together. All of our spare time was spent at home or with our friends in local pubs and clubs. I introduced Kenz to the joys of darts (yes, I know, I'm a geek but I don't care) and we often went on pub crawls around Brentwood together: one such crawl ended with me giving Kenzie a blow-job in a pub toilet and being so sick afterwards that he had to hold my hair!

I had a big TV show lined up for that summer. I'd already signed contracts and was looking forward to doing it. The show was called *Trust Me I'm a Holiday Rep*. There were to be six celebs on it: three boys, three girls. While having meetings with the producers, I suggested that they consider having Kenz on the show. The producers agreed and when I told Kenz he was delighted. We thought it would finally be the happy ending we needed. We could show everyone publicly how happy we were – and have a great time doing it. The only problem was Kenzie's manager. If we put the show through him, he would take 20 per cent of Kenzie's fee. In my eyes, he didn't deserve it as he hadn't done anything to get him the show in the first place. Kenzie tried to pluck up the courage to tell his manager that he was doing the show – and that he had arranged it off his own back – but each time he went to do it he chickened out. He knew that all hell would break loose and that his manager would immediately demand his 20 per cent. As the deadline loomed for me to fly to Cyprus to film the show, I realised that Kenzie didn't have the guts to tell him. Not only that, I realised that for as long as we were together Kenzie was always going to be torn between me – the girl he loved and wanted desperately to be with – and the other most important people in his life, his mum and manager, neither of whom wanted him to be with me.

I loved Kenzie so much that I made the decision to end it. You know when you hear people say that, if you love someone, you have to let them go? Well, I truly know what that means now. I couldn't carry on any longer. I was miserable, I couldn't share in any of Kenzie's happiness when something good happened in his work, and my presence in his life was creating rifts between him and his friends and family. It was breaking my heart to watch him running around desperately trying to please everyone. All he wanted was for everyone to be happy but it was never going to happen – not while I was his girlfriend anyway. The night I ended it with Kenzie, he was at mine. I sat him down on the bed and told him the full truth. I explained how much pain I was in over my decision and that I didn't feel I had any choice. He fully understood – after all, he'd been through it all as well, living a double life for the past six months – but all the same he begged me not to end it. Both of us cried our eyes out for hours and hours. We talked and talked, until there was nothing left to say. Eventually, one of his friends came to pick him up. He left in floods of tears and I cried myself to sleep. Two days later, I flew to Cyprus.

Even though I had ended it, I felt like I was the one who had been dumped. I hadn't wanted to end it and my heart was broken. Kenz and I agreed not to have any contact while I was in Cyprus. He, too, was well and truly heartbroken and we thought it would be better if we tried to move on with our own lives for a while. I knew that we would always remain friends and I needed some space to get my head straight. I still didn't know if I had done the right thing. Kenzie was by far the best boyfriend I ever had. My family and friends all loved him and he loved them. He is quite possibly the only boyfriend I've had who really knew me at all.

CHAPTER TWENTY-ONE

Trust Me, I'm Scott Wrong... Sorry, Wright

When I arrived at the airport, I met the other celebs who were going to be joining me as holiday reps. They were: Jordan Knight from New Kids on the Block, Scott Wright from *Coronation Street*, Syd Little from Little and Large, Nina Myskow, the journalist and broadcaster, and Jasmine Lennard from *Make Me A Supermodel*. From the outset, I knew I was going to have a lot of fun and I knew that I was going to get on like a house on fire with the others. There was a really nice vibe straight away. Jasmine had bought my book to read on the plane and Scott put all the girls' luggage in the overhead compartments. Before we even left England, Jordan had told Jasmine and I that we were beautiful and Syd had made us all laugh with his jokes. Nina was warm and friendly. I was very excited.

We got to Cyprus and arrived at our multimillion-pound villa to discover that we only had five bedrooms between six of us, so Jasmine and I agreed to share a double bed.

Everyone was happy and relaxed. We all took to our new jobs extremely well – apart from Jasmine, who went home after a few days. We were left to our own devices on the evenings that we didn't have an airport run or bar crawl to organise. We became like a little family. Syd and Nina were nicknamed Mum and Dad by the younger members of the crew and we all made an effort to enjoy every minute of our time there. In fact, I'd never had such a good time at work. I bonded with everyone so much that we all cuddled every day. We looked out for one another; we all opened up about our lives and listened to each other's stories and problems.

I messed around for the first few days just because I could, but after getting in trouble for it a couple of times I took the job more seriously. I wanted to prove to everyone that I could be trusted with a position of authority and that I was capable of doing the job properly. I nicknamed our boss from the holiday company 'The Dragon' because she took an instant dislike to me and gave me a hard time. She made me cover up all nine of my tattoos with bandages – so that I looked like I'd been in a car crash – and screamed at me if I so much as forgot to wear the blue hair scrunchie we'd been given. Nevertheless, I had a ball. The sun, nice people and hard work were just what I needed. Even when they brought in an old enemy of mine to replace Jasmine, I wasn't bothered. Nadia – from *Big Brother* and sex-change fame – joined us halfway through the show.

By then, the rest of us were living like a little family and I wasn't about to be fake-nice to someone I had never met but who had called me a 'dog', 'minging' and 'ugly', among other things, in the press. When Nadia arrived, she tried to shake my hand. Before I took it, I asked her if she actually wrote the columns in which she had said all those horrible things about me. When she said that she had, I told her, 'Well, fuck off away from me then.' I wasn't about to shake her hand without an apology. A huge row ensued and Nadia ended up in tears. But I refused to budge unless she said sorry. I told her, 'Of all people, Nadia, you should understand how awful it is to read such nasty things about yourself, so you shouldn't be writing them about people you've never met!'

She refused to see it from my point of view and even tried to joke that I should be happy that I was being talked about in a national magazine. Syd, Nina, Jordan and Scott all took my side, in private and on camera. Jordan said he 'loved' me and totally understood my point and was backing me all the way. Syd said he loved me 'like a daughter', and he too said he wouldn't speak to Nadia if it came to it. Nina didn't like all the arguing but she was on my side as well.

Nadia and I did make up after things calmed down, but I never did get an apology from her. Still, there was no point in holding a grudge or in continuing to make it miserable or difficult for everyone else. Even so, I didn't want to share my newly single bedroom with her. It had been a nightmare sharing with Jasmine. She'd had no respect for anybody being asleep and thought nothing of banging around and making noise in the middle of the night. Scott joked to me that he would give Nadia his room if he could come and share with me. The idea didn't sound that bad. What with the sun, sea and romance of Cyprus, I quite fancied Scott, and I knew and liked him a lot more than I did Nadia. I told he could come in with me if he wanted – and a few hours later he had moved all his stuff in.

That night, Scott and I weren't tired. We lay on the

balcony, watching the stars and talking. It got cold late at night so Scott went to get a blanket to wrap us in. I was starting to have feelings for him – or at least what I thought were feelings. Looking back, I think what I was experiencing were purely rebound feelings. I was still missing Kenzie and hurting, too. Scott had backed me up when I needed it against Nadia. He had been a gentleman the whole time we were there, he had made me laugh and now he was wrapping me up in a blanket under the stars. That night we ended up kissing and from then on our relationship progressed very quickly. I was keen to forget about Kenzie and I got carried away with the holiday romance of it all.

Within a day, we were a couple. Everyone was really happy for us and encouraged it. But once we got together we were outrageous. One night, we had sex on the balcony while the production crew filmed the others below us. They had no idea what we were up to just a few feet away. I was on his lap stark naked with my legs spread and my feet on the balcony railings for balance. If anybody had looked up, they would have got a real shock! We spent the rest of our time in Cyprus having sex anywhere we could – all over the villa and the patio and swimming-pool area.

I revelled in being as naughty as I could on camera but without them actually seeing anything. One day, I pulled Scott all round the swimming pool by his cock while the crew interviewed him on camera. He squeaked his way through the interview! Another time, one morning, the film crew burst into our bedroom while we were in mid-session. Luckily, we had the sheet over us. Scott was spooning me, so we managed to appear normal for the interview but we did the whole thing while he was still inside me. I couldn't get enough.

I'd never had a proper holiday romance before and I loved it. I hadn't forgotten about Kenzie but Scott had definitely taken my mind off him.

The only problem I had with Scott was that he partied too much – even for me. I thought everything would be different when we got home. I even called my mum and Kyle to say that I had met someone and that I would be bringing him home with me. I asked my mum to make sure I had clean sheets on my bed! She laughed and said, 'I suppose he's "The One", isn't he?' I told her that he might just be and she laughed again and said, 'Yeah, until the next one!'

I did take Scott home with me. He changed his ticket so that he got the same flight as me, instead of one to Manchester where he lived. He ended up staying for a week and I introduced him to all the family. Kenzie phoned me the minute I got back and demanded to know if it was true that I was seeing someone. The papers had got hold of it while we were out there. I couldn't admit to him that it was true. I skirted around the issue and said that I would talk to him soon. It broke my heart all over again to hear his voice and I knew that it would kill him to know I had met someone else so quickly.

In my defence, I was hurting so badly myself after Kenzie that I was on a self-destruct mission – and Scott was my first mistake. When we got home, it didn't take me long to realise that Scott had brought his partying lifestyle back with him. I hated it. I asked him to stop, but he didn't see that there was a problem. It was normal for him. It all came to a head when I was filming a show called *The Big Call* for ITV. Julie Goodyear from *Coronation Street* was also on the show and Scott came to watch the recording. We planned to go out clubbing afterwards and, as I'd hit it off with

Julie, I asked her to come, too. We met up at the Wellington, where we got quite merry, before deciding to move on to Kensington Roof Gardens. There were about eight of us out that night. Kyle, Jonny and Emma were with me, amongst others.

When we arrived at Kensington Roof Gardens, there were paparazzi outside and quite a big queue of people. We walked straight to the front and, as we were about to go in, a guy in the queue shouted, 'Jodie, are you still with Kenzie?'

I was about to answer 'No', when Scott shouted nastily in front of everyone, 'No, I'm fucking her now.'

I could have slapped his face. Instead, I kept my cool and walked inside, only to totally ignore him when we got in there. He went off to the bar with one of his mates and by the time he came back to me he wanted an argument. He started shouting that I didn't care about him and that all my friends were bastards. He called me a c*nt and some other nasty things, before storming out of the club. Julie witnessed the whole thing and told me I deserved better. She had taken a real shine to me and was totally disgusted by Scott's behaviour. I didn't chase him; I was happy for him to go. He had really overstepped the mark and I knew I didn't want to be with him any longer.

Shortly after that, I left with Kyle to go home. On the way, Scott started calling me. I had no interest in talking to him so I didn't pick up the phone. He must have phoned more than 20 times, and because I wouldn't answer he left a few nasty messages, again calling all my friends bastards and generally giving me a load of abuse.

When I got back to mine, he was still calling and eventually I picked up. I wanted to go to sleep but knew he wouldn't leave off. Also, his car was still at mine, so I knew

I'd have to talk to him at some point. As soon as I picked up, he started crying down the phone. I couldn't really understand what he was saying but managed to get something about him getting into a fight and then being in a taxi. He wanted my address to give to the driver. I gave it to him and said that he could come and sleep at mine, but that I didn't want to talk to him. He arrived a few hours later, at seven o'clock. I let him in and put him on the sofa in the lounge. Kyle was in bed with me by then (not in that way – he's gay, remember!) and all I wanted to do was sleep. But Scott wanted to 'talk'. I told him firmly that I had nothing to say to him and that we could talk later.

'Get some sleep,' I told him. He started crying again and asked me not to shout at him. I hadn't even shouted – or said anything nasty at all to him! All I wanted was for him to get some sleep and go home. He then proceeded to cry, shout and whimper in the corner of the room for half an hour. He wasn't making sense. He said something about 'telling his mum and dad' about me, and kept saying 'Don't be horrible to me', even though I hadn't said a word. Kyle was listening to the whole scene from the bedroom and couldn't believe what he was hearing – nor could I. Every time I tried to walk away, Scott cried out as if in pain and begged me not to be nasty to him.

Until now, the only cross words we'd had were over his partying lifestyle. I thought he did too much of it and he didn't think he had a problem. We'd only had small arguments and I had never said a nasty word to him. I'd gently suggested that he might want to cut down if he was serious about being with me, but other than that we had been having a nice time together. I had no idea where all this 'Don't be nasty to me' was coming from and I didn't stay to find out. When I couldn't take any more, I walked out and went to bed, leaving him crying by himself. Eventually, he went to sleep.

When he woke later that morning, he wasn't even embarrassed by his behaviour. He strolled into the kitchen where I was standing chatting to my mum and dad and said hello to them as if nothing had happened. By then, of course, I had told them about the night before and my dad had decided to give him a talking to. He took Scott out into the garden and told him that he should calm down his lifestyle. I don't know what else was said but Scott left soon after that. I told him I needed some space to make my mind up about us, but I had no intention of ever speaking to him again.

Scott drove home to Manchester and proceeded to send me about 50 texts begging me to give him another chance. I ignored all of them. He then took to sending me picture messages of his face looking really sad with the text beside it saying, 'Marry me?' He even sent one text saying, 'My future is with you, I love you and I love your family. I'll stay at home and look after the dogs while you go out to work if that's what you want. Please marry me, I can't cope without you.' He couldn't have been more wrong if he'd tried. Everyone knows how much I love my dogs, but the last thing I would ever want is a bloke offering to stay at home and look after them for me while I went out to work. What I really wanted was for him to leave me alone. After two days of my ignoring his texts and also ignoring the huge bunch of flowers he had delivered to my house, Scott turned up. He'd made the four-hour drive from Manchester to sit outside my house and refused to go away until I went out and spoke to him. He sat and cried as I told him that it was over and that I'd be happier if he left. He begged me to give it another shot and I told him I wouldn't. He ended up driving all the way home five minutes after he arrived. That's eight hours driving in one go. Wrong!

Eventually, he got the message that I wasn't going to give him another chance and I didn't hear from him again for a while. The next dealing I had with him came a week after he had sold a story on me to the *Sunday Star*. He told the paper that the sex with me was 'all right'. Funny that, because he admitted to me – and on camera on *Trust Me I'm a Holiday Rep* – that he hadn't had a proper erection in three years and that I was the first girl in that time to have given him one! The utter cheek! If sex with me was 'all right', then I'm a nun and he's a Hollywood actor. He wishes. It was the best sex he's ever had and he knows it. That's why he begged me to marry him repeatedly after we split.

The day I read the story, I sent him a text. It simply said, 'If you tell one more story about me to anyone, I will give all of your texts and sorry pictures and voicemails you have sent me or left me to the papers. Then everyone will see how pathetic you are. Don't fuck with me 'cos I'll fuck with you ten times more and you'll wish you had never bothered.' I then had the pleasure of seeing him that weekend at the *Trust Me I'm a Holiday Rep* wrap party. He stayed well out of my way. I think he had also remembered by this point that I had a load of dirty pictures of him that I had taken in Cyprus. I had come to realise that, if I took dirty pictures of people and kept them, I could use them against them later on when they tried to sell stories, as they inevitably would.

Kyle and my mate Sarah came with me to the party and I had a good old catch-up with everyone else that was there. Halfway through the night my phone started ringing with a number I didn't recognise. Whoever it was called about five times and I didn't answer it. The sixth time it rang I decided to answer. A male voice shouted that it was 'Rob' and I hung up immediately. I only knew a few Robs and I had all their numbers stored in my phone, so I thought it was just some stalker. A few seconds later, it rang again. I answered again and this time I made more of an effort to hear what he was saying over the noise of the nightclub. He shouted even louder, 'It's Rob, Robbie, Robbie Williams, Max's mate; go somewhere where you can hear me!'

It was all I needed to hear and I was outside in about 20 seconds flat. I then had a ten-minute chat with him. He asked where I was, what I was doing and even what I was wearing. He said that he'd got my number off Max and that he had been watching *Trust Me I'm a Holiday Rep* on TV and was enjoying it. He asked if I had the whole series on DVD and when I said yes he asked if I would bring them over to his and we could sit and watch them together. When I asked why he would want to do that, he replied, 'Well, I really just want you to come over. What do you reckon? Leave the party and come to mine.'

The previous week, I had been at the first recording of Ant and Dec's *Gameshow Marathon*. Robbie had turned up to support them and had made a beeline for me at the after-show party. He had spent pretty much all of his time at the party talking to me. I was in a corner with my mate, Chloe. I always keep myself to myself at celeb events, so wasn't really mingling with anyone else. I think he liked that and stayed to chat for ages. During the phone conversation, he said that I'd looked gorgeous at the party and that he'd really enjoyed chatting to me.

To cut a long story short, I told him clearly that I would

be up for going over to his but that I didn't want any 'funny business' and that I would come over for a chat as friends only. I didn't want him to think I was going over to have sex with him or that I was some sort of booty call. He told me that he was on his way back from playing football and that he would call me when he was nearly home so that I could get in a taxi. I then slipped back into the club. I waited almost an hour, which is how long he said he would be, and made the decision to carry on drinking at another club down the road. I hadn't heard back from him and didn't think I would by then so I wanted to make the most of my night.

As we got to the door of the club, I saw a gorgeous man stepping out of a car. He looked me straight in the eye and I recognised him instantly as Jennifer Lopez's ex-husband, Cris Judd. I smiled at him and he smiled back, undressing me with his eyes. We entered the club at the same time and on the stairs I bumped into my mate Patrick – who also turned out to be a friend of Cris's. He introduced us properly and we grinned at each other with the knowing smile of two people who have immediate and obvious chemistry. Patrick walked with us to a table and then left us to our own devices.

At one point, I was called up to dance on the stage in front of everyone. I got up there, wearing the tiniest black see-through dress and long black boots, and gave the sexiest performance I could, knowing full well that Cris was watching every second of it. When I finished, he practically climbed over the table to sit beside me. He asked me to dance and I spent the next hour being thrown around the dance floor by this gorgeous man. He's an amazing dancer and I later found out that he has choreographed for Michael Jackson and has even won awards for choreography. When we had had enough, we sat back down to get to know each other. We discovered that we both rode motorbikes and had a long chat about that. When the night came to an end, he asked if he could come back to mine and I happily agreed. My publicist Jo had driven me into London so we bundled him into the back of her car and made the trip back to Essex.

Once back at mine, we started kissing. There was a wild animal attraction between us but I was determined to control myself. I didn't want him thinking I was easy, although I could have happily shagged his brains out there and then. Instead, we stuck to very passionate kissing and some groping and dry humping. It sounds hideous when I put it like that, but we actually had a very nice time. It was very erotic and extremely passionate. He kept looking into my eyes and saying, 'You're so beautiful', and we stopped our sexy fumbling for cigarette and conversation breaks every now and then. We didn't go to bed; in fact, by seven o'clock we were still at it on the sofa. He asked me what I was doing that day but, unfortunately, I had a job on miles away. We were both gutted that we couldn't spend the day together as we had hit it off so well. So, at eight o'clock, we kissed goodbye on my doorstep and he took a taxi back to London.

Cris called me about five times that day and even called me at four o'clock the following morning. He kept saying how he wished that he could be with me and we decided that he should try to change his flight. It was booked for the next morning and neither of us wanted him to go back to America so soon. He had been on the phone all day trying to change it but wasn't having much luck. With every call he made to his agent or the airline, he called me afterwards to give me an update. He told me that, if he could change it, he would come and stay with me for a week and I promised that we would go out riding on my motorbikes. I would have happily cancelled work for the week to be with him – he's gorgeous! Unfortunately, the following morning, he called to say that he hadn't managed to change his flight and that something important had come up for him work-wise anyway. He promised to be in touch soon and made me promise to visit him in America.

I never did hear back from Robbie – although I did have a voicemail from him, which I got the next day, asking me yet again to go over to his. Maybe it's because I told him I would only go over as friends. Perhaps he was only after a shag for the night. Who knows? Never mind, with Cris and his huge hard-on writhing around on my sofa, I soon forgot all about Robbie anyway!

CHAPTER TWENTY-TWO
Shakey Times

A few days later, I was asked to go and work at the Moto GP. The Moto GP is my favourite sport of all time. I'm obsessed with Valentino Rossi and have followed him and the GP with my dad for years. I've never been so excited as when I got the call asking if I would walk one of the riders out on to the grid at Donington; I screamed down the phone! I took my dad with me on the day and we walked around grinning like idiots. We met nearly all the riders and had the best day ever.

Halfway through the day, I was introduced to the British rider Shane 'Shakey' Byrne. Shane took an instant liking to me and offered to take me round the track on the back of his scooter. I couldn't say yes quickly enough. He then took Dad and me on a tour of the garages, and after that took us back to the motor home that he lives in during the GP. I even got to stand next to Valentino at one point in the Yamaha hospitality tent but my legs went weak and I couldn't speak. I walked Shane out on to the grid at the start of the race and nearly wet myself when they started the bikes up.

At the end of the day, my dad and I were walking back to the car when we heard a screech of tyres behind us. It was Shane on his scooter, asking for my number. When we got in the car, my dad and I had a bet on how soon he would text me: he said by the end of the night; I said before we even got home. I won. Shane texted me within 15 minutes of getting my number. We flirted via text for the next few days, then he invited me to go to the GP in Germany. I jumped at the chance. It's such a big passion of mine. I flew out and spent four days living with him and his best mate in his motor home. It was amazing. We spent all our time at the track and ate in the hospitality tents every day. We were treated like royalty. I was in my element. Again, I walked him out on to the grid for the race and I loved it. I took a million pictures of all the bikes and riders and called my dad a few times. He was very jealous. The weather was really hot, so we spent our spare time sunbathing on the roof of the motor home. All in all, I had a great time.

When the four days were up, Shane asked if I wanted to drive down to Austria with them. They were going to drop the motor home off at the KTM headquarters and fly home from there. I agreed and Shane got me a ticket to fly with him from Austria. The motor home was top of the range and very luxurious so the long drive was really comfortable. I read a book practically the whole way while lying on a sofa. In between reading, we played silly games and even managed to get Shane's best mate dressed up in one of my underwear sets for a laugh.

By now, it was obvious that something might happen

between Shane and me. We were having such a good time and I did fancy him. He had the most amazing blue eyes and was a real cheeky chap. He had a funny charm and made me laugh lots. When we arrived in Austria, we had a whole day to play with until our flight that night, so Shane took us to a posh restaurant overlooking a huge lake for lunch. We went rowing on the lake afterwards and had a great time. Back in England, we had a few days over at Shane's house on the Isle of Sheppey and he flew me around in his helicopter. He even flew me over my own house so I could take aerial pictures. Things were great.

After a few days, Shane asked me if I wanted to go to Switzerland with him. He had another house out there and wanted to go and furnish it. I said yes, and the next thing I knew I was lugging a three-piece suite into the back of a white van and setting off on what turned out to be a 14-hour drive. At the other end, we dragged the massive suite out of the van and up the stairs into his house. The place was beautiful. He said he wanted a woman's touch in furnishing it and we spent a few days going round the shops looking for nice things to buy.

One day, he had a meeting and left me to go round the shops on my own. Hardly anyone spoke English and I began to feel a bit lost. I started to miss my family, friends and dogs. I had been away in Barbados with Kenzie, Cyprus for *Trust Me I'm a Holiday Rep*, Germany for the GP and now I was in Switzerland. Suddenly, I felt like I wanted to go home. When Shane finally came back for me, I wasn't in the best of moods. We went back to the house and I told him how much I was missing everyone. He had planned to stay out there for an extra day but said that we could leave sooner if I wanted. I was really grateful and the next day we left for home on another 14-hour drive.

On the ferry back across the Channel, I asked Shane if we could go straight to mine when we got back to England. He said no. He had some things to do first, *then* he'd take me home. 'If you don't mind then,' I said, 'I'll order a car to pick me up at Dover and I'll go straight home. You can come and meet me whenever you're ready later on.'

Shane flipped out and called me selfish. I knew right then that he wasn't the one for me. Selfish? What? I'd flown to Germany on my own to see him; I'd accompanied him on the 14-hour each-way drive to furnish his house; I'd lugged a massive three-piece suite in and out of a van; I hadn't seen my friends, family or dogs for what felt like ages and now, just because I wanted to get a taxi home, he was calling me selfish. If I wanted to be selfish, I'd have demanded he take me home, not offer to get a cab.

I knew then it was time to move on again. We had a big row on the ferry and I refused to talk to him for ages. Eventually, he offered to take me straight home and I was pleased. We half-heartedly made up and he drove me to my mum and dad's house. That night, he was staying with me and we crawled into bed. I was exhausted from all the travelling and was asleep as soon as my head hit the pillow.

I can't have been out that long before I was woken by Shane prodding me in the side. Paddy was asleep at the end of the bed, so Shane started with: 'I can't sleep with his snoring.'

Half-asleep, I answered, 'Babe, if you just shut your eyes I'm sure you'll fall asleep.'

He wouldn't have it, though, and kept on that he couldn't sleep with Paddy in the room. Because I was so tired and I just wanted Shane to shut up, I got up and put Paddy in the kitchen for the night.

When I climbed back into bed, he said, 'So what's going on with us then?'

It was three o'clock in the morning and I was knackered. I said, 'Babe, I just want to get some sleep, can we talk about this in the morning?'

'No,' he replied, 'I want to know what's going on. Are we together?'

I had already gone right off him when he called me selfish and was also now angry at having to put Paddy in the kitchen. 'Babe, I'm not going to have this now, I need some sleep,' I said.

He wouldn't let it lie and in the end I had to shout at him that I was working in the morning and would he please let me get some sleep. He came to work with me the next morning and it turned out to be a really long day. We didn't get back until late at night and I was knackered again. We got into bed and I fell asleep as soon as the light went out. But, true to form, he woke up again. 'I waited to see if you were going to fall asleep and, when you did, I woke you up. I can't sleep with Paddy on the bed,' he said.

I had brought the dog to bed again, thinking that Shane would just have to get used to him. I couldn't believe it: Shane had actually waited to see if I was going to fall asleep and, when I did, he woke me up to have a go at me for it! I argued that Paddy had always slept on my bed and that Shane would have to get used to it. If any man thinks he can come between me and my dogs, he's sorely mistaken!

Shane then jumped out of bed and turned on all the lights. It was two-thirty in the morning. 'It's me or the dog, babe,' he shouted. 'I can't sleep here if he's sleeping here!'

You can guess what happened next. 'Bye then!' I said cheerily.

He packed up his stuff and began throwing it in the van. Just as I thought he was going to leave me and Paddy to get a decent night's sleep, he came back into the bedroom and said, 'So, what *is* going on with us then?'

Aaaaaarrrgggh! 'Babe, I'm tired. I will NOT talk about this with you at two-thirty in the morning. We'll talk about it tomorrow,' I said and he left.

I didn't answer his calls the next day. He had already confessed to me in Switzerland that he thought he was in love with me and I didn't want another Scott on my hands.

Instead, I went and got a tattoo on my leg saying 'Heart-Breaker'. I'd broken three hearts in a row – unintentionally – and it summed up how I was feeling. I hate the feeling of having to dump someone; in fact, I'd rather be dumped than be the dumper. I got the tattoo as a warning to all nice men. I'd realised that after years of abusive, cheating, nasty men I wasn't willing to put up with crap from anyone any more. My fuse was short and blokes had to watch their step with me. They only had to call me selfish, not like my dogs or drink too much for my liking and they would be out the door. I had a zero-tolerance policy. All I ever wanted was what my mum and dad had: a long and happy marriage with the love of my life – whoever that might be. When I got the tattoo, I realised that maybe what I'd been looking for wasn't what I needed. What was good for my mum and dad wouldn't necessarily make me happy. I decided that I would carry on having fun and if a nice man appeared then I would give it a go – after all, you don't know until you try. If any man pissed me off along the way, he would be sacked immediately. I also realised that even if I never met 'The One' it didn't matter. If I get to be 70 and still single, I won't mind as long as I've got Kyle, Lauren, all the people that matter and 20 dogs; then I'll still be happy. Having a man is not the be-all and end-all. But, in the meantime, it doesn't hurt to have some guy-candy on the go for fun. Everyone needs an occasional bit of man-joy in their life!

CHAPTER TWENTY-THREE

Cheating and Depressed

I stayed single for a while and partied with my mates between jobs. I was happy and relaxed. The next bloke I got with was a builder. It was only really a short fling but, for the first time ever, I cheated! I was doing a club opening one night and, by coincidence, my ex Scott Sullivan was there. As soon as I saw him, I fancied him again. He looked gorgeous and I was feeling naughty. He was at my side within five minutes of my arrival and we stayed like that for the rest of the night. We moved on to a club in Essex and as soon as we arrived and settled into a booth Scott leaned over and kissed me. The sexual tension had been building all night and it was obvious we would end up doing something together. I hadn't mentioned the fact that I was seeing someone and he hadn't asked. The kiss was the best I'd had in a long time. Not only did I know Scott and feel comfortable with him, but also he looked amazing and I wanted him. Within minutes, I was playing with his cock and he had his hands inside the cute little pilot outfit that I'd bought from a sex shop.

The passion between us was too much and I pushed him back into the booth and unzipped his flies. I bent down to him under the table and took him in my mouth. He loved it – we'd always had outrageous sex and both of us got off on it – but I wanted more. I pulled my thong to one side and sat on him, in the middle of the busy club. People were dancing all around us, oblivious to the fact that we were shagging. I did try to make it look as if I was innocently sitting on Scott's lap, bouncing up and down in time to the music. The only people that clocked on were two of my best mates, including Kyle, who danced wildly in front of us to distract people's attention. God love my mates!

When the club shut, we decided to take a cab back to mine. There were five of us, so we ordered a seven-seater people-carrier. Scott and I wasted no time jumping straight in the back and shagging all the way home. Our mates all knew what we were doing but didn't turn round to look at us. A couple of them passed out on the way home anyway and we made full use of the big back seat. Even in the car, we managed three different positions.

Back at mine, we had sex for hours. We made the *Kama Sutra* look boring as Scott threw me round the bedroom and I took him from every possible position and angle. Exhausted, we slept for a while, before waking up and going at it again. Later that day, I dropped him off at his mate's house and then went home to end it with the builder. I felt really guilty for cheating, but Scott had given me an amazing and memorable night of sex. It was what I needed. When I thought about it, it was exactly what I hadn't been getting.

Work was going well: I had a small part in a film called *Are You Ready For Love?*, I'd worked at the British Super

Bikes (great fun) and I'd done some wicked photo shoots for a few lads mags. My website was growing fast due to the daily blog that I wrote for it and I had signed the contract to do *Celebrity Big Brother*.

Even though my personal life was great and I'd had a couple of little flings – including one with a photocopier salesman – being famous was starting to take its toll. I was feeling really down and wasn't even sure if I wanted to do the whole celebrity thing any more. I wrote a blog for my website that my brother posted for me the day I went into the *Big Brother* house. This is what it said:

My Blog

Friday, 6 January 2006: I'm in *Celebrity Big Brother*

Well, if you are reading this now you probably know that I am actually in *Celebrity Big Brother*... The main thing I want to do is apologise for either lying to you (if you are somebody that knows me personally) or for just not telling you that I was doing *CBB*. Obviously it was written into the contract that I couldn't tell anyone (including immediate friends and family). I have been telling all my close friends that I am off to America to see Jordan Knight (which they all believed – again, people, I'm so sorry! I'm actually surprised you didn't clock on anyway as I'm so crap at lying!).

Right now I am terrified. When I say terrified, I mean terrified to the point that I haven't slept for a week, I can't eat properly, I feel nauseous

My Blog

(I've been gagging constantly throughout the day), I haven't been able to think properly (in fact, I've been walking around like a zombie for a week). I have been so stressed, I've given myself migraines. That TERRIFIED!

After turning down the likes of *Love Island* and *I'm a Celebrity* (and not even giving *Big Brother* a second thought as I have never been offered it before), I had always thought I would never do a show that involved sitting around doing nothing like the above mentioned. I did *The Games* ('cos it was for charity and I got given a personal trainer for four months – joy!) and I did *Trust Me I'm a Holiday Rep* 'cos I'd always thought that, if I hadn't ended up doing what I'm doing now, it is probably what I would have ended up doing and I wanted to try my hand at it. Also, I was paid to work in Cyprus for two weeks – not bad, if you can get it! *Big Brother*, however, is a weird one. I've never really watched it until the one that Kenzie was in. From the first moment I watched it, I was hooked. Not just on *BB*, but on Kenz. His personality had me gripped and actually it was in the middle of an episode that I said to my dad, 'I want to be with him!' I fell for him on screen and was going out with him a week after he came out of the show. Alas, our relationship didn't last, but we remain extremely close. I love him like a brother and we speak at

My Blog

least once a week on the phone (I normally see him once a week as well). *BB* did wonders for Kenzie. Everyone got to see how amazing he is and got to know the real him. Until then, unless you were a Blazin' Squad fan, you probably didn't even know who he was. Now, he has gone on to do well with Friday Hill and is enjoying the love from his newly made fans. He already had a good career ahead of him and doing *BB* has made it even better.

Now, for me, I too have a good career. It is still going as strong for me as the day I stepped out in the army belts and was front page of three national newspapers. Most of my income comes from TV work, appearances and photo-shoots. I enjoy what I do; no, in fact, I LOVE what I do. It's something I've wanted since I was five years old (and grew to want even more desperately when I was bullied at school for being ugly). Throughout my teenage years, I was rejected time and time again by modelling agencies and newspapers that I sent my pictures to. I didn't give up, though, and after a stint as a lap-dancer at Stringfellows, and with renewed confidence, I finally made it to where I am now. However…

What I didn't know (or perhaps 'realise or think about' is a better way to put it) about being famous is that you put yourself up to be

My Blog

abused, criticised and slated for everything you do, say or wear. I stupidly and naively assumed that if you were a nice person then people would like you. Not so. I have been slated for pretty much every aspect of my whole life since becoming known. I have been called 'ugly', 'a slapper', 'a minger', 'a freak', 'trashy', 'trampy', 'thick', 'pointless', 'a bimbo', 'without class or style', 'hideous' and 'vile'. My boobs have been described as being like 'spaniel's ears' or 'saggy', just because they are real and don't touch my chin like silicone ones. My face alone has been described as 'hideous', 'ugly', 'deformed' and 'scary', to name a few. My nose (which I broke playing hockey at school) has been described as 'vile', 'bent', 'scary', 'deformed', 'misshapen', 'a monstrosity', etc etc. Every inch of my body has been scrutinised by those who have delighted in pointing out my cellulite repeatedly. I have been made to look like I don't have a brain, I'm cheap and useless, I don't do anything good and I have no talent, personality or skills. I've even been called a 'bully' (the most hurtful of the lot) for having a go back at the people who abuse me on a daily basis!!!!! I have been slated for wearing a 'Bollocks to Poverty' top (which I was asked to wear by the charity that designed it) when I hosted an event for Action Aid. I have been

My Blog

accused of using my best friend's murder to gain publicity for myself (I only gave interviews in her memory to not let her death go unnoticed and be just another statistic, with her mum's full knowledge and consent and all money made went into a trust fund for her baby, who was 10 weeks old when she was killed). It has been written that my brown hair doesn't suit me and I should 'leave that look to Angelina' (even though it's my natural colour). I have been in the 'Blinging' section of a magazine's 'Minging or Blinging' section only one time that I recall in three years of being in 'Minging'. If I do go out wearing normal, nice clothes (which is actually quite often), the pictures don't ever seem to get printed. I have been called 'ugly', or something very similar, publicly by Ulrika Jonsson, Jade Goody, Garry Bushell, Goldie Lookin Chain, Jordan, Elize Du Toit, Michelle Heaton and Nadia from *BB* (people who at the time of calling me ugly were also in the public eye – so should have known better – but who also had never met me, apart from Jordan) and these are only the ones I can remember off the top of my head at four o'clock in the morning as I write this. I have been accused of being an attention-seeker (when I don't even go to a quarter of the red-carpet things I am invited to), I have been accused of showing flesh to get in newspapers

My Blog

(if you look at the pictures in my autobiography, you will see that I have been dressing the way I do since I was 15 years old – I didn't get famous until I was 23). I have been written about nicely so few times that I actually remember each and every one of the articles (no matter how small) and the journalists' names that wrote them and I beat Christina and J-Lo one year for column inches – that's a hell of a lot of nasty press when you think about it! I have been publicly humiliated over and over again. I have had days where I can't get out of bed because I have been so depressed. I have been laughed at and mocked for three whole years. It is as bad as, if not worse than, the bullying I suffered at school (and I wanted to kill myself over that). All of the above nasty things have been written in every magazine and newspaper, they have been written all over the internet and they have even been said to my face on many an occasion (from a drunk guy outside a nightclub to a sober girl yelling insults in my local High Street).

After three years of it and three years of loving what I do, but hating the abuse and being depressed behind closed doors, I've had enough. I physically can't take any more. The way I feel right now is that, if it's going to be like this for me forever, I'd rather not do this job any more. There is only so much abuse a person can

My Blog

take and, although up until now I have tried to be as thick-skinned as a rhino (and nearly got there), just recently I have come to realise that nobody can be expected to hear and see all of these nasty things about themselves and not feel like they are going insane or want to curl up and hide from the whole world. If you think I am being dramatic or over the top here – think again. Try and put yourself in my shoes. Imagine what it feels like to read abuse about yourself or have abuse shouted at you in the street EVERY day for three years. It's vile. It's more than vile – it's soul-destroying. Sometimes, I feel like I'm going mad, sometimes I cry, sometimes I get angry, sometimes it doesn't bother me at all and I rise above all of it. But one thing remains consistent: every day, without fail, I think to myself: 'Is it ever going to be good?' I'm ashamed to admit that, when people approach me in the street or in a bar or wherever, I'm scared and nervous of what they are going to say. The reason for this is that half the people are nice and half the people are vile. Because I am scared and nervous, I often act coldly towards them and it's only after they've said something nice that I loosen up and am able to chat to them. Until then, I am sure people who meet me think I am cold and rude. It's not really 'cos I don't want to talk to anyone that I act this

My Blog

way; it is simply because I have had so many people be rude to my face and say nasty things that I seem to always expect the worst now.

So, it is now crunch time. Judgement Day. Make or break. Like I said, I don't know if I can carry on doing this job if it's going to be this abusive forever. I don't want to let these people beat me but I don't know if I have the strength or energy or will to fight them any more. I started my own blog to try to fight them (at the very least I get to set straight the lies, voice my opinion and let people see the REAL me on it) – but even that didn't work! I now have a spate of internet forums slagging me off even more for being honest in my blogs every day. No matter what I do, I can't win. I even got turned down by ChildLine when I offered to do a tour of schools giving talks on bullying to the kids because I 'didn't have the right image', due to what the papers were saying about me (full story in my book). At times, I couldn't even use my fame to help other kids that wanted to kill themselves, like I once did, because the press were making me look so vile. OK, let's look at the facts, because I KNOW that there will be people reading this going, 'Yeah but you ask for it, wearing all those skimpy outfits.' Well, if I was tall enough or beautiful enough to be a catwalk model, I would have been. If I could sing or play

My Blog

an instrument as well as my brother, I would have done what he is doing. If I had been lucky enough to make it as an actress, I would have done that too. Instead, I am 5ft 2in with the same curves as my mum (which, by the way, I AM proud of) and I have an outrageous and daring dress-sense. I only ever had a figure for glamour modelling, not catwalk, and, after going to every audition and casting under the sun and never being picked, I was happy to eventually get somewhere.

The outfits I wear are partly to do with my job (they help me to be noticed and make people talk about me) and partly to do with the fact that I have always wanted to stand out and be different in a sexy and fun way. Every time I go out, I treat it like I'm going to a fancy dress party (it's much more fun that way) and I dress to please myself. When I went to the *Dodgeball* premiere (pic on back of my book) in bra, knickers, fishnet tights etc, I had decided I wanted to look like a Pussycat Doll for the night (at the time, the Pussycat Dolls weren't really known over here, they were just a very sexy all-girl dance troupe in America). I put together an outfit that most resembled what they wore on stage and I loved it. I didn't go out in bra and knickers because I'm a slag or any other hideous reason that someone might have come

My Blog

up with. In the same way a normal person on the street might go and buy a pair of skinny jeans 'cos they've seen them on Sienna Miller and want to copy her style, I, for one night, wanted to look like a Pussycat Doll, as I thought they were all gorgeous.

I could go on forever about why I do the things I do and I could still be called a liar and other nasty things. The true fact of it is that I have been and always will be different to everyone around me. I have never followed fashion (preferring to make up my own) and I have done nothing illegal (apart from last week, when I took my mini-moto out on the road).

I don't want pity, I don't want praise. I just want to be given a fair ride and for people to stop being so nasty. All of these things are what have made me agree to go on *CBB*. Right now, I feel like it is the only way to reach out to the masses and show them that I'm nothing like what I have been portrayed to be for the last three years. I feel like I have nothing to lose by going on it and it is the only option left for me to be given a fair trial (short of changing my whole identity and moving abroad).

Yes, I have cellulite. Yes, my boobs droop a bit as they are not made from silicone. Yes, my nose is wonky and slightly on the large side. Yes, I use sun-beds, which I know are not good

My Blog

for you, but I feel better with a tan. Yes, my teeth are veneers, but a TV show offered to pay the twenty grand it cost to get them done and I love them. Yes, my lips are really thin but I have a phobia of needles, otherwise I'd get them done too. Yes, my voice is annoyingly deep but I can't help that. Yes, my hair is helped along with extensions and, yes, they fall out everywhere and annoy people, but I love the way they look and hate my own thin hair. Yes, I get spots like everyone else and, yes, I have love-handles. I am not stunningly beautiful. I know all of these things. Without make-up I feel as minging as people say I am (that comes from years of being bullied for my looks and also from honestly thinking that I do look better with a bit of slap). I can be annoying as I am so highly opinionated and I can be hell-on-earth for everyone around me when I'm depressed. But I am also a hyperactive, fun, caring, kind, thoughtful, diplomatic young woman who wants to live life to the full and enjoy as much of it as possible as I truly think that life is way too short.

All I ask is this: if you like me on *CBB*, then please vote for me. The money from the phone calls goes to my charity and I REALLY, really don't want to be out first!!!!! Give me a chance. If *CBB* edit me to look like a total bitch or weirdo then fair enough – I'll probably want to slit my

My Blog

wrists for a bit, until I pick myself up and either move abroad or stay here and go back for a second round of mental battering from all around me. I don't know what's going to happen in there. There could be people I don't get on with, there could be people that are so mad they make me look boring. All I do know is this: I will be honest and I will be myself throughout. I don't have a game plan, I haven't got a clue what the public will even want from me. I can only treat it like the TV show that it is and I will either love it or hate it. My friends will now be taking over my blog for me for the next week or three, depending on what happens. I might be chucked out after a day anyway, so all this writing might be pointless.

I hope you enjoy the show and I hope you understand why I am doing it. I have never been so scared in my whole life as I am right now. It's only a TV show, I know, but to me, with such a huge point to prove, it's much, much more.

I will now leave you in the capable hands of my friends and family for a bit.

Lots and lots of love (and happy viewing)

Jodie
xxxxx

CHAPTER TWENTY-FOUR

Celebrity Big Brother, 2006

C*nts...

CHAPTER TWENTY-FIVE
The Future

Things got better for me after *Big Brother*; not in the way I had hoped to change public perception, but because three nasty 50-year-old men were so horrible to me that the public felt sorry for me. Regardless of why things changed, they did and it was a good thing. Suddenly, everywhere I went people were nice to me. The first premiere I went to after I got out of the house was amazing. I stood on the red carpet for nearly two hours signing autographs and the crowd went wild for me. I loved the love. For the first time since I'd become known (with the exception of my fans, who have been amazing from day one), people were behind me and being nice to me. I hated *Big Brother*. I hated the people in the house (even the ones I thought were nice turned out to be as fake as you like), I hated the way it was edited (not that I will ever watch a single episode, but I've been told how I was made to look) and I hated the fact that I felt I had no choice but to do it in the first place. It was the third anniversary of Kim's death while I was in the house and it wasn't a good time for me. But there were positives: I raised public awareness about the evils of the fur trade, and I showed that adult bullying exists and can be a major problem. Oh, and I also raised £50k for my charities. Not bad going for a week's work!

But I'm feeling great now. I've been in a video for The Streets, I've got at least three big TV shows lined up and I've bought my first house. The house is the most beautiful thing I've ever seen and I've turned it into every girl's dream home. I have a huge walk-in wardrobe, a dressing room and make-up room (complete with giant mirror surrounded by lights) and I have a stripper pole to keep fit on and entertain men. Life's amazing once again. I'm annoyed at myself for getting through so many blokes since my split with Kenzie, but after that relationship I really hit the self-destruct button. Kenz and I have remained very close friends. I even had a call from his mum when I came out of the *Big Brother* house to say that she felt awful for the way I was treated in there. You never know, there may be a reunion at some point. I love Kenz like a brother and speak to him and see him all the time.

I have been on loads of brilliant TV shows recently, including: *A Bear's Tale*, *Trisha* (as the resident sexpert) and *Celebrities in Therapy*. PETA, the animal rights charity, made me their British ambassador and I posed naked for their anti-fur campaign – following in the footsteps of the likes of Pamela Anderson! I've had a whale of a time and made some amazing new friends. Kyle, Lauren, all my other friends and my family and dogs are still making every day a living joy for me; I have nothing to complain about. I no longer care what people think of me. I have come to realise that, for every one person that loves you, there's always one that hates you – whether they've met you or not. I'm living only for myself now. I've given up trying to please everyone; I only want to have fun. I won't make excuses for my behaviour and I don't care how many lies get told about me. I am a young girl enjoying life. I don't always get it right, but I haven't done badly. I'm 27, I haven't been married or divorced, I don't have any unplanned kids and I've never done drugs. I have manners, respect and a feeling of self-worth. That, to me, is important. I haven't had the best or easiest life so far, but I haven't had the worst either. The two things I desperately need to give up are smoking and men; only time will tell if I ever manage it!

On a positive note, I did end up meeting and becoming friendly with my two idols: Paul Weller and Steve Craddock (who works with Paul and who is also in Ocean Colour Scene). My brother's band are doing brilliantly and he even managed to get former Stevie Wonder producer Narada Michael Walden to come and play drums with him in a pub in Brentwood!

On 11 February 2006, I took my six closest mates on a 3,800m (12,500ft) sky-dive in aid of my charity Refuge. It was one of the things on my 'Things To Do Before I'm 30' list and I loved it so much I've already booked another jump. It was *almost* better than sex! Paddy is still the one big love of my life and luckily he loves the new house as much as I do. I hope you are all having as much fun as I am and I hope you've enjoyed my story. Until the next timeÖ

As you continue pushing through fear and doing it anyway, you learn to trust your ability to handle whatever life may hand you.

SUSAN JEFFERS, *THE LITTLE BOOK OF CONFIDENCE*

Thanks to

Alan Strutt, Alex Sibley, Angie Jenkinson, Aroon Maharajh, Barney Monahan, Big Ben Ofoedu, Calum Best, Carlee Harrod, Chad (Adam Child), Chris Parker, Chris Quentin, Cleo Rocos, Costa, DT, Damian Bowe, Dan Kennedy, Danny Manville, Darren Lyons and Martin and everyone at Big Pictures, Dave McConnell, Dave White, Dean Gaffney, Debbie Manley, Debbie Woodcock, Derek Moran, Ed Sayer, Ernie Smith, Father Ed, Fathom and Daniel, Fenton G, Fiona Thompson, Fleur Hicks-Duarte, Gary Lucy, Gary Smith, Jai Gates, Jake and Christian Panayiotou, James Alexandrou, James Hewitt, James Perry, Jamie Lorenz, Jo Lacey, Jo Marsh, Jo O'Meara, Joe Leftbridge, Joe Swash, Jon Bowler, Jonathan Simpson, Jules Stenson, Kate Pierce, Katherine Mcaloon, Mark Parker, Mark Rubenstein, Mark Sutton, Martin Cullum and Sous, Matt Ellenby, Max Michael, Mehdi Sunderji, Michael Payne, Nadia Brooks, Natalie Cassidy, Nick Ede, Nicola

Dunn, Nikki Tabarn, Nikki, Brooke, Saskia and Biba Kirsopp, Paul Elysium, Peppe, Piers Adams, Paul and Gill, Polly Graham, Rachael Coote, Rav Singh, Ray Panthaki, Rebecca Wade, Richard Blackwood, Rick Parfitt Junior, Rob Chiltern, Rod Brown, Sam Brown, Sara Nathan, Sarah May, Scott Sullivan, Sean O'Brien, Selina Doyle, Shane Lynch, Spencer Murphy, Stef Aleksander, Steve Humphries, Steve Nash, Sue Evison, Tasha 'Chicken', the Bickerdykes, Tom Hawes, Tony Nicholls, Veronika Damiani, Vicki Duffy, Victoria Newton, Vince Humphrey.

Everyone at: *Zoo* magazine, the *Sun*, the *Sport*, the *News of the World*, MCN, Ducatti, Formula One and Playstation, X Box, World Wildlife Fund, Battersea Dogs Home.

To all the paps: Jason Mitchell, Ali Chapman, David Abiaw, Dean Cranston, Jeff 'the mod' Walker, Joe Kerr, Jules Annan, Ben Melvin, Louis Wood, Stephen Walters, Charlie Pycraft, Stuart, Nikos for having a laugh with me in the ridiculous world of showbiz.

To everyone on Ward 5 at Harold Wood – for making me better enough to finish writing the book and for looking after me.

To Yvonne Delane and Nikki Benezra at Fight For Life – words don't describe how amazing you are.

To Emma and Sarah at Beat Bullying – for not passing judgement and for allowing me to join you – it's an honour!

To Sandra Horley, Lisa King and everyone at Refuge – together we will fight this all the way. Thank you for your support and kindness.

To everyone at the RNIB – thanks for having me on board!

Lucian Randall, Rosie Ries and John Blake – for allowing me to do it my way, for putting up with me and for helping me beyond belief.

Sherry Adhami – for understanding me and letting me go with my mad ideas.

Linda Robson – a true inspiration and a wonderful person.

KG – for always playing Eminem.

Ricardo Ribeiro – for being my partner in crime.

Danielle Elkeslassy – for providing hours of fun and great conversation.

Rob Evans – my favourite homo... Bender, faggot, gaylord, arse bandit, fudge-packer, ring-raider, queen, mincer... Good snog though!

Mohammed George – for just being you.

Zoe Williams at *Now* magazine – for writing the nicest unrequested piece about me I've ever read.

Giuseppe Anzalone – for being the best dancing partner I ever had and for being a wonderful person and inspiration to me.

Louisa Backhouse – for looking after my babies while I was in *The Games*.

Max Beesley – 'allo, sugar, never did get the signed Rob picture, muppet!

Dane Bowers – for calling me an arsehole.

Sadie Hewlett – for being a great bird and the biggest diva I've ever known!

Chris Carey – for making me shine and pushing me.

Lady Isabella Hervey – for being a great friend and for being my strength when I was weak.

Linsey Dawn Mackenzie – for always being there when I need you.

Paul Brooke (Pro Bike) – for allowing me to smash up your bike, for getting me through my test, for being a great friend and for listening to all my problems.

Emma Silverman – for being my absolute rock throughout the last two years.

Dave Courtney (and Storm) – for protecting me and for being the softest bloke I know (sorry, I mean hardest). Love you, you sexy beast!

Lauren Adams – for making me cry laughing – flat squirrel.

Chloe (Wish) – for telling it like it is and never failing to make me laugh.

Jeff Weston – for believing in me from day one.

Jo Leigh – for helping me and understanding me and always getting me a smoking car.

Russell Ellenby – Mary! My wife. We'll get married if we're both still single at 30!

Alex Taylor – for being a great friend and amazing entertainer. You should have your own TV show!

Emma Greenwood and Jonathan Lipman – for being amazing friends to me and for all your support. For being groupies with me and for ghost-hunting with me!

Adele Newell – for being a true friend and for your love.

Emily Dubberley – for giving me the inspiration to carry on writing.

Rebecca Hipwell – for always making me laugh and being there through all the tough times, even Black Saturday!

Michelle Foreman – a true friend. I wouldn't be here today if it wasn't for you! I owe you everything.

Kyle Kaine – curl on a stalk, wig and gown, my soul mate, stylist and gorgeous best friend. I love you more than black eyeliner. I can't imagine life without you!

Lauren Roberts – for mentoring me through this book, for endless debate and insane waffle, for being the best friend a girl could have and for truly knowing me. Thank you so much. I love you.

James MacKenzie – my little chimp, I love you with all my heart.

Big Nan – for always loving me.

Little Nan – for providing me with hours of entertaining stories and for loving what I do.

To Cheeky, Bella, Rebel, Pixie (RIP), Teddy, Tommy, Baby, Bean and Paddy – the little rays of sunshine in my life.

To Kim, may you rest in peace forever until the day we meet again – and look after Pixie for me!

The biggest thanks go to my true friends (you know who you are) and most importantly to my mum Kris, dad John and brother Jordan. For sticking by me through thick and thin, for picking up the shattered pieces so many times, for putting up with my mad schemes and plans, for allowing me to make my own mistakes, for standing up for me, for encouraging me, for making me laugh and cuddling me when I cry, for never failing to be there, for putting up with my mess, for helping me through hard times and for making the most of the good times, for keeping me sane, for understanding me, for putting me in my place, for helping me to tidy my flat, for listening to my problems and helping me to solve them, for chatting to me for hours on end when I can't sleep, for kicking me up the butt when I needed it, for going out of your way for me and, most importantly, for loving me with all your hearts. I love you more than all the grains of sand in the world.

Web sites

OFFICIAL JODIE MARSH WEBSITE
www.jodiemarsh.tv

PEOPLE FOR THE ETHNIC TREATMENT OF ANIMALS
www.peta.org.uk

BATTERSEA DOGS AND CATS HOME
www.dogshome.org

WORLDWIDE FUND FOR NATURE (NOW KNOWN AS WWF)
www.wwf.org.uk

BEAT BULLYING
www.bbcclic.com

REFUGE
www.refuge.org.uk

24-HOUR NATIONAL DOMESTIC VIOLENCE
HELPLINE: (freephone) 0808 200 0247

ROYAL NATIONAL INSTITUTE FOR
THE BLIND (RNIB)
www.rnib.org.uk

FIGHT FOR LIFE
www.fightforlife.org